CALL ME TAI TAI

CALL ME TAI TAI

THE ASIAN ADVENTURES
OF A TRAILING SPOUSE

SHELLY ASCHKENASE

WINDY CITY
PUBLISHERS

CALL ME TAI TAI
THE ASIAN ADVENTURES OF A TRAILING SPOUSE

Windy City Publishers
2118 Plum Grove Road, #349
Rolling Meadows, IL 60008

www.windycitypublishers.com

Published in the United States of America

ISBN#:
978-1-941478-95-0

Library of Congress Control Number:
2020905144

WINDY CITY PUBLISHERS
CHICAGO

CONTENTS

章 章 章 章 章

INTRODUCTION

"You lived in Shanghai?" people say. "It must have been awesome! We had such a great time during the two days we were there on our tour."

"Of course, you had an amazing time," I think. "Safely ensconced, pampered in a luxury hotel, you likely experienced only the city's best when you ventured out." Instead, I shoot them a big smile that belies the bevy of less attractive or crazy stories in my repertoire and nod approvingly.

The take-away Shanghai stories tend to unfold somewhat differently for people who have actually attempted to live there. Tourists, stuffed with "real" Chinese food, happily shuffling through the crowds at the Yu Yuan, trying to figure out how much to pay for cheesy trinkets that have a 50-50 chance of breaking before they're given to the delighted recipient, know nothing about the challenges of living in Chinese-built housing, strategies for dealing with local household help or Chinese employees at work, the drama of making friends, the marital stresses of expatriate life, or the difficulties of shopping for household necessities on a daily basis.

To be fair, arguably few expats knew much about the "real China"—how the local population actually lived. But that's not a story I'm qualified to tell, either. The story of my Tai Tai (a privileged, married woman who doesn't work) life lies somewhere between that of pampered hotel guest and permanent resident. Of course, some of the events will have casual visitors or business travelers nodding their heads in agreement, while other events transcend both

1

foreigners' and the Shanghainese's experiences, representing something altogether unique and remarkable, occurring only within the exclusive expatriate world. The highs and lows, the craziness, the follies, the drama, the glamour, the indulgence, and the delights of that life remain the rarified domain of the Shanghai Tai Tai. During the early 2000s, when I lived in "The Paris of the East," the city resembled a wild buffet, believable only through extensive tasting.

So, when I choose to dive under the surface of Shanghai, regaling my cocktail party or gym conversation partners with tales of my Tai Tai life, their eyebrows raise, their jaws droop a little. "You should write a book," they respond.

When I thought seriously about this idea, I realized that while countless journalists, teachers, and service mission representatives have described their experiences of living in China, no one has revealed the daily dramas and details of pampered executives' wives' (or husbands') lives. Thus, *Call Me Tai Tai* was born. Lest you think we floated down Huai Hai Lu in a glorious, impenetrable dragon-shaped bubble, let me assure you that not a word of this book would have been key-stroked had the unusual not replaced the usual in our extraordinary Asian-expat version of *Dallas*.

"Don't blink," they say in Shanghai, "everything will change." One day you're looking out the window at a row of picturesque old houses, the next you're watching them bulldozed flat to make room for the next record-setting skyscraper—which will undoubtedly rise magically to completion within weeks. A favorite restaurant stands on the corner one week, replaced by an illegal DVD business or a quick market the next. So, before the incredible Tai Tai world I witnessed vanishes or morphs into something unrecognizable by my generation of expats, I hope to bring my experiences to life in these pages.

WE INTERRUPT THIS LIFE TO BRING YOU...?

I n the fall of 2004, I was well aware that to most outside observers my life appeared quite privileged. In fact, in my own head, my existence felt more satisfying than any of my childhood fantasies about my adulthood. Who could have imagined a better lifestyle than the *Brady Bunch* had? The mom, Carol—with her shapely figure and bunny-blonde stylish pixie haircut—had recently married a tall, dark-curly haired, hunky architect. At their trendy split-level house in sunny California, Mike rolled up every evening in his sporty convertible, parking next to Carol's mom-chic, wood-paneled wagon. They smoothly parented an ideal, blended family of six above-average-in-every-way children and could afford to maintain sanity by splurging on a faithful live-in housekeeper. The whole family was good looking, wore groovy clothes, and excelled in whatever they did. I couldn't see any room for improvement.

Yet, now I found myself lady-of-the-house in a large, charming 1920s Georgian home—complete with swimming pool and English garden—in the upscale suburb of Shaker Heights, Ohio. I had my own two above-average children; a Brazilian au pair; and a tall, handsome, very fit spouse pursuing a hot career. We took annual ski and beach vacations, traveled abroad, and generally enjoyed a satisfying, enviable upper-middle-class existence. No offense, but Carol Brady had nothing on me.

Of course, no lifestyle exists problem free. While Carol Brady dealt with issues easily and always remedied in twenty-four minutes, I found myself facing the unique challenges of running a management consulting partner's household. Consultant's lives are complicated. For starters, they're gone four to five days a week, *every* week. Sometimes, their work requires a week—or more—away from home at a time. Hello, long-distance relationships! Because my husband traveled so much, I also necessarily single parented most of the time. Hence the Brazilian au pair. What's more, even when consultants work in the home office, the job demands long hours, including weekends. While Mike Brady rolled into the driveway at the same time every day, early enough to help the kids with their homework and help problem solve, my husband regularly made odd-hours conferences calls to Europe or Asia, fired up spreadsheets on the computer at all hours, entertained clients in the firm's suite at a Sunday afternoon baseball game, or hosted tables at Saturday evening charity functions. With most of his emotional and physical time and energy spent on business and his own personal tasks, he seemed to parachute in only for random appearances in our lives. What else could I call such a spouse but… Planet.

Another thing Carol Brady never had to trouble her golden head over was moving. Consulting families sometimes move in the interest of serving a client, for the good of the firm, or for a better offer at a competing firm. As a result, becoming a "trailing spouse" (a spouse who follows in a move) came with the turf. Until now, I had handled this deal just fine. I cheerfully, dutifully packed up my life numerous times, changed careers, put my own ambitions on hold, and even managed to mostly enjoy the new adventures that trailing created. For the record, I faithfully supported Planet's career by enduring seven moves in thirteen years. As a result, the phrase "we interrupt this life to bring you another one" rang through my brain more often than I would have liked.

And now, when my spouse came home from the road, suggesting yet another move, I waited for the name of some other benign American city to emerge from his lips. Instead, I heard…

"What would you think about moving to Shanghai?"

He may just as well have said Zimbabwe! I was fully prepared to move to some other part of the US. In fact, even Europe I could get a handle on. I could picture teaching my kids to ski, learning Schweizer-Deutsch, and pigging-out on chocolate and fondue in Switzerland. Absorbing Italy's history and culture while indulging in its legendary cuisine? No problem. But *China*? A densely populated, dangerously polluted, communist, third-world country on the other side of the world? He had to be kidding!

"Um…is there a choice?" I replied, testing my joke theory.

"No." My chances of blithely packing up and reinventing my life once again seemed to blow apart like a firework. China? And NOW, when the kids and I were positively thriving in Shaker Heights? What could China possibly offer any of us that would be worth giving up the life we currently had?

Remembrance of China Past

My issues with moving to China primarily stemmed from my memories of traveling there in 1989, just after the legendary, secretive Country's reopening to the world. In the late 1980s, Beijing's roads swelled with an unbelievable sea of bicycles. The few busses and even fewer cars fought their way through the mob of clean cut, serious-looking people pedaling about in their identical dark blue or grey Mao-style suits. The same short, pixie hair cut crowned the heads of both men and women, and since they were also dressed alike, it seemed hard to decipher which gender was which.

The landscape also felt disturbing. Despite the majesty of the Forbidden City, the Summer Palace, and the Great Wall, Beijing appeared a city of drabness. Like a bad science fiction movie, city skies loomed grey above ashy cinderblock buildings. The people dressed in grey, their faces expressionless, looked like an army of robots in a surreal post-modern world—Orwell's *1984*, come to life.

Another stand-out memory involved personal space. One day, after we came off a Great Wall sightseeing tour, nature called, and I set out to find a toilet. Fortunately, this was relatively easy, because I could smell the facility about a quarter mile before I could see it. The ladies' room was a concrete and peeling, sea-green plaster affair. Around six enclosed stalls hid long rectangular porcelain troughs a couple feet deep. I took a deep breath, went in, shut the door—which didn't lock—and proceeded to get business underway as quickly as possible. Imagine my surprise when the door suddenly burst open and in ran two frantic-looking Chinese ladies. With bladders clearly afire, they shoved their way into *my* stall and proceeded to attend to their own business right behind me! I subdued the temptation to shout, "Don't you think this is taking communism just a little bit too far!"

After my unintended foray into local culture at the Wall, Planet and I went on to the Summer Palace. Strangely, amid the splendor of the palace and grounds a sizable population of beggars camping out there created a disturbing contrast. I felt horrified by their filthy clothes and bodies, often revealing hideous disfigurements. Some of them held sleeping toddlers, many missing limbs. I didn't understand the begging at all. Wasn't the point of a communist government to provide all basic necessities for all citizens? Didn't everyone have a proper job, housing, and health care? Wasn't the revolution all about producing a chicken for every pot?

And speaking of food, our travel package included meal vouchers for the hotel we checked into, but when we tried to collect them, nobody seemed to know what we were talking about. After much ado, Planet finally convinced the desk manager to pony up two free breakfasts, but we never did get the rest of the pre-purchased meals. Some western currency would probably have made them magically appear, but Planet remained stubborn about applying American ethics to the situation. Inside our hotel room, the desk chair leaned sadly to one side on its broken leg, and we quickly discovered the desk lamp had a burned-out bulb. The hotel staff could have cared less how many calls we made to maintenance. It took a while for my husband to realize that nobody ever intended to come up and fix them. In addition, giggling clean-cut young prostitutes, trolled the hotel lobby, claiming to be students who "just wanted to practice their English" with you *in their rooms*. Never mind that I was standing right next to my husband: hands over their mouths they chortled and invited me to come, too.

Based on this long-ago trip, China seemed a fascinating place to visit, but to *live* there? I couldn't see breaking out the champagne and party hats. No, this trailing spouse felt much readier to hang up her title and retire the suitcases and moving boxes.

Facing the Unknown

Haunted by visions from my previous trip to China, a plethora of concerns plagued me. A list of everything great about Shaker that I'd have to give up ran through my mind. For starters, I didn't want to give up my house, my town or my car. Nor did I want my children to lose their home, their schools, their friends, or their activities.

Shaker Heights truly felt like a "forever" home to me. The town was one of America's first planned suburbs, filled with stately Tudors and genteel Georgians. I had worked on creating a warm, cozy home and building a life for my family there. My kids were thriving and happy. The schools were excellent, and a notable portion of the high school's graduates matriculated to the country's top colleges. My daughter attended an all-girls private school. The school's second grade consisted of two classrooms of twelve girls each. One day when I asked Alexis, "who's your best friend?" She answered, "Mommy! We have to love them all equally!" A priceless reply! My son attended the local public school, where students' families came from thirty different countries. So, why leave the country to have an international school experience?

The Shaker community served my family well in many other ways, too. As a Junior League volunteer, I enjoyed the numerous community service projects I served on and the women I met. In addition, Cleveland serves as home to the nation's third largest Jewish population. As a result, my family had no idea how spoiled we were. My kids had started their religious education—which they actually enjoyed—and I had fulfilling volunteer opportunities and the women's organization at our Temple. Our kid-friendly suburb also offered a plethora of well-run kids' activities. Alexis took gymnastics, dance, and was becoming quite a skater. Anders was working his way through every sport the parks and recreation district offered. Both kids spent the summers playing in our backyard pool and attending the outstanding summer camps the local private schools offered. They also loved their music classes at the well-known Music Settlement. The concept of health and medical care in China also vexed me. Shaker Heights families lived privileged lives because we had the Cleveland Clinic and Case Western Reserve Medical School. It scared me to contemplate how antiquated or inadequate medical care might be in the Middle Kingdom. In addition, healthy foods and an intense gym were two essentials that I never took for granted. What kind of healthy food options existed in China? Did they have diet anything? What about all the time I'd spent at the local gym and with my personal trainer toning my body and maximizing my cardio capabilities?

My trainer, Big Ben Bradley lived up to his name. He was a six-foot, ripped he-man. Like the famous clock in London, he loomed larger than life. Lately, he had become a minor local celebrity for his occasional contributions to a popular national sports and health magazine. His trainees believed he got his thrills out of making our workouts resemble near-death experiences. In fact, he theorized that we should hate him at least once per work out and preferably for the duration. We did! In the throes of doing a thirty-second wall squat while doing bicep curls with a ten pounder in each hand, I'd slap on my best murderous look for Ben's benefit. As I groaned in agony, the trainer would simply look me in the eye, smirk, and say, "Whaʼd ya say about cheesecake, Cupcake?" He got results, and we always came back for more.

After faithfully adhering to Big Ben's regimen, I looked better than I had before I'd had children. Now, I pictured my achievements flying away as fast as The Concorde bound for London.

The area's many bike trails and lovely places to walk were also very important to me. Anytime I exercised outside, I appreciated the rows of charming old houses with well-landscaped yards as well as Shaker's wide tree-lined boulevards and abundant parks. Hence, I couldn't get my head around having to live in a concrete jungle, black clouds of pollution floating above and swimming through festival-sized crowds on the ground. Considering how my life might change brought my brain to crisis level. Yet, I couldn't ever let my kids know how upset I felt. What could I do?

Well, suddenly the slightest unpleasantness in my day caused the car to detour to the Cold Stone Creamery or my favorite bakery. If the kids attended a birthday party, I began saying "yes" to a piece of cake. Eating out now seemed so much more appealing than shopping, cooking, and kitchen clean-up. I put on ten pounds faster than a canoe over nearby Chagrin Falls' falls.

Stress eating, I coached myself, would save my children—and Planet—from knowing just how much I detested the idea of moving to China. Following that logic, by August I'd gained twenty pounds and found myself buying new clothes two whole sizes larger than I'd worn in May!

It wasn't simply the China concept causing my distress, it was also the accompanying challenges. First, in early June Planet left to begin working in Shanghai, leaving me to single parent until late July. A record six weeks of single parenting certainly broke some consulting-spouse records, I'm sure. During that time, I also held the dubious honor of undertaking all the move preparations. Alone. While the kids trooped blissfully off to camp with their friends, I descended into my own special circle of hell and began to divide a 6,600 square-foot dwelling, pool shed, and garage filled with eighteen years' worth of accumulated stuff into five categories: donations, long-term storage, ship cargo, air shipment, and suitcases for immediate use during our first two weeks abroad. A daunting project on its own, but made worse by the fact that our domicile was now for sale and needed to appear in *House Beautiful* shape at all times for potential buyers. I also had to tackle the real estate agent's *and* the City-generated repair punch lists. Simultaneously, I had to keep an eye on the calendar, as the kids and I needed an extensive series of vaccinations to become Shanghai residents. Some of them involved serial injections, spaced out over the a few months. The craziest day of all was when we got *eight* vaccinations in one day. The kids were impressively brave! In my mind, was this the nightmare before the nightmare? Why exactly *were* we moving to a country rampant with foul diseases?

Despite my shattered heart, each day I put on a brave mask for the kids. But, I began to share my real feelings with my friends, who remained supportive and positive. My Italian friend was actually an expat in Shaker Heights herself, so she understood exactly what I was going through.

"What can you do?" she said. "You have to support your husband's career. You will find something you like to do there, you'll make friends, and you'll be fine."

Another friend had lived in Africa as a child. She had fond memories of her family's adventures there and assured me it would be great for the kids. A third friend, Penny—who hailed from Scotland and her husband from Singapore—had moved to Shaker Heights after a few years in Thailand. She advised, "The first year will be hard. But by the time you leave, you'll never have made better friends in your life or cried so hard to leave a place. The more challenging the place is to live in, the stronger your friendships will be." I hoped that this would ring true. Penny also told me that the only thing she regretted was not having shopped more. "There is *so* much great stuff to buy and the prices are so reasonable! My best advice is to just keep shopping!" At the time, I had no clue what she was talking about.

When I went to the July meeting of my temple's women's group, I received more opinions. Some of the ladies suggested that the kids and I should stay in America, letting my husband go alone, maybe just for the first year. Others thought it would be a good experience. One woman advised me to think about the move as my husband's midlife crisis. "It's way less painful and whole lot cheaper than a mistress!" she said. This concept held interesting possibilities for mentally dealing with the situation, but the one comment that made a difference came from a middle-aged lady I didn't know. "Think of it as a gift to your husband and children." Her idea startled me out of my misery and made me think. I had been concerned only with how much my family would losing by leaving Shaker. Listening to Planet natter on about how this move would advance his career and how he was excitedly setting up our lives there made his gains obvious. But it never occurred to me that my kids…or I…might benefit. The heavens opened wide. Enter angels singing. While I still couldn't embrace the concept of a new life in Shanghai for myself, miraculously I suddenly saw the proverbial light of what a few years spent abroad could do for my family. It didn't lessen my own trauma significantly, but it certainly improved my attitude.

章

2

HOME IS WHERE YOU KEEP YOUR PASSPORT

Finally, the big day arrived: Sunday, August 8, 2005. A small jet ferried us from Cleveland to Chicago, where we planned to stay overnight in preparation for our Monday morning flight to Shanghai. Despite my spouse's careful planning, Murphy's Law prevailed. On Monday morning, we learned that a typhoon had rolled into Shanghai, delaying our flight for about six hours. A typhoon? Just what were we getting into moving to Asia? Blizzards and heatwaves I understood, but what exactly happened in a typhoon? Was this a bad omen?

When flight time finally arrived, we faced the minor drama of maneuvering our dozen jumbo-sized bags from the hotel to the airline counter. Oh, did we look like "*those* people." Except we weren't. We were just a crazy family trying to move immediately necessary essentials across the world to our new home. I wondered how many people in O'Hare that day were relocating, like us. With enormous relief, I watched the agent hoist all twelve huge pullmans onto the conveyor belt. Now we just had two children and four carry-ons to worry about.

The flight time is about fourteen hours, but the captain can cut off some time if weather permits traveling over the polar cap. We got lucky, arriving in thirteen and a half hours. Shanghai lies twelve hours ahead of Shaker Heights, so when we landed, we'd basically lost a day. It felt completely bizarre walking off the plane knowing that this was our new home—a place I'd never before laid eyes on. About 10:00 pm Shanghai time, we made our way through the passport control line, then we garnered our ridiculous stash of suitcases and managed to work our way through customs. The bored agents seemed not to give two hoots that the American family with a dozen suitcases had nothing to declare. As we snaked through the exit area, Planet scanned the crowd for the driver he'd hired, Mr. Zhou. After a few minutes, amidst a sea of ebony-haired beings, a thin, relatively handsome man sporting silver glasses and dressed in a blue suit suddenly began waving. He appeared very professional, surprisingly tall for a Chinese man, his thick, raven hair neatly styled.

"There's Mr. Zhou!" Planet cried out.

My weary mind attempted to process the situation. We now *lived* in *China*. We had a driver—our own for-real chauffer.

"*Ni hao*. Welcome," Zhou called to us, smiling.

"'Ni hao' means 'hello,'" Planet explained.

"Ni hao" the kids shouted back, pleased.

I wondered what Zhou thought of us four exhausted Americans with an embarrassing three whole trolleys piled high with luggage.

We waited near the door while Mr. Zhou retrieved the car and brought it around to the passenger pick up area. Planet had selected a silver Chrysler minivan for our family. "That way it's easy for me to tell which car is ours when Mr. Zhou pulls up to get me," he explained. I nodded, not comprehending.

Why did it matter? Well, at this time about ninety-five percent of the approximately 70,000 expats in Shanghai had leased either a blue or a silver GM GL8 minivan. With most drivers dressed in navy suits and white gloves, standing next to the nearly identical vehicles, it was sometimes hard to tell whose car was whose. Mr. Zhou seemed proud to drive the outlier vehicle.

"To the Westing, Mr. Zhou," my husband advised.

"Westing?"

"Chinese for the Westin," he informed me, pleased with his Chinese vocabulary.

I nodded, eyebrows raised. We planned to stay at the Westin Hotel at The Bund because our new house wouldn't be ready for us to move into for another five days. Hotels in Asia often have apartments, and since Planet had lived in a Westin apartment over the summer, he still had the lease.

Enroute to the hotel, I entertained the over-tired kids by tasking them to name our new car. They came up with "the Shang Hai-Ho Silver." *Ha ha!*

When we finally arrived, I couldn't wait to get some sleep in a real bed. The Westin's "heavenly bed" lived up to its reputation, and I remained grateful for the seven hours the kids and I managed to get that night, especially since our bodies thought it was 12:00 noon Ohio time. The world had already literally and figuratively flipped upside down.

Day 1

I never dreamed my life would involve waking up to a new home in Shanghai, but yet, here we were. That morning, the crazy adventure that comprised our two and one-half years in China began. From now on, just call me *Tai Tai* (a rich businessman's wife).

Our adventure began with an elevator ride downstairs to the hotel's main restaurant to check out the sumptuous buffet breakfast. Not a bad start! We strode across the cream and butter colored marble floors, past walls trimmed in dark wood and chrome, dotted by glamorous modern Asian-style furniture. At the buffet, we discovered both standard Western favorites—like eggs, bacon, and toast—and the much more interesting Asian selections: brown tea eggs, a variety of steamed dumplings, congee with all of its accompaniments (peanuts, dried fish, seaweed, and such), miso soup, several types of fish, huge steamed buns filled with red bean paste or pork, several types of fried noodle dishes, and, of course, plain and fried rice.

Unfortunately, we didn't have the pleasure of lingering over the lavish spread. We had business to handle. After breakfast, we planned to venture out to Pudong to see the compound (the name for Shanghai's exclusive gated communities where most expats lived) and our house.

At 10:00 am sharp, we found our new ayi (it means "auntie," but is how you address your housekeeper) waiting for us in the hotel lobby. I noticed Xiao Ting wore her hair in a short pixie—a Mao-era hold over, seemingly still popular with middle-aged Chinese. A short, thin, serious-looking woman whose skin appeared stretched too tightly over her face, she strolled over, neatly dressed in jeans and a red blouse. The ayi would work for us from 10:00 am to

6:00 pm, Monday through Saturday. She would shop, cook, clean, do laundry—including ironing!—babysit the kids, run errands…pretty much anything and everything required to run a household. I could hardly keep from performing a quick Cha Cha Slide around the Chrysler for joy. We'd basically hired a wife!

We introduced ourselves, then ducked through the Westin's revolving door to see if Mr. Zhou had pulled up outside yet. There stood the shiny, brand-new minivan, with Mr. Zhou properly standing at attention, patiently waiting.

"*Ni zao*," Zhou called, smiling.

I assumed Mr. Zhou meant good morning. "Good morning," I called, as I waved like a typical friendly Midwesterner. As he smiled back, I noticed the array of caramel and black dots on his teeth, some of which were completely colored. *Oh, my!* My mind reeled with the sudden reminder that many people in the world have never had the privilege of dental care. One day, a few months later, Anders commented, "Mommy, Mr. Zhou's breath could stop the Maglev!" Indeed! Poor Mr. Zhou. Maybe now that he was an expat driver, he could finally afford to see a dentist. We introduced Zhou and Xiao Ting to each other; then the two slid into the front seats of the car, while we climbed into the second and third rows. It felt very strange sitting in the back of the car instead of in the driver's seat or the passenger seat. It seemed even weirder to know we now had two employees, and protocol required that *they* sit up front.

As we pulled away from the Westin, I noticed many old buildings and interesting antique shops. Within a couple of blocks, we passed the legendary Bund. I craned my head to take in the beautiful old buildings lining the roadway, the Huangpu River winding its way through the city just beyond. Just looking at this scene, I thought we could easily have been in any European city. This looked nothing like the China of village huts and red-tile-roofed Shikumen buildings I expected. A few moments later, the Chrysler rolled onto a high, long bridge heading out of the Puxi side of Shanghai into Pudong, the metropolis' "new" area. There, I noticed mammoth buildings towered over both sides of the highway, layered row upon row in a mind-boggling display. I marveled that the earth didn't tire of holding them up and simply implode. I could not imagine living in an apartment building housing as many people as a small US city, potentially requiring its own zip code! Although recently built, these industrial-looking mint green, Pepto-Bismol pink, tarnished yellow, and smoke-colored buildings stood covered in rust stains, appearing tired. I thought they'd been built in the 1960s or 1970s, but Zhou proudly announced that they were "new." Well, here's to cheap and quick construction: they looked like the Dollar Store version of apartments! To complete the scene, from every window, the laundry that so embarrassed Chairman Mao flew proudly.

The children were not as interested in the view as I was, so I asked Mr. Zhou and Xiao Ting to teach us some Mandarin. We should probably get started. So, our assistants decided the best lesson for today was numbers one through ten. One and two were easy to say and remember. *Yi* (one) and *er* (two) sound like "e" and "r." Sounds like the room in an American hospital, the E.R. Maybe that would help me remember it. But three, *san*, didn't connect to anything in my mind. Four, *si*, sounded like a buzzing bee and felt difficult to say. Five, *wu*, seemed even harder. It sounded like a ghostly moan: "oooo."

Then, Mr. Zhou announced that hand motions accompanied each number. *Interesting.* I assumed this came in handy for children who babbled or Americans with bad accents. Apparently, the hand gestures represented a homonym—meaningful in Mandarin, since each word could have four different meanings based on tone. So, for example, *ba's* (eight's) hand posture was to pose your index finger outwards and your thumb up, like a gun, because *ba* is also the word for gun. The kids found this very impressive.

After our language lesson, I returned to checking out the scenery. Shanghai at this time was a city of a just over seventeen million—slightly more than double New York City's population. The thought of providing infrastructure for that many people, in a city attempting to emerge from second world status, seemed mind boggling. I could scarcely imagine the mammoth task of handling the city's sewage and garbage. The further we moved away from the river and the Lujiazui area, the lower the buildings stood. Most of the structures appeared beat up and dingy. They formed a mix of industrial-style, cheap modern concrete squares and ramshackle strip malls seemingly wrought from old mud. Small patches of grass poked out near the curb, where the ground wasn't taken up by vendors' stands. A few trees and random flower plots provided a splash of color. Pudong generally looked brown and dusty, wherever it wasn't filled with grey concrete, sidewalk vendors, bicycles, and motor scooters. An abundance of billboards and neon signs accented the otherwise drab scenery. Pudong looked nothing like the China of my imagination, which was filled with quaint ancient villages where I rode my bike on my daily errands, waving a hearty American "hello" to the locals.

As we progressed toward our new house, I noticed the sea of bicycles dominating Chinese roadways in the 1980s had given way to throngs of cars, busses, motorcycles, mopeds buzzing purposefully down the roadways, with only a smattering of travelers still pedaling two wheelers. I marveled as families of three happily zoomed along on scooters. Most people wore surgical-style masks to combat the serious pollution. Some of the ladies also wore detachable sleeves on their arms to protect their skin from the sun.

In Pudong, two-wheeled vehicles and pedestrians out-numbered cars and busses. With lanes so filled, traffic necessarily cruised at a leisurely pace. There was much to see besides just buildings and vehicles. One moped rider had dozens of melons strapped to the back of it. A man dangled six live chickens by their feet from the handlebars of his bike. Another man had strapped flattened cardboard boxes to the rear of his bike, nearly four feet high! How did he keep it from tipping over? Inside crowded passing busses, some passengers napped, some looked stressed, and some stared back at the funny-looking western family in their Chrysler minivan.

Pudong hustle-bustled. Along the sides of the roadway, vendors held their turf, hawking their wares: fruit, hair ornaments, socks, sweet potatoes, plastic kitchen ware, and a variety of other small items. Chinese life seemed to happen in the streets. Nearly every person appeared in motion, except for the random person sleeping or the occasional pods of men squatting on their haunches for a quick conversation or a smoke. Everyone moved purposefully, on some mission or another. After a solid forty-five minutes of driving, we finally reached The Pearl compound—our new neighborhood.

Having a place to call home in Shanghai actually denoted an accomplishment, the result of months of nail-biting work. Renting a dwelling in Shanghai did not simply amount to browsing advertisements, touring the properties of interest, and then signing a contract. At this time, *waiguoren* (foreign people) renters had to cope with poor-quality construction issues and corrupt landlords. China seemed to have few rental laws, and the ones that existed favored the landlords, of course. So, once Planet selected a house, the games began.

The first housing challenge involved figuring out where in this vast metropolis to live. Since our kids would be at Shanghai American School (SAS) Pudong, we decided we needed to live on that side of the city. Back in the 1980s, any self-respecting Shanghainese would die rather than admit to living in the backwater shantytown that lay opposite the Puxi side of the Huang Pu. But in the early 2000s, the government opened up the "Pudong New Area" to development. Before you could say pot stickers, the iconic Oriental Pearl Tower, the stately Jin Mao Building, five-star hotels, and the Shanghai World Financial Center emerged along the "other" side of the Bund—now quaintly named *Bin Jiang Da Dao* (the River Promenade). The Lujiazui Finance and Trade Zone, the Shanghai Stock Exchange, and a plethora of foreign businesses sprang up as well. The swampy farmland transformed into a commodity as hot as the old French Concession, equally international, and boasting some of Shanghai's most expensive addresses before you could down a lukewarm Tsing Tao beer. Suddenly, Pudong was "in," and we were jumping on the opportunity along with a plethora of other Chinese and foreigners from all reaches of the globe.

Over the summer, from across the Pacific Ocean, I had sent my spouse lists of the compounds I viewed on the internet that seemed suitable choices for our family. In his free time, he checked them out. I grew puzzled by how many times Planet told me the pictures of the compounds I'd seen on the internet didn't mirror the photos. He found the poor-quality construction and cheap appearances of the houses very disappointing. At this time, expats on a "good" package could expect to pay about $4,000 per month for a well-furnished apartment in an upscale compound. They could expect to pay anywhere from $5,000—$15,000 per month for a furnished villa. (For real. If your eyeballs just fell out of your head, put them back in.) Planet grew increasingly irritated to think of paying Neiman-Marcus prices for Walmart quality.

Finding a villa that came anywhere near worth the rent seemed as elusive as locating a unicorn. In no time, my husband had ruled out eighteen of the twenty compounds on our list! Finally, he toured The Pearl compound. He concluded that this compound's houses seemed the best constructed of any he'd seen—which wasn't saying much. So, he made an offer on a four-bedroom, approximately 4,000 square foot home that actually had an American-sized yard. The compound offered 24-hour security guards, English speaking on-site management, numerous community amenities, and a bus to Shanghai American School (SAS). Thank G_d the company would be paying the $8,000 per month rent required to fund all this "luxury."

Now we just had to wait for the Firm to handle the negotiation details. It already seemed an adventure: how odd that we had to wait six to eight weeks to find out whether our contract would fly. How hard could it be to barter for a house and hammer out the details?

Real Estate Fun & Games

During the housing search, we learned some fascinating unpleasantries. For starters, even desirable properties in swanky neighborhoods had mold, plumbing, electrical, paint, and other construction issues to plague potential renters. Before having the dubious pleasure of renting one of these abodes, renters had to endure the "who will pay most" game. In this sport, landlords hung onto a bid for a while to see if they could find another renter (or company) who would pay more. The lucky souls whose contracts actually went through and who finally moved into their desired villas often found themselves facing unexpected surprises. There were two main reasons for this situation: low or non-existent industry standards and, of course, corruption. Often, construction projects were run by people put in charge because of their *guanxi* (relationships and the resulting social status), not because they had project management or engineering skills. Even projects run by competent developers or contractors remained questionable, as they stood to make significant amounts of extra money by using inferior or even illegal materials. Since it was well known that most expats stayed only two to five years, and there was so much money to be made from construction and rentals, the government, the construction industry, and the landlords remained indifferent to housing problems.

A few of my friends lived in Pudong's Jin Qiao area in a beautiful, Spanish-style compound, which looked like a picture-perfect California neighborhood from the outside. Inside the homes, however, things were far from ideal. The compound remained notorious for its plumbing issues. One night an acquaintance named Monica decided to try out her Jacuzzi bathtub. She ran the water, added fragrant bath salt, grabbed her book and her glass of wine, and waited eagerly to step in for some R & R. Suddenly she saw her husband running toward her. "Turn the water off!" He shouted. "Turn it off NOW!" The pipes were leaking through the ceiling, all over their home office where the husband had been working below. By the time Monica had turned off the tap, her husband's laptop lay ruined, water pooling in sad puddles all over the desk and the floor, and the ceiling drywall falling down in sorry chunks. In addition to the physical mess, they fought their landlord for months to cover the costs of that disaster. Other foreigners had tried to take their landlords to court for such incidents, but mostly without luck. When this couple's multi-national corporation got involved, the landlord finally gave in and paid half. *Half!*

Another woman I knew in that compound woke up one night to a hissing sound. She followed her ears to the dreaded basement. Hardly daring to look, she discovered water spraying wildly out of some pipes. "I woke up my husband out of a dead sleep without even feeling guilty, because you just had to see it to believe it," she told me. Apparently so.

Other compounds had electrical issues. My own brush with electrical mishaps happened one day when I walked into my home office and turned on the light switch. I heard a pop. Sparks shot out of the plate! Then, I smelled smoke. In a panic, I phoned the management office, shouting "fire!" The young lady answering the video phone looked confused. "Fire," I shouted again. "Send help."

"OK," she nodded and hung up. I waited. About ten minutes later, a maintenance worker rolled up on his decrepit bicycle and detached a rusty ladder from it. I could hardly believe my eyes! What if the house had been engulfed in flames? Hadn't I said "fire" clearly enough? I led the man upstairs to my office, where he looked at the now silent but smoky-smelling switch. His face showed no expression. "OK," he muttered, peddling away toward The Pearl office. I had twelve heart attacks wondering what the maintenance worker planned to do. Would he tell the management company to replace the switch? Had he gone to get fire prevention of some sort? Would he simply do nothing? Place your bets! My major immediate concern was whether the house might slowly, stealthily burn down from inside the walls while we slept. So, I called a friend's husband, an electrical products company executive. He explained to me that since most of the contractors in China use sub-par materials, these shorts happened all the time. The good news was that the house was not about to smolder to a crisp or suddenly blow up like a roman candle. I just needed the faulty switch replaced.

I encountered two other electrical issues at my house. Heated floors had grown very popular in Shanghai as newly well-off homeowners tried to save money on heat by using these upscale items in the winter. Whatever the case, our heated floors had shocked the previous inhabitants enough times that they had insisted maintenance disconnect this feature. So, no cozy warm bathroom floor for us in our "luxury" villa. I doubted this missing item generated a rent discount.

My other story involves the Jacuzzi tub in our master bathroom. One night I filled the tub, anxious to get in and relax. When I switched on the jets, nothing happened. (I guess in hindsight I should have been glad I didn't get electrocuted!) The next day I called the management office about the issue. They sent over a repair man. He fussed over the jets for about an hour, and then told me the tub was fixed. A few nights later, I fired up the tub. Again, no jet action. The next morning when I told the management office, they told me I'd have to wait a week until the "senior" repair man could look at it.

When the senior repair man came out, he spent about an hour fiddling around the tub area with his various tools. "It's fixed, Madame," he announced, and off he went. Repairs round two, but still no jacuzzi action.

Over the next year, I requested repairs for this appliance a total of five times (I kept going partly just to see what would happen) before I gave up. When I mentioned the situation to a friend, she explained that apparently status items like Jacuzzi baths were sometimes installed in the villas just to give the homeowner "face" (prestige). The other lesson in this story is that yet again, someone without any knowledge or training got a job because he was owed a favor.

After surviving all this K-Mart quality at Ritz prices, Shanghai expat renters sometimes endured one last surprise when ending their contracts: the repatriating game. Chinese landlords earned an unsavory reputation for developing sleazy money-grab schemes for completed contracts. In a classic example, my neighbors were loading the children into their ubiquitous GM minivan, preparing to drive to Pudong Airport to repatriate back to the US, when their landlord roared up in his imposing Mercedes 550, parked in front of the van, and jumped out raving like someone had just killed his mother. He vociferously insisted they broke furniture, damaged the walls, and stole a table. Surprise,

surprise, all these offenses added up to an amount equal to their deposit plus an additional 1,500RMB (about $220 at the time). Of course, my neighbors had committed none of these crimes. The landlord obviously hoped to scare them, capitalizing on the fact that they were unlikely to risk missing their flight just to argue with him. Luckily, they still had 1500RMB in their pockets. As predicted, the landlord won and the shell-shocked family made their flight. So, when Mr. Zhou rolled the Chrysler through The Pearl's gates in August of 2005, I literally had no idea how fortunate we'd been to get the house we wanted and to face only minor construction issues.

110 The Pearl

As the Shanghai-Ho-Silver rolled up to The Pearl's gate house, a Chinese guard in a crisp blue uniform and a Marine-style hat stepped out of his hut, addressing Mr. Zhou in Shanghainese. After a few minutes of interrogation that sounded like two angry dogs barking at each other, the guard finally agreed that this driver and this car belonged to house 110. A white-gloved hand reached out holding a placard for Mr. Zhou to put on the front dashboard of the car, designating our vehicle as part of the community. Then the guard primly saluted us, and we wound through the compound, slowing making our way to our house. The whole scene seemed quite impressive, a much bigger deal than gated communities in the US!

As we drove, I noticed the red brick houses crisply lined up in precision order, all exactly alike. Did the concept of all houses looking the same—except for the three variations in size—stem from communist sensibilities or a lack of builder imagination? What a contrast to the variety of sizes and styles in Shaker Heights. The smaller houses provided about 2,900 square feet, and the largest ones, about 5,000 square feet. The rents at this time ranged from about $6,000 US a month for the smallest houses, to about $8,000 a month for the mid-sized homes like ours, to a whopping $12,500 US a month for the big villas with private swimming pools. As these were not quite the posh, high-quality villas lining desirable avenues in the heart of New York City, London, or Paris, I found the prices absurd. When I questioned Planet, he replied, "This really isn't 'expat gouging,' simply a matter of supply and demand."

I looked at him quizzically.

"How many expat wives would want to come live in China if the houses didn't look reasonably similar to those at home? They're not going to live in Chinese apartments or villas, no matter how upscale by Chinese standards." Well, he was right about that, but I still thought the situation crazy.

Grace, our landlady, met us at the door, and we stood face-to-face with Shanghai's new real estate elite. She was pulling in enough rent from this house—which until now she'd been living in—to purchase two other homes across the street. Now, she could afford to move to Hong Kong and rent out this house.

When we got out of the car, a wall of thick air and its aroma confronted me. The air was old, musty, damp, earthy, like the dewdrops and mist of 1,000 centuries. I could smell the heat of the day, plus an unidentifiable odor. When I entered the house, I noticed damp overtones of mold and old cooking oil. The foyer floor was laid in a caramel and pearl marble. An impressive curved marble staircase, adorned on one side by a filigreed wrought iron rail, graced the right side of the foyer. To the left lay the living room/dining room. The dark wood flooring looked like it came from a Walmart fire sale and might warp with the next rain. To keep up with Western-style luxury, a fireplace with a white marble mantel stood at the far wall. A cheerful, bright bay window made up the back wall. The furniture consisted of two 1980s-style flowered couches, three comfortable arm chairs, and a coffee table. I noticed inexpensive-looking texturized gold wallpaper in the room. How much mold had accumulated behind that paper? I couldn't allow myself to think about it. In the dining room a traditional Western-styled brown wood table with six matching chairs stood atop a traditional Chinese wool rug. From Aaron Rents? At the far end of the foyer I entered the kitchen dinette, where a glass-topped wrought iron table adorned the smoky salmon-colored tile. Imitation Mexican tile? For show? In the attached family room, the worn, Saturn-red couch cushions felt and smelled like they had been filled with sawdust. I started to get excited when I saw a fireplace on the far side of the room, until I realized it was fake—another just-for-show luxury item. Though small and cheap by American luxury standards, the kitchen was surely posh by Chinese standards. As I examined the K-Mart-quality cabinetry, my spouse's words about The Pearl's housing quality—better than any of the other compounds— rang in my head. During our tenure in Shanghai, the cabinet doors constantly fell off.

In imitation of American luxury, the kitchen lay outfitted with a tile backsplash and some type of faux-granite countertops. A small oven dominated the far end of the room. I quickly discovered it was too small for most of my cookie sheets, and with only one shelf, it took twice as long to get any baking done. That was, if I got lucky in reading the temperature, which was labeled in Celsius with the numbers mostly rubbed off. On the kitchen dining area wall, I noticed a video-intercom and another on the wall outside the master bedroom. All we had to do was pick up the receiver to interact with the management office or to talk to people at the front door. The only question was, could they see me, too? What if the intercom rang and I was in my pajamas! I never did find out whether the staff could see us, but I felt safer assuming they could.

On the side of the house opposite the living room and dining room, I found the main floor powder room. Just beyond it lay the laundry room/mud room. As I wandered, I discovered a separate bathroom and a tiny bedroom for the ayi. Though the ayi room was about the size of an average-American walk-in closet, it housed a single bed, a chair and desk, and a shelf over the bed. I continued my tour, making my way to the second-floor landing, which was basically a small room. While some people used this area in their homes for an office and others for a second TV room, we remained the only expat family to turn ours into a gym. Yes, at Planet's insistence, we shipped our treadmill and elliptical trainer along to China! The room had a sliding glass door, which thankfully let in lots of light. The wood floor presented cause for concern, however. Constructed of cheap laminate, it had started to warp from the damp air.

Flanking the sides of the foyer/gym, I found three ample bedrooms, a massive master suite, and an office. The master suite contained a dressing room area complete with built in drawers under the window and a walk-in California-style closet opposite that. From there, the room gave way to the gratuitously-wasted space of the master bath. Oddly, the room featured attractive caramel and pearl marble on the floor and the walls, but then the builder had installed cheap, smelly dark-brown cabinets and inharmonious grey marble counter tops. Builders' special leftovers? Or actual modern Chinese style? A

Jacuzzi bathtub, his and hers sinks, a toilet, a fancy French bidet, and a grey marble shower completed the bathroom. What a hodge podge.

Overall, the house seemed reasonable. We had plenty of space. But would it ever feel like home, filled with someone else's discount décor? The marble staircase worried me. It looked great, but what if someone slipped? I had visions of Anders going downstairs to get a drink of water in the middle of the night and suffering a terrible crash. Speaking of which, how would we get to a hospital in the middle of the night? Was it within boundaries to call Mr. Zhou for a midnight emergency? So much to think about!

Outside, we found the yard more than adequate. As an unexpected bonus, our landlord announced that she loved her garden so much she planned to pay out of her own pocket to have landscapers come twice weekly to care for it. While we lived in that house, however, I noticed that the landscaping was a strange process. The grass stayed reasonably green, but didn't grow despite the fact that it was never mowed. Not once in 2½ years. In fact, when the landscapers came, they showed up without any tools at all. One day, as I peered out the window, I saw two men and a woman—dressed in the traditional sky-blue pajama pants and tops and large bamboo-wok hats on their heads of Chinese garden workers—down on their hands and knees in various parts of the yard. Shockingly, they spent about an hour and a half just randomly pulling out fists full of grass. Twice a week, every week. You had to see it to believe it.

Our garden tour completed, we walked back toward the house's front door. My eye fell on the mailbox. I couldn't resist taking a look. Inside the box, we already had mail. Hey, Sunday mail delivery! I picked up the single sheet of white paper addressed to the "new resident."

The notice read as follows:

REGISTER WITH THE LOCAL POLICE WITHIN 24 HOURS OF ARRIVAL
All foreigners (tourists, visitors, and long-term residents), including returning Chinese holding foreign passports, must register their place of residence with the local Public Security Bureau within 24 hours of arrival. If you are in a hotel, registration is usually done as part of the check-in process. Those staying with family or friends in a private home must also observe this requirement. Failure to do so can result in fines and/or detention. Please consult with your nearest police office for more details.

"Wow!" I said, handing the paper to Planet.

"Oh, yeah. The office told me we'd have to register with the local police. My assistant will get that done next week." Planet seemed completely unfazed. Maybe he thought this registration would actually protect us if something happened. Maybe it would. But it would also make it easier to keep tabs on us. Welcome to Communism.

While processing the details of our new Chinese house, my mind reeled back to our wonderful old house in Shaker Heights. In sharp contrast to The Pearl's abodes, Shaker's architectural gems had been built to last and filled with all the charm that rendered them classic. Our bright, sunny home comprised about 6,600 square feet on four levels. The first floor had a cavernous living room/dining room embellished with charming moldings. The ample kitchen, floored with authentic, expensive Mexican tile, opened into the family room, which featured floor-to-ceiling windows along the back wall. The cozy library had wood-paneled walls and a fireplace. A back staircase led from the kitchen to a large guestroom with its own bathroom that lay above the three-car attached garage. Pre-World War II, the room had housed a live-in couple who made up part of the home's staff. A few steps up from the guestroom stood the main staircase leading to the other three bedrooms. The generous master bedroom had a working fireplace, perfect for curling up in bed with a book and a glass of wine on snowy winter nights. My Shaker master suite also included a sizable sitting room. The main closet itself was large enough to be a glam bathroom, stocked with well-designed shelves and drawers. Of course, the master suite included its own bathroom. The third floor's completely finished rooms and full bath—designed to house a trio of maids—I turned into a wonderful play zone for my children. In the basement, we used the large main room as a gym. Several smaller rooms served as a laundry room, a wine cellar, a ping-pong table and play area, and an ample storage space.

So far, the only real advantage I could find to living at 110 The Pearl was the ayi. Would this exorbitantly expensive Walmart-quality marble palace ever feel like home, or would I always feel like a hotel guest?

It's a Beautiful Day in My New Neighborhood

After seeing the house, Planet walked us over to see the compound's clubhouse, the basketball/roller hockey court, and the pool. On the way to the clubhouse, we passed The Pearl office, where we would pay our utilities bills. Apparently, I had dodged a bullet here as well. Over time, I heard horror stories of expats standing in line for hours to pay utility bills or make withdrawals at the bank. Thankfully, I had only to drop off the bills and the payment here, where the agents could even give me a receipt.

As we left the management office, we noticed a roller hockey and basketball court. Anders had always wanted to play hockey, so we promised to find out how he could sign up. When we reached the clubhouse, I saw a customer service desk, an ATM—another worry off my mind, a small gym, some classrooms, and a playroom. I also noticed a small library with a piano, meeting rooms, and a restaurant. Finally, we reached the far end of the complex, which housed the indoor pool. The pool was much larger than I expected, and the complex even offered locker rooms and a towel desk. I felt relieved to have places to entertain the kids and have dinner onsite.

Having the clubhouse would have been enough, but across the road the compound had built a recreation center. This building housed a large indoor gym, spacious party rooms, and a huge patio surrounding a small but charming outdoor pool. A miniature waterfall splashed down the substantial rock formation emerging from one end of the water. As we would discover, the recreation building remained constantly abuzz with local weddings and expat community events and parties.

I guess hosting a wedding at The Pearl held great prestige for the locals, because at least two blazed through every weekend. I found it surprising we were always allowed to use the pool regardless of the fact that there was a formal occasion happening right next to us. Who wanted half naked, soaking wet foreigners in their wedding photos and videos? Well, neighbors explained to me that some Chinese really liked having "Western friends" inadvertently attending their special day. They said it was good luck and that we added character and face to the event.

Some people actually even took photos of their family and friends purposely including us waving in the background from the water. Go figure! Eventually, it just grew very annoying to try to relax in the pool on weekends with a boisterous Chinese wedding taking place right next to me. Sometimes the MCs and the music were so loud, and the guests' gawking so awkward, that I just went home. Soon, I felt glad that I didn't live close by. A neighbor who lived near the pool told me that she had issues with party guests who wandered off to investigate the "lifestyle" in this wealthy community. Multiple times she found wedding attendees *inside her garage* (unfortunately, accidentally left open) scrutinizing her possessions!

Next to the school, the compound had its own small convenience store. Whoever was in charge of purchasing for the little shop did a very good job, as the store managed to sell almost everything I'd want in my kitchen within its tiny confines. Thank goodness for this 7-Eleven plus!

We had one last task in our tour of The Pearl today: we needed to stop by the management office and get our first *ming pian* (personal cards) made. The business-style cards had the compound name at the top, then our family name, our address, and our phone number. On the back, they conveniently and helpfully printed both The Pearl's name and a miniature map in Mandarin. This was sometimes a life saver in case you had to take a cab or show someone else's driver how to get you home. These very useful cards were exchanged by everyone everywhere in China.

Compound Life

The Pearl, like most other compounds in Shanghai, arranged activities to keep its denizens happy. The management held farmers markets, holiday bazaars, kids' parties, family parties, and whatever other events they thought would keep us paying the insane rent. Even the residents themselves sometimes held get togethers. Regardless of the reasons, having a convenient way to meet people and to socialize definitely made living 7,000 miles away from home easier.

One of the best things about living at The Pearl was the weekly Thursday Market. I so enjoyed being able to bike to the clubhouse for a farmers' market experience. Of course, the standard fruit and vegetable ladies showed up, but the Frenchman with the most wonderful fresh yogurt caught my attention. His product tasted nothing like the cultures found in Western grocery stores. He churned out his product in the wee hours of the morning and poured it immediately into small glass jars. He even offered home delivery. This stuff, we soon discovered, served as the magic elixir that cured "Shanghai Stomach" (the bouts of diarrhea or upset stomach that plagued newcomers). An Italian vendor sold wonderful red and green pesto, sauces, bread, and pasta. A variety of other vendors sold small household items like candles, silk boxes, oils oil burners, and such. It was all good, but the aspect I loved best was the variety of beautiful, inexpensive flowers. I could fill four large vases and several small ones for around $15-20. Spreading around fresh flowers brought cheerfulness to my borrowed house and in my mind counteracted the polluted air.

In addition to the farmers' market, The Pearl management held several shopping bazaars throughout the year. During these fairs, about thirty vendors would set up their tables in the banquet hall. A popular Chinese silk guy always came, numerous jewelry vendors, a German botanical body products shop, the basket man, a grandma selling knits, two Pearl neighbors who made greeting cards, and an ever-changing variety of other artsy-craftsy shopkeepers. I appreciated these events because they required no sitting in traffic, no searching out various items, and no wasting time haggling with Chinese vendors.

THE HELP

Household helpers served as an indispensable part of any Shanghai expat home. Because they were so affordable and covered basically all the tasks that usually make up a housewife's life, most Tai Tai's enjoyed Shanghai life almost stress free. Almost. When I arrived, I found myself amazed to have a full-time housekeeper and a driver, leaving my entire day (and night) free to do as I pleased. But nothing wonderful is ever easy, and, as with so many other aspects of China-expat life, Planet and I were on a learning curve about dealing with the help.

Driving Mrs. Expat

Having learned the hard way that multi-national companies did not come out ahead in traffic accident situations, most firms no longer allowed their China-based employees to drive. Thus, though the transportation packages differed, nearly everyone I knew had a driver. Some firms provided company cars and drivers, some provided compensation equivalent to what the employee would have paid at home for a car, and others left employees to fend for themselves. Planet and I had to lease a car and driver on our own. We found it expensive, but much more convenient and much safer than using cabs.

Having to depend on someone else's driving—and in this case a Chinese man's—made me incredibly anxious. When Planet was in the process of hiring a chauffeur, I gave him very strict instructions that I wanted a slow, careful driver. Quite honestly, I wanted a chauffeur who would drive like an old lady, as having a car accident ranked number one on my list of experiences to avoid in China. Planet assured me he had made this clear to the translator, who had in turn impressed my wishes on the candidates. As a result, Planet had chosen Mr. Zhou as our driver.

He, like many private chauffeurs, had worked his way up from driving a taxi. From what he told me, cab driving in China was its own unique brand of hell. The cabbies worked ridiculous hours for terribly low pay, their lives frighteningly similar to the rickshaw runners of old. Comparatively, his new job as expat driver—with a fancy car, great pay, and a free phone—must have seemed like Heaven on Earth. It's socially acceptable to ask people their salaries in China, and Mr. Zhou proudly told us his take-home pay was 1500RMB per month—about fifty-percent more than the average person's salary at the time. In addition, I noticed he made about seventy-five percent of an ayi's salary, yet his job seemed to involve about twenty-five percent of the work. Zhou merely had to maneuver the prestigious Chrysler all day, and when he had down time—which was most of the day—he could stand around smoking and chatting with his driver friends, drinking tea, or reading the newspaper while he waited for me or Planet. We found it a little hard to figure out reasonable working hours, since in effect, Zhou was on duty 24/7. When we asked him about this, his polite, proud, enthusiastic, and very Chinese answer was, "Mr. Zhou is *every* time service to you!" When I asked around, I found out that most people gave their drivers time off only one Sunday a month. Ditto for their ayi. *Wow! Turn the clocks back to "Downton Abbey!"* This seemed a bit extreme, so Planet and I agreed to give Mr. Zhou all Sundays off, with the understanding that if something came up for us, we'd give him advance notice, and he'd drive us.

I heard through the grapevine that Tai Tais often had trouble with their drivers in the beginning, as apparently Chinese men did NOT like women giving them orders. In fact, I had some issues with Mr. Zhou during our first month in China. If he didn't want to run an errand for me, he'd say, "Ohhh… Tai Tai, is ah-nooo parking there!" Or he'd tell me "Ohh! No, no, no! *Tài guì le!"*—the parking was too expensive (meaning more than $1!). In general, he gave off some attitude about driving me around. I finally told Planet to have someone from his office call and translate. His job was to drive BOTH me and Planet. This wasn't a household where the husband got dropped off at work and then the driver had all day to do as he pleased until evening pick up. Basically, Mr. Zhou would be driving *me* around ninety-nine percent of the time. If he didn't like it, he should move on. Zhou wasn't happy, but he understood, and we made our peace.

Over time, I learned some reasons why Zhou may not have been completely happy driving the Tai Tai around all day. The Chinese have an old saying: if you don't know at least two ways to make money, you're stupid. Some drivers translated this adage into respectable businesses. Being an expat chauffeur paid well, so a frugal man could save up to open a restaurant or start his own chauffeur service. Other side jobs were less ethical. One acquaintance told me that she was having trouble getting her driver to take her places after he dropped her husband off at work, and when he did agree to drive her, he was always late. Somehow, they figured out that the man was picking up cab fares whenever he wasn't with them! Another woman kept finding used condoms in her minivan. When she hired someone to spy on her driver, she learned he was running a brothel out of her car!

Fortunately, I had no issues with Zhou's driving. In fact, I came to respect his skills in dealing with Shanghai traffic. Considering how orderly and rule-bound Chinese life is generally—Confucian principles and all that—the chaos of the roadways came as a surprise. Out in the wilds of Pudong, traffic seemed less a problem than the driving. Each person—and ninety-nine percent of the time it was a man—drove like he was at a high-performance track and had to prove his skill and power to other drivers. Suddenly two cars shared a lane, jockeying for position, neither one willing to give up any turf. Minivans changed lanes without signaling—sometimes darting across several at a time! Sedans cut each other off as closely as a Gillette razor shave. How was it possible there wasn't a wreck a minute on these roadways? A rhythm and a method of predicting driver behavior seemed to exist, understood only by the Shanghainese. I suddenly had a whole new level of respect for Zhou's job and realized that I had *no* desire to brave this insanity. Within a week of our move to the Middle

Kingdom, I had officially gotten over not driving. My anxiety remained at a reasonable level if I didn't look out the window at the craziness, and I resolved to maintain my sanity by reading, taking notes, or making phone calls. I found the extra productivity a bonus.

Another aspect of having a driver I grew to appreciate immediately was not having to worry about parking. What a stress buster to simply be dropped off in front of a building and then picked up again at the door, whenever I was ready. No hunting down a parking space, braving weather, and walking in traffic to my destination. Mr. Zhou paid all our parking expenses up front, kept all the receipts, and gave us a bill at the end of each month. I found it charmingly Chinese that Mr. Zhou took offense when parking required an "outrageous" 10RMB per hour (about $1.25). Zhou made it a badge of honor to find the cheapest parking spaces, and we appreciated his mentality and his efforts.

As with ayis, a driver's job had certain boundaries and responsibilities. Zhou kept the car's exterior spotless at all times. He even kept a special brush in the trunk, and often when we came out to the car, he was giving the Chrysler the once over. I quickly started to appreciate never having to worry about running low on gas, finding a filling station, or pumping gas. I also liked not having to worry about taking it in for service.

A driver also had some duties I wouldn't have guessed. It was Zhou's job to push the grocery cart if I went to the supermarket. Very quickly, we dispensed with that formality, however. Yet other responsibilities, he insisted on keeping. Every time I reached the supermarket checkout lane, he magically appeared to maneuver the cart to the car, unlock the door for me, and unload the contents into the trunk. He also refused to allow me to help unload. "No, no, no!" Zhou protested, striking the strong-man bicep pose. I could hardly keep from laughing aloud: Zhou's arms and legs resembled Rubber Man's and he smoked about two packs of cigarettes a day. At seven years old, Anders probably had bigger biceps! Back at The Pearl, Mr. Zhou also refused my help unloading the car. Yet, he held no qualms about bellowing into the house for ayi to come out and help, as there were certain things he considered *her* job. He also tried, unsuccessfully, to get ayi to clean up the inside of the car. She, however, clearly considered anything to do with the car *his* job. Because of this tug-of-war, during Xiao Ting's tenure the inside of our car remained a mess.

One of Mr. Zhou's other duties was to run certain errands. So, soon after we arrived in Shanghai, we sent him to the fish market to pick up some halibut for dinner. I loved not having to spend all morning schlepping into Puxi, trying to navigate through a foul-smelling market, figuring out which fish was which, and trying to negotiate a non-rip-off-the-Westerner price. Being able to send Zhou to pick up clothes at the tailor also saved me a lot of time and aggravation.

The Vacuum

During our first few months in Shanghai, Mr. Zhou got the chance to play hero. My vacuum cleaner broke, though it was nearly new. I asked him what to do. My driver explained to me that I needed to have the receipt in order to get the machine repaired. *Oh, no! I had zillions of receipts sitting in a stack, all in Mandarin characters that I had no hope of deciphering!* I asked him to come into the house and help me sort through them. Fortunately, the numbers were written in English as well as Chinese, so at least I had that to go by. When we finished, Zhou pronounced those dreaded words, "*mei you le*" (don't have it).

Crap! Now what?

Suddenly, my driver's face brightened. "IIII know, I know, I know!" his voice rang out gleefully. He did his best to explain that his wife worked at a local department store where they sold that model vacuum. He had an idea. He skipped out the door toward the car, useless floor cleaner in hand, saying he'd be back soon.

Zhou met up with his wife at the store, where they enacted their plan. They switched out my broken vacuum with the floor display! The store wouldn't know it wasn't theirs, repair it for free, and then put it back on the floor as a model. No one would be the wiser. Zhou's face could have lit up all of Antarctica during a January midnight when he returned, functional floor sample vacuum in hand. Chinese ethics never ceased to amaze me.

I didn't know whether I was supposed to reward him or consider this guanxi. So, I paid Zhou 100RMB (about $12) for his trouble. He left the house whistling.

A Rented Wife

When we first arrived in Shanghai, we weren't comfortable having a live-in Chinese helper, so Planet and I agreed to hire an ayi who spoke English, would live out, and work five and a half days a week for us. In these days, employers had to pay a higher rate for household helpers who lived out, since the worker then had to pay for her own food and housing. Fair enough. While Planet was in Shanghai on business prior to the move, he learned from people in his office that the best way to find a hard-working, trustworthy (relatively speaking) ayi was to snap one up from someone who was leaving. Since we didn't know anyone yet, his co-workers advised him to ask in The Pearl's management office. I thought this sounded like a great idea.

Planet sent me word: yes, they had a woman—Xiao Ting—whose current family was repatriating. The ayi had spent several years working for an American couple, so presumably they had trained her to Western tastes. This also meant she wanted 2200RMB per month (about $275). Princely, I thought, considering the average Chinese person's salary at the time was about 1000RMB a month and she was only working forty-four hours a week. Planet, however, liked what he heard and wanted this task off his list, so he didn't even negotiate. When my family finally met Xiao Ting, I found it ironic how her name sounded like "shouting" in English. I soon realized how perfectly her name suited her sour disposition.

In the beginning, I felt relieved to have a domestic helper. My house remained spotless any time she was on duty. My laundry was not only clean on a daily basis, but ironed and put away. Let me tell you, ironed underwear feels great! My dinner arrived hot on the table promptly at 6:00 pm, and all the dishes were washed and put away before she left for the day. *Wonderful!* I could send my ayi to buy food at Chinese markets and on errands. She would pack our clothing for vacations, then unpack and launder everything when we returned. She served as a built-in babysitter at any/all times. When Xiao Ting babysat for us after hours, she charged us time and a half—a whopping 15RMB per hour (about the equivalent of about $1.95). Whoopee! No hunting down a local teen, begging, and paying $10 an hour plus proving snacks and drinks!

Before long, I noticed that trying to get Xiao Ting to cook proved difficult. We often asked her to make Chinese food. Crankily she explained that Chinese cooking took time. We had to tell her early in the morning if we wanted Chinese for dinner and leave her money for the market. I was happy to provide money for her to shop at local markets any time, though I quickly learned what that meant. She would get a better price from the vendors than I would as a white foreigner, but she would pocket some of the savings for herself. Apparently, this behavior was apropos Chinese ethics in the ayi world.

To her credit, Xiao Ting asked me to teach her to cook the Western dishes that we liked. Though she agreed to write down the steps and ingredients, she didn't. She just stood there watching me cook, wearing a pained expression, pretending her English wasn't good enough and the steps were too challenging. She grew surly when asked to make dinner on a daily basis. After weeks of showing her repeatedly how to make the same dishes, she still insisted she wasn't ready to make them on her own. She watched me make myself a vegetable salad nearly every day for lunch, yet she still would never make me my lunch. *Really?*

Eventually, I found out why she behaved this way. Ayi finally got up the nerve to tell me directly that her previous employers had hired a cook, and I should do the same. *What!* At the salary I was paying, she was lucky I didn't have her doing the gardening and ten other things as well! "No. Sorry, Xiao Ting. That's not in our budget," I told her, even though I knew that she, like every Chinese employee, thought their employer had a bottomless well of RMB stashed somewhere in the back yard.

Possibly one reason why Xiao Ting remained sour about cooking "American" had to do with the grill. I thought this was certainly easier than stir frying, but Xiao Ting wasn't crazy about it. She believed she had to give the grill a thorough cleaning every time she used it—nearly daily. I ignored her snarling.

One Sunday—ayi's day off—I decided to make us some burgers for lunch. Xiao Ting had scrubbed down the grill meticulously after dinner last night, so I was surprised when…booosh! A big orange flame shot up from the piece of meat I'd just laid onto the steel. This seemed odd. Maybe the fancy imported Australian beef was especially juicy? Hmm. I carefully laid another burger onto the grates. Boosshhh! Same thing for the next two pieces of meat. Well, this incident certainly gave a whole new meaning to the term "flame grilled"!

"Holy Cow," I shouted to Planet, who was busy playing with his Blackberry at the kitchen table. "I just about got crispy-crittered putting the meat on! What's wrong with the grill?"

"I don't know," Planet replied distractedly. "Call the grill man, and have him come out and check it."

Fortunately, I finished grilling our lunch without any more potentially life-threatening moments, and on Monday, I rang the grill man. The good news was that Xiao Ting got to stay home and play the appliance-repair-service waiting game, while I went out. Later, I called the repair service to discuss the technician's findings. He said he'd checked the gas line, the ignitor, etc. He couldn't get the machine to flare up. So, he concluded there was nothing wrong with our grill. I felt tempted to do an angry bear dance around the living room. Did this guy actually know how to repair the grill? Or what it another case of the jacuzzi repair men? In China, you never knew. Well, at least it was Xiao Ting's turn to risk blowing up next.

The following weekend, I attempted to grill chicken for dinner. As soon as the chicken hit the grill rack, boossshh! This time I nearly singed my eyebrows and torched my hair! Xiao Ting had given the grill a thorough cleaning after its last use, so what in the world was wrong with this thing? Suddenly, I realized the common denominator. Cleaning! The next time Xiao Ting came to work, I asked her to show me how she scrubbed the grill. Sure enough, she was putting some type of industrial heaven-knew-what on the racks.

"Xiao Ting, *bu hao*," (no good) I said waving the combustible liquid. "Only soap and water, please!"

She looked skeptical, but complied. It worked. The next time I attempted to grill, I no longer had to dodge balls of fire. Xiao Ting didn't seem any happier about grilling, but she wasn't complaining any more than usual, either.

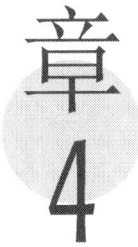

GETTING UP & RUNNING

In our first weeks of Shanghai life, we had much to accomplish to get our lives up and running. Basically, everything! For starters, we had to get a government physical, we needed bikes, I had to learn how to grocery shop, and we wanted to explore some local restaurants and spas.

One of our first tasks was to complete the required Chinese government physical. All foreign residents had to comply within a week a week of arrival. Apparently, they took both the physical and the deadline very seriously, so Planet and I made this a priority. I found it baffling that incoming Americans had to leap this hurdle. Really? We have the world's best medical care and are probably the most vaccinated people in the Western world! Saudi princes arrived in their elegant private jets to receive heart care at the legendary Cleveland Clinic, for goodness sake. It also seemed bizarre that only adults had to pass the physical. Kids—veritable walking petri dishes—didn't!

As Planet and I signed in and took our seats in the waiting room, we had no clue what our physical might involve. I wondered how often the government sent people packing if the physical revealed they had certain diseases. Were you allowed in if you had VD, but received a penicillin shot? While I mused, a nurse called my name. For the next forty-five minutes, the staff efficiently hustled me from station to station. First stop, the blood draw. From there, an assistant led me to the EKG room. Then, bizarrely, came an ultrasound of my abdomen. Was this in case I had hidden gems or bags of opium in there? If they found a hernia, what would happen? Next, a tech motioned me over for a chest x-ray. Well, that at least seemed sensible. Who wants someone bringing TB into the country? If I turned up carrying pneumonia—or SARS (rampant at the time)—would they quarantine me or immediately escort me to the airport? Whatever the case, I thought the government would have been much better served by spending the day x-raying Chinese citizens' chests!

One day, about two weeks later, I went out to my mailbox to discover we had a lovely gift from our host country—copies of our health status reports. Though the reasons for the physical remained a mystery, thankfully, Planet and I now both had the government's official stamp of approval. Look out, Shanghai, we were licensed to stay!

Welcome to Spa Life

Since we already had ayi babysitting the kids, Planet rewarded us for enduring the physical with lunch and then a foot massage. He wanted to introduce me to a foot massage place that the Chinese people in his office had recommended called Taipan. Although not as posh as the major hotel spas, Taipan had mid-level *feng shui* ambiance. In the massage room, we were seated in large, comfy La-Z-Boy-style chairs with small tables in between. Menus stood on the tables encased in plexiglass. A hostess seated us and then told us to order whatever snacks and drinks we wanted, as everything was included in the massage price! I perused the drink menu. Watermelon juice, pear juice, tangerine slushy, iced coffee, chrysanthemum tea…endless interesting possibilities. The snacks included pork on a bun, toast, curried beef noodles, pork over rice, and other local favorites. I noticed the Asian version of Jell-0 (exotic-flavored gelatin set in a flower-shaped mold) and serradura (a Chinese version of tiramisu). I ordered an iced coffee, and then our massage got underway.

The treatment began by placing our feet in plastic tubs of hot tea strewn with red rose petals. While our feet soaked, the therapists kneaded our backs, necks, and arms. I loved that although we had signed up for a foot massage, we received almost a full body massage already anyway! Fortunately, the "footie" itself felt surprisingly relaxing, and ninety minutes absolutely flew by. When we emerged, sleepy and blissed out, I learned the crowning glory: this whole ninety-minute slice of Nirvana cost us only $138RMB each (at the time, about $15), and with Zhou driving, we could grab a nap on the drive home!

A Gym!

Planet and I had always been serious about fitness, so we made joining a gym in Shanghai a priority. One morning, we packed up the kids and had Zhou drive us to a place my husband had scouted in nearby Jin Qiao: MegaFit. Mega, it was! This had to be one of the biggest fitness centers I'd ever seen. The first floor housed the check-in desk, a sales office, a weight room, the pool, the locker rooms, and a spinning room. One the second floor we discovered the weights and cardio equipment room, the aerobic rooms, a café, and an attractive babysitting area. The babysitting area had a play structure with a ball pit (similar to a McDonald's Playland) a video/TV area, and—best of all—kid-sized fitness machines, just like mom's and dad's! On the third floor, we found offices, classrooms, and a spa. Then we took a look at the class schedule. All the popular types of classes seemed to be covered. Planet and I nodded to each other in agreement. We joined immediately, and I checked finding a decent gym off my list of things to worry about.

The first day I went to MegaFit on my own, Mr. Zhou taught me the Chinese name while we drove: *Mei Ga Fei*. Once there, I had a good workout, but it felt strange to not know anyone. When I finished, I hustled into the locker room. The attendants gave members exactly two towels: one hand-towel sized, and the other a Chinese-person-sized bath towel. The fabric felt incredibly thin, and the towels smelled a little moldy. Later someone told me that MegaFit didn't dry the towels completely because the managers believed that would make them last longer. Well, that explained the smell!

The shower proved an experience. The stalls reeked of mildew, so strongly that I had to hold my breath. Under the water, the temperature seemed comfortable until someone flushed the toilet! Zap! I nearly boiled for a few minutes! In my future experiences with the MegaFit showers, I noticed that one of the showers had overly hot water that didn't get cool, others had cooler water that never got very hot. Some of them had clogged nozzles, making the water dribble out in a thin line. Another Shanghai construction special!

I showered as quickly as possible. Then I stopped off at the toilet. Amazingly, though attendants cleaned the area regularly, it actually smelled *worse* after cleaning than before, like they had used old, dirty water to clean the floors. Then I went over to dry my hair. It took forever with the incredibly low-powered dryer in the damp air! My locker room experience left much to be desired, but at least I had a gym.

When I got into a routine, I worked out at MegaFit four or five days a week. Before long, I noticed that the classes never varied. The series of exercises and even the music for each class remained exactly the same for the entire time we lived in Shanghai. How different from the US, where instructors prided themselves on varying both the workouts and the music! Well, at least I'd found a way to stay fit and meet people.

The Waiguoren Bike Show

After joining a gym, my family's next mission was to buy bikes. Pearl bike club members recommended a visit to the Giant bike store in Jin Qiao. When the kids had chosen the bikes they liked, it was time for a test drive. Alexis rolled out the shop door onto the sidewalk on a cherry red one, followed by Anders on a shiny black one. A grandpa wearing boxer shorts, a wife-beater tank, white gym socks, and classic red plastic sandals stopped dead in his tracks. Within seconds, a few young men also gathered. I wondered why the kids were attracting attention, until I realized I'd never seen a Chinese child on a bike— only children riding on their parents' bikes.

Fortunately, my kids remained so absorbed in testing out their potential rides they didn't notice the slowly thickening crowd. My nerves, however, began a slow rattle. Facing the wall of Shanghai's heat and humidity, I had chosen to wear a skirt today. *Crap!* Well, I'd seen Chinese women in dresses and such on their bikes and scooters, so maybe I didn't look too weird. I took a deep breath and bravely wheeled out on a splashy purple and white model.

The locals chattered among themselves. What were they saying? I deeply wished I had learned to speak Mandarin before we arrived in China so I could understand. I felt sure the crowd knew much more about bike prices than we did. What if they were giving out pricing clues that would have helped us?

The kids tried a couple more bikes, until Alexis finally settled on a purple model and Anders found a red one that met his approval. I took the purple and white one, which seemed fine for getting the kids to the bus stop and picking up groceries at the compound store. Planet, however, wanted a high-tech, glamorous model for his Sunday morning bike club rides, which had to be special ordered. The gathering of locals watched in awe, still chattering as Mr. Zhou helped the shopkeeper's assistants load our new wheels into the rear of the Silver. I breathed a sigh of relief that our *waiguoren* (foreigners) show had ended.

Comfort Food?

After bike shopping, everyone had worked up an appetite. So, Planet instructed Mr. Zhou to drive us to the Jade Leisure Center. Jade Leisure Center housed about eight restaurants, each with a different type of food. Planet suggested the Blue Frog, which had American diner-style fare.

When we arrived at the restaurant, I noticed the modern, woody, California décor, and the sizable menu included about three-quarters Western style food and one-quarter Asian style food—a little something for everyone. I hoped the place would become our go-to when we needed a little American comfort food. Unfortunately, this was not the case. I found the food quality on par with a high school cafeteria, and the prices outrageous, considering.

Despite the over-priced, mediocre food, "The Frog" remained a popular place for Tai Tai volunteer committee meetings and other expat gatherings. Thankfully, the tuna melt, which appeared on the menu during the week, tasted decent and became my go-to order. Yet, bizarrely, this sandwich didn't appear on the weekend menu. Well, one Saturday after working out at MegaFit, I wanted my usual. When I asked the waiter for a tuna melt, however, a panic-stricken grimace of horror appeared on the man's face. The answer was no. *Huh?* This was one of the weird quirks about Shanghai dining: special orders *will* upset us. You couldn't add or subtract ingredients or make substitutions. If you didn't want tomato on your sandwich, you either didn't order that item or you received tomato and picked it off. What exactly made a tuna melt a "weekday" item? Who knew! But alas, there'd be no tuna melt on the weekend.

Grocery Shopping Learning Curve

Once we moved into our house, we needed to stock it with food. Of course, I could simply have sent Xiao Ting to the grocery store, but I wanted to know what kinds of foods were available and experience buying groceries in China. Imagine going to stock up your new house with everything from toilet paper to dish soap, but you don't know where anything is located in the store and all the labels are in Mandarin characters! I thought I solved the problem by taking Xiao Ting along to translate and show me which products to buy.

Mr. Zhou ferried us into Jin Qiao, and I hoped the enormous, two-level French hypermarket, Carrefour, would be the place to get everything I needed in one stop. The place seemed like an American warehouse store on steroids. Little restaurants and tiny storefronts made up the first floor. Random vendors had thrown up sets of shelves housing their wares. I needed nothing there, so I put my cart on the cart escalator and rode up to the second floor. There I waded my way through the electronics, the shoes, the clothes, the bed linens, until I finally reached the food. Already, I felt very distracted and nearly over-whelmed. I couldn't believe it took this much effort to reach the food. Clearly there was no such thing as quickly running in for one item!

Although I thought bringing ayi along was a genius plan, in actuality she couldn't have been less helpful. I couldn't tell the dish soap from the window cleaner from the shampoo, so what was up with Xiao Ting's reluctance to make suggestions? Did she really not understand that I needed every type of potion for her to clean the house? Was she afraid I'd fire her if I didn't like her suggestions? Was it the Confucian rank thing, where a subordinate can't tell a superior what to do? Argh!

As I stood wondering how to proceed, we came across a store "guide." Oh, happy day! Apparently, these attractive young ladies would translate and help English-speaking shoppers find products. Without this kind, cheerful young lady, it may have taken me all day to stock my kitchen. I hoped my ever-crabby ayi was taking notes! I left that day having only successfully purchased basic cleaning supplies and a few food items.

With my kitchen still sorely lacking, I planned my return to Carrefour. This time, I came alone, figuring I could get much more done without ayi sulking and Mr. Zhou trotting along behind us. When we arrived, I told Mr. Zhou he could just wait in the car for me. He looked concerned, but he stayed put. I had already learned that no self-respecting Tai Tai wanted to mark herself as a newbie by having her driver push the grocery cart. It was a mistake everyone made, but only once.

At last I was free to take my time and absorb. First, I made my way to the fruit. I saw nearly every kind imaginable from around the world, and the prices seemed very reasonable. As I cruised along, I noticed a huge wooden display housing about thirty kinds of fresh honey in big glass jars. I thought it would be fun to work my way through them all. Then I spied an entire row and a half devoted just to Chinese tea—the equivalent of the American cereal aisle. I had no idea which tea to buy, but I enjoyed guessing. Another aisle stood stocked with a huge variety of single serving fruit juices, including aloe and sugar cane. What health benefits did they possess? Endless streams of processed snack foods made up another aisle. Chip-type snacks and pretzel-type snacks came in the most interesting flavors—corn, shrimp, aloe, seaweed, and pork, for example. What I really needed, however, was protein. But what could I count on to be safe? Chicken might have Bird Flu. With beef, I risked Mad Cow. Who knew how much mercury (or whatever else) was in Shanghai's fish? That left pork, likely a good choice as it was a Shanghainese favorite. Plus, I hadn't heard of any pig diseases going around. But the Aschkenases weren't really pork fans. Planet and the kids weren't about to eat tofu or seitan. So, where did that leave me?

I sighed. I'd just have to cross my fingers and hope for the best. Fortunately, the signs describing the various meats and their cuts were in both English and Mandarin, as were the prices. I settled on the fancy imported Australian beef and chicken. The man at the meat counter looked very amused by what must have been my obvious confusion. He could probably tell by the look on my face that I was new. He spoke to me, but I have no idea what he said. Perhaps, "be a real woman and try the pork trotters!" Standing at the meat counter, I spied a meat-cutting room off to one side. Unlike in the US, whole sides of animals hung from hooks in the ceiling, pigs' ears, intestines…if you could imagine an animal part, it seemed to dangle there. Duly noted.

When I got to the bakery, it looked very similar to those in American supermarkets. Pastries, cakes, rolls, and many types of artisan breads lay attractively arranged. There was even something resembling pizza bread. I saw some rolls I thought the kids would like and picked up two of them.

"Ho jab jab ho, zzz na," a bakery clerk buzzed at me. My eyes widened. "Blabber blabber, jibber jabber," she insisted, holding up two more rolls.

I stared at her, totally confused, feeling like a stupid American.

"No, thanks," I said, shaking my head side to side. Then I smiled, waved cheerfully, and zipped off, with the woman still fussing at me. I thought I'd escaped, but at the checkout counter, the rolls remained an issue. I didn't understand what the clerk said, either, but finally she gave up and rang up the next food item. Later, when I told a friend this story, she explained that the rolls are *four* for 10RMB. In China, the rules are the rules. No wonder the bakery lady and the clerk freaked out: they didn't want me to leave paying full price for only half the goods!

Anders pretty much lived on cheese, so when I arrived at the dairy cooler. I felt pleased to have choices of a great variety of cheeses from around the world. I grabbed a French brie, some Kraft American Singles, Danish feta, and Australian Cheddar cheese. Glancing at the labels, these dairy treats were shockingly expensive. Cheese seemed to cost about fifty percent more than at home. Standing in the dairy aisle, it seemed odd that I couldn't find the milk. Well, milk isn't a staple in China. So, it came unrefrigerated, in pint-sized boxes, stored logically with the other boxed drinks, of course. The biggest selling brands here were Nestle and two from New Zealand. I saw one French brand and a ridiculously expensive organic European brand. I had no idea which to choose, so I grabbed one of each New Zealand product. We could taste test. Then I returned to the refrigerated area for butter. Oh, how swish! Products from France, Denmark, and even Kerry Gold. It seemed cool to have the world as my grocery provider.

Next, I sought out that crucial American staple, cereal. While the US has a reputation for offering a ridiculous variety of brands and flavors, here only a paltry quarter-aisle stood dedicated to the crunchy comfort food. I looked at the prices, shocked. Did I calculate the exchange rate correctly? The cereals cost a whopping 75RMB a box (about $10.75)! Between cereal and cheese, I could clearly picture my hardship allowance from the Firm literally and figuratively eaten up in a hurry.

I looked at my watch. Already I had spent about ninety minutes roaming and learning! Mr. Zhou probably thought me insane. Oh, wait—I was! A mild throb began beating at my temples. Clearly, I'd have to speed things up.

As I rounded the corner, trying to pick up my pace, I discovered a freezer holding a large selection of Nestle ice cream products. Next to that stood a freezer full of Asian- and European-brand ice cream bars. As I looked closer, some of these frozen treats came in surprising flavors like Japanese sweet potato, red bean paste, green tea, and avocado. Wow, we now lived in a part of the world where people viewed vegetables and plants as dessert!

The tiny but skilled warriors in my head were beating out a steady rhythm around the top of my throbbing head as I then cruised past a fresh fish display, a series of large tanks stood in my path. I knew Asian people liked their food very fresh, but it hadn't occurred to me that they bought their seafood live. In this miniature version of Sea World, all types of fish swam excitedly around in their aquariums—live frogs, turtles, eels, and even…snakes? Snakes!

What was the protocol? Did the shopper bring the fish or snake home live and kill it there, or did the grocery clerk do the honors? Oh, my aching head! Suddenly, it all seemed too much. I raced with my overloaded cart to the checkout. I could have whooped for joy and gratitude as Mr. Zhou magically appeared out of nowhere to help me unload. What a relief to have him push the cart to the car, pack the load, and drive through the crazy traffic home. I tipped my head into the headrest, closed my eyes, and imagined myself fading into a Provencal field of lavender. I hoped my next grocery run would be much less noteworthy!

The Ruijin Complex

Now that we had a built-in babysitter, Planet and I scheduled a date night. Shanghai had no shortage of interesting dining options. From fine dining establishments to Uighyur street food, if you could imagine a cuisine, you could find it in this city. As a foodie, I looked forward to sampling my way through this vast metropolis of culinary delights.

Planet suggested dinner at one of his favorite restaurants. Mr. Zhou picked us up, and we made our way to the former French Concession. There, the city stepped back in time as we rolled past interlocking tree canopies and charming old mansions on the peaceful, sophisticated streets. What a difference from the hustle-bustle of the city's other districts! As we pulled through the gates at the Ruijin Guest House Complex on Ruijin Lu, I immediately fell in love with the property. This old estate provided a welcome refuge from the forces of the city's millions and jungle of high rises. Though several homes remained on the site, it also had a charming boutique hotel, two restaurants, and the popular Face Bar. La Na Thai and Hazara Indian restaurants quickly became two of my favorite places.

The two restaurants resided in one of the old houses at the back of the property. Inside, the décor boldly mixed eastern and western elements, creating a unique charm. Proceeding into the Face Bar, which seemed really hip, a large wooden bar reigned over one end of the room, while several "Bali beds" (or opium beds) provided decadent nooks for imbibing. A hostess seated us on the patio, secluded by a tall green hedge and surrounded by a vast lawn. Strings of star-shaped lights on the trees enhanced the ambiance, giving it a romantic flair.

Inspired, I ordered a champagne cocktail. Though quite delicious, I found the drink prices as high or higher than any fancy bar in London or New York. As I sipped the strong, savory-sweet bubbles, the hostess appeared, to guide us to our table at Hazara Indian. As we walked, I noticed that outside the bar area, in the mansion's large foyer, stood a bakery counter stocked with fancy, European-style pastries and chocolates. Apparently, it was now trendy for upscale restaurants to sell chocolates. Then I spied…a humidor? A large glass-walled case filled with cigars (including Cuban!) occupied one side of the room. Forget political/social correctness, this place seemed to offer every indulgence for an evening's revelry. After a delicious and relaxing dinner, I couldn't wait to return to check out La Na Thai and spend another tranquil evening in this charming venue. I also left glad to know that the city offered significantly better restaurant food choices than The Frog!

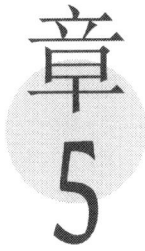

SCHOOL DAYS

One of the first questions many people ask is whether my kids attended a local Chinese school. The answer is no. First, even if we had wanted to make such a bold move, I doubt the Chinese government allowed foreign passport holders to enroll their children in local Chinese schools. The other reason is that most expat families planned to return to their home countries or knew they would move to other countries where they'd need a country-compatible educational background.

Fortunately, Shanghai offered no shortage of private, international educational opportunities. Pretty much the same as with foods of the world, Shanghai had schools of the world: American, French, British, Singaporean, and German. There was a Christian academy and an experimental school. For those determined to raise bilingual children, Yew Chung offered a Mandarin-English option and had a sister school in California. The list went on and on. We chose a school providing American curriculum, since we felt pretty sure that we'd return to the US.

Before we moved, Planet started asking around at work about school options. He discovered that getting into the school of one's choice wasn't exactly easy. Even with price tags at around $22,000 a year per child, spaces in all the schools remained limited. Some families found themselves with children at two different schools or even two different campuses of the same school.

Anxiously, Planet decided to apply the kids at SAS before our assignment was even a reality—just in case. Even though the experimental school—Shanghai Community International School (SCIS)—lay at the edge of our compound and claimed to have derived their program from the best curriculums from around the world, he thought SAS had a better academic reputation and was more established and organized. For this privilege, our kids would spend forty-five to sixty minutes a day (each way) commuting. They were only seven and eight years old, so I wasn't crazy about this idea at all. But nearly every family faced the same travel hurdle. There had to be safety in numbers, I hoped.

During the third week of August, SAS held its orientation. Finally, the kids and I had the chance to visit their new school. My heart pounded as Mr. Zhou whisked the silver minivan down the Lingbai Highway. How would Alexis feel about being in classes with boys again? Would it be easier or more difficult for the kids to make friends here? I hoped Planet had made the right choice and that our children would leave campus excited about their new school!

Mr. Zhou banked the car off the highway and onto a side road, which sloped into steep ditches on either side, filled with water on the right. Not a comforting thought. Beyond the treacherous ditches, small storefronts stocked with household goods, hardware, and even golf clubs stood waiting for customers. The shopkeepers chatted with their neighbors and passersby. Street vendors tended their portable woks, hawking all types of breakfast foods: fried onion pancakes, steamed buns, and other types of appetizing fare. Further down, on the left, stood a building that looked like a school, next door to a makeshift barracks for transient workers. On the right, I noticed the remnants of a housing development. The concrete blocks of outer walls for large houses loomed, abandoned, tall grasses and weeds now protruding from the space intended for windows and doors. What story lurked behind that abandoned mess?

When we arrived at the Pudong Links compound, Mr. Zhou had a chat with the security guards, impressively clad in elaborate olive-drab uniforms, US army-style hats, and the requisite white gloves. They handed him a cardboard pass for the car. We felt like VIPs as we drove off to a two-guard salute.

Winding our way toward the school, I took in the scenery. The Pudong Links neighborhood looked just like a new home community anywhere in the US, complete with an attractive golf course and a club house. The yards were sizable, and the houses looked so inviting, I immediately felt at home. Here, it seemed easy to shut out the crazy whirlwind of Shanghai. We passed the golf course and made a left at the dead end, where we found the school. The architectural style reminded me of the American Southwest, with its beige paint and red tile roof. It sprawled like a ranch house made of connected squares. The various squares were connected by ugly, rubbery, orange covered walkways; courtyards filled in the centers of the walkways. The school's architectural style certainly seemed more functional than aesthetically pleasing. Nevertheless, I found the outdoorsy, open feeling of the school pleasant. I took the palm trees as positive sign of mild winters. I definitely wouldn't miss the Shaker snow belt!

Today, volunteers and vendors had set up their tables to distribute various types of information to the new families: a couple of multi-national banks, the Community Center, the Boy Scouts, health services and the local hospital, the PTSA, two children's sports organizations, and many other such groups. I felt lucky to gather so much information all in one place at one time.

Laden with brochures, my newly purchased dual-language cookbook, and a copy of *Shanghai for Kids*, we worked our way to the cafeteria for the orientation. As we sat listening, I concluded that this hardly qualified as an introduction, the event was so disorganized and the scene so chaotic. One of the three principals welcomed us, pointed out the places to find our bus route, where to find out our teachers' names and room numbers, where to get IDs made, and where to buy smart cards and load them with lunch money. No welcome speech, no pep talk, no tour.

As a mom, I freaked out wondering why the school hadn't mailed bus information to us a week ago, like any normal US school. Thus, we made our first stop the cafeteria. Jam-packed with families, we felt like salmon swimming upstream. Finally, we squeezed our way toward the poster showing Alexis' and Anders' bus information. The kids would board the bus at 7:00 am to arrive in time to get to their classrooms and get settled by 8:00 am. The bus time was much earlier than they were used to, and the commute time was exponentially longer.

For our next task, Planet and I decided to divide and conquer. Planet stood in the massive line to pick up the lunch cards, while I led the kids over to the wall of people perusing the classroom lists. *Really, they couldn't have mailed this information to us, either?* Standing on my tiptoes, I saw Alexis' name on a third-grade roster. Her teacher, an older woman named Mrs. Hyatt, hailed from Canada, and her husband served as the high school division principal. Mrs. Hyatt seemed grandmotherly, wise, and fair. Then, pushing politely—if that's a thing—we made our way over to the second-grade roster. Anders' name appeared on Mrs. Thompson's list. She had moved here from Michigan, and SAS was her first teaching assignment. Her husband taught grade three. Although young and inexperienced, the Thompsons were kind and full of enthusiasm.

Reading through the kids' class lists surprised me. I had thought that an "American" school would have a primarily American study body. Instead, to my delight, school statistics showed that only twenty-five percent of the students held American passports. The student body represented forty-five countries! Well, that was a one-up on Shaker Heights! I considered the international diversity one of the best aspects of SAS. I felt really excited about that idea as we made our way back to Planet. He still had a long wait in the lunch cards line, so I walked the kids over to the ID line. When I saw the line there, I knew this day would require all of us to draw on all of our patience. The kids behaved like veteran travelers, without even one complaint. When we got their IDs, the clerk informed me that parents had to wear ID badges while on campus. Now I had to wait in yet *another* line in a completely different building!

Next challenge? Finding our way through the labyrinth of corridors to the kids' classrooms. Luckily, the younger kids' rooms were located nearest to the main door and were the easiest to reach. We found Anders' classroom without much trouble, and Alexis' classroom nearby. With all missions now completed, we made our way back to the front of the school to ring Mr. Zhou. There, Planet showed me the treasure he had snagged while waiting in the cafeteria line: this month's lunch menu. To my delight, I saw that each day the students had a choice of an "Eastern" or a "Western" style meal. With pleasure I scanned the list.

MONDAY
Chicken slices, fajita style
Peruvian sautéed beef slices
Mexican rice
Mixed sautéed veggies
Potato gratin
Banana bread

TUESDAY
Pork steaks baked with cheese and mushroom gravy
Xinjiang Lamb sautéed
Beef tacos
Potatoes and chorizo/ rice
Veggie lasagna
Profiteroles in chocolate

WEDNESDAY
Spaghetti Bolognaise
Macaroni and cheese
Sautéed French beans
Cabbage roll
Crème caramel

THURSDAY
Burgers in tomato sauce
Hainan chicken with rice
Chicken drumsticks
Chicken fried rice/Steamed rice
Sautéed bok choy
Condiments
Grilled vegetables with cheese
Brownies

FRIDAY
Fish steaks curry
Stir fried chicken with garlic and cilantro
Sautéed Asian veggies
Steamed rice
Veggie fajitas
Apple butter cake

This was great! I pictured my children watching all the other kids eating these dishes and liking them, positively influencing Alexis and Anders to expand their palates and eat more adventurously. The move to China would be worth it if Anders ever ate curried fish!

Moments later Zhou rolled the Silver up in front of the school. He dropped the kids and me at The Pearl, and then chauffeured Planet to his office at the Bund. I looked forward to our international school experience.

6

WELCOME BACK TO COLLEGE!

After setting up our home, adjusting to the household help, and getting the kids settled at school, next we focused on making friends. Well, welcome back to college! Making friends in Shanghai closely resembled the college experience: living away from home and trying to create an inner circle who could serve as a lifeline. We foreigners tried each other out, then figured out who to keep and who to politely distance ourselves from. As with college, most expats would only share space and time for a limited period (the average stay in Shanghai was two to five years). So, relationships were necessarily short and intense. I'll never forget a comment one lady made to me at a coffee morning. She said, "I've been here for six years now, and I've been through three sets of friends. It must be time for me to leave." At the time, I didn't understand. I just knew I needed to develop my own group as soon as possible. I figured I'd learn how to deal with the expat-friendship revolving door by observing.

What I discovered was this: living thousands of miles from home and the relatively short Shanghai-friend lifespan tended to create two types of people. Some foreign residents were "collectors," who added people to their silk ming pian books the way other people collected coins or stamps. They could never have too many and always made room for one more. Other expats were cliquish. They established a small circle of pals, and while they always acted friendly to others, they allowed no one else to penetrate their inner sanctum. Whatever the case, the first few months of friend shopping felt like online dating: trial and error until you found out who would stick. I experienced the highs of finding people I wanted in my friend group and who also wanted me in theirs. I suffered the lows of trying to distance myself from those I'd vetoed and being avoided by those who had relocated me to their "no" list. I wouldn't wish the task of moving and trying to establish a new friend group on anyone, but that aside, Shanghai seemed a far easier place to get established than some of the US cities I'd lived in.

In search of my circle, I spent time out and about in my neighborhood, going to MegaFit, checking out the Jewish community, attending Shanghai Expatriate Association (SEA) and The American Women's Club of Shanghai (AWCS) functions, attending Parent Teacher Student Association (PTSA) meetings, and volunteering at school. It was absolutely exhausting to walk into rooms full of people I didn't know, courageously approach a group, and start a conversation—nearly every day, for months.

The good part of this crazy life was that there were always many other people looking for friends. The collector style definitely suited me, and I set out to meet as many people as possible.

Getting Neighborly

The first few weeks at The Pearl, I tried to spend time at the pool or taking the kids for bike rides, hoping to score some acquaintances. We had a few good experiences at the pool. It felt great to have neighbors notice we were new and make a point of introducing themselves. The compound seemed like a ghost town when we arrived, and thankfully on our first trip to the pool, we discovered a group of Finnish, Danish, and Dutch moms and kids.

"Where is everyone?" I asked.

The Danish neighbor replied, "The American schools start the earliest, followed by the international ones, and then British ones about two weeks later. A lot of people aren't back from their home countries yet."

I nodded. "Oh, I see. How long will it take for the kids' lessons and activities to start?"

"Oh, nothing starts until September, after all the schools start," the Finn answered.

Panic set in. This was only the second week in August. I worried the kids and I might die of loneliness and boredom before Shanghai ever got cranked up for the fall! Yet, the afternoon went well. Seven-year-old Anders easily fell in with the European boys. I felt relieved to see them all playing happily together. Thank goodness you could just pop boys into a pool with a ball, and all would be well, no matter what language they spoke. Things went significantly less well for eight-year-old Alexis, however. The girls were either too young or too old to really become long-term friends, and she was acting uncharacteristically shy. She didn't complain, though, and I knew she felt happy just knowing there were actually kids around. Although the pool group remained friendly all afternoon, surprisingly no one asked for my ming pian. I came away a little disappointed. Later, I heard via the grapevine that the Scandinavians were lovely, but very clannish. In all fairness, the same could be said of many groups, and at times, all of them. We'd just have to try again.

The next time the kids and I ventured over to the pool, I met a very nice American lady, Angela Templeton, playing with two cute little girls, about three and five years old. As we got to know each other, I found out these were her two youngest. She looked so young and had such a fit figure, I could hardly believe she it when she confessed she had eight kids! Eventually, she mentioned that she belonged to a special type of religion, about which I knew almost nothing. So, the super mom offered to give me a copy of their holy book. I said I'd take a read through it. Why not? It could be interesting. I'd just put on my literary critic hat and treat it like another book review project.

Angela seemed like such a kind and good person, and I wondered how she had time to cultivate friendships while running a household of ten. Already I respected and admired her, but I also felt worried that maybe her special religion would prevent us from being friends—with Jews historically not exactly winning any worldwide popularity contests. I hoped to add her to my friend group, but only time would tell.

When school finally started in late August, I learned that the clubhouse bus stop made a great place to meet other moms and to gather information. On day one, we arrived first and stood anxiously waiting alone, until a blue GM minivan zoomed up. Four energetic platinum-haired boys, who looked like carbon copies of each other, leapt out after their contrastingly calm older sister. Their mother emerged from the front passenger seat, where she'd been balancing a younger sister on her lap. What's this? Six children…and pregnant, too? We moms introduced ourselves. Noelle Hamburger and her brood hailed from the Midwest, by way of France. Her son Wesley was in grade 3 and in Alexis' class. Sarah was in 10th grade, Will was in 9th, Warren in 7th, Wayne in 5th, and Wyatt was in 1st. I could hardly handle China with two kids, so I thought this mother must be some kind of parental rock star. I wondered if she'd met Angela.

As we stood getting acquainted, a tall, sporty blonde, who looked like she just stepped off a tennis court, approached with her two stately Boxers and two sleepy-looking high-school-aged kids. No surprise, Jody Chesney called California's Bay Area home. Her family had arrived here after living in Japan and Singapore. Standing there, I started to think I might eventually enjoy living in Shanghai if all the moms had such interesting backgrounds. "I'm not sure we're staying," Jody informed us. "I think we might be moving to back to Singapore. I'll know by the end of the week."

You could have blown me over in one shallow breath. I couldn't imagine arriving in China—after all the moving drama, the shots, etc.—and then having to pack up and move again right away. How did these ladies with career-expat husbands manage to keep their sanity?

To my relief, the three of us exchanged ming pian. *How many more moms would show up?* I looked back at the clubhouse door, where I spied a tall, pretty blonde girl—about sixteen—standing next to a smaller version of herself, camped out on the steps. The younger girl's golden locks lay neatly braided. Her large azure blue eyes assessed the group. She resembled Gretel from the Grimms' fairy tale. No parent accompanied the two. Since the younger sister looked about Alexis' age, I decided to check them out.

"Good morning," I began. "I'm Mrs. Aschkenase. We're from Ohio. What's your name?"

"I'm Therese, and this is Bianca," the older sister responded.

"This is Alexis. She's in third grade at SAS this year."

Smiles rolled from face to face. "I'm in tenth grade, and Bianca's in fourth. We lived in the US, once."

Close enough! A potential friend for Alexis!

Bianca finally spoke. "Our dad is from Germany, and our mom is from Spain."

"Wow!" My brain exploded a little at discovering another global family. No wonder the girls looked like they'd just stepped out of a Swiss Chocolate ad. I wondered where else they had lived.

"You can sit with me on the bus…*may…be*," Bianca teased Alexis. "Maybe. I'll think about it."

My opinion just deflated. Did this child really just say something so rude right in front of me? Just then, two children, obviously cutting it close for the bus, burst through the clubhouse doors. When they saw the bus hadn't arrived, they stopped short, panting.

Bianca gave the girl, who was about the same age, a hug.

"This is Bella," she explained. "She's my *sister*," she announced.

What? The girl was clearly half Asian and had skin at least three shades darker than Bianca's. My face must have given away my thoughts.

"No really. She really really really really is!" Bianca insisted, grinning charmingly.

I stared at her, my right eyebrow raised. "And who's this?" I couldn't resist asking, pointing toward the boy, wondering what story she'd tell next.

"That's her brother, Anders."

Another Anders? I thought my Anders might faint from joy. He'd never met another child who shared his name. Anders number two was also in second grade. Though they weren't in the same class, the boys bonded instantly because of their names and stood chatting away. The Lindstroms' father, we later learned, was Swedish, and their mother was Chinese. Mrs. Lindstrom had an exotic job as a fashion show event planner, so she spent a significant amount of time away in Paris and Milan. I felt stunned to discover Mrs. Lindstrom regularly left the children home with ayi while she traveled, even when her husband was also away. I couldn't imagine that, but apparently here in China it wasn't uncommon. I even heard of people who went on vacation, leaving their kids home with ayi. What a different world!

As I stood thinking that thus far my morning seemed to have all the ingredients for a heck of a reality TV show, the bus rolled up. To my surprise, a spotless, relatively new, European-style coach suddenly stood before us—a luxurious touring chariot, curtains and all. The door whooshed open, and a stocky, middle-aged Chinese woman in a flowery dress wobbled down the steps. She waved her hand to indicate that the kids should board. Apparently, all the foreign private schools had bus ayis. These ladies spoke little or no English, yet their job required them to keep order and chaperone the kids. From the stories my children told me over the years, these women remained much abused by their young passengers. Nevertheless, I felt better knowing that an adult bus monitor would accompany the children on their long rides to and from school.

"Bye," the gang of kids collectively called, waving as they maneuvered up the bus steps.

When the coach started pulling away, I saw Alexis waving, but looking a little sad. Then I noticed Bianca's eyes boring impishly into mine from the window of a seat a few rows back. I thought I could just make out Bella sitting next to her.

About a week after SAS opened, my across-the-street neighbors returned to Shanghai. I had heard their children attended the British school, even though they were American. Clearly, news traveled the expat grapevine quickly, because Eden Oberlander had also already heard of *our* arrival. Excited to have American neighbors, she made a point of coming over to meet us as soon as possible.

Eden grew up a quintessential California girl, but with a twist. She wasn't just another fit, blue-eyed blonde: she was a career expat, a community service volunteer veteran, a get-it-done person, and a devout Christian.

"I was *so* excited when people said an American family was moving in," Eden announced, as she zipped across the street into my front yard.

For fun, I asked, "why?"

"Because I know Americans are going to be nice."

Well, that seemed a bit simplistic, but after only a couple weeks in the Middle Kingdom, I was starting to comprehend what she meant. While it's fantastic to hang out with women from all over the world, sometimes you just want to share a moment with someone who completely understands the nuances of your culture. Americans definitely seemed likely to have certain characteristics—nice being one of them. Sometimes, diversity just required too much energy. Sometimes you just wanted to tell a joke in your own language without something being lost in translation or compare notes without risking offense to anyone else's culture.

"C'mon over to my house. We can have a cup of tea and talk," she offered. "I have about a half hour before my driver gets here." One thing about Eden, she was always rushing off to somewhere, always deeply into multiple projects.

"OK. Sounds good." I smiled.

We walked across the street to her house, where instead of going to the front door, Eden opened up the garage door. She had transformed the space into a game room/tv room for her kids. The walls surrounding the couches stood completely lined with shelves and boxes, ceiling high. She noticed me gaping.

"This," she explained, matter-of-factly, waving her hand like a magic wand across the area, "is what happens when you downsize from a castle in Scotland!" Then she grabbed a small box and a tote bag from one of the shelves, clearly central to today's mission. Eden told me that the Oberlanders had moved here from the UK a year ago. Her son, Pierce, was Anders' age and grade, and her daughter, Priscilla, was three years older.

"We kept them in the British school system, since that's what they're familiar with," Eden explained. "We thought the move might be less traumatic that way."

She went on to tell me Priscilla had been born in France, and Pierce in Poland. My mind wandered from what it would be like to have lived in several countries already (including in a Scottish castle!) to the experience of giving birth abroad. It seemed mind boggling that her kids were American, yet they had never lived there, plus they attended The British International School of Shanghai (BISS). Boy, I had met some gutsy, interesting women in the past few weeks!

As we continued getting to know each other, enjoying Chinese green tea served by Eden's ayi on the beautiful traditional china she'd collected in Poland, my neighbor said,

"I have some errands to do for the Cub Scouts and some other shopping to do tomorrow, so I'll take you with me, if you can go. I can show you around the markets a little. And I'll let you know when my language lesson group starts again. We're waiting for the Australians who live down the street to get back. The Australians are always the last ones back."

My eyes as large and round as a harvest moon, I replied, "Thank you!" I felt truly grateful. Finally, my Pearl world was beginning to turn!

True to her word, Eden stopped for me the next morning. In the car, my neighbor showed me a Cub Scouts uniform from the US. Our first stop was the fabric market in search of a vendor to copy it for all of the troop members. I couldn't believe a person could just walk into the market with pretty much any item of clothing and get it copied exactly. *Amazing!*

Once there, my neighbor quickly succeeded in finding someone to copy the uniforms, making everything seem so easy and so cheap. I watched in awe. Next, we set out to find a vendor to create the project badges and other patches that adorn the uniforms. *You could do that too?* We hunted through the stalls for about an hour with no luck.

"Oh, well," Eden commented. "I'll have to try a different market or ask around. The right place has got to be here somewhere. *Everything* is here in China, *somewhere*. You just have to figure out where." *Incredible!*

We left the fabric market in pursuit of other items on Eden's list. The Shanghai markets seemed very interesting and exciting, rife with possibilities. By the time we returned to The Pearl in the late afternoon, however, the day's experiences had grown so overwhelming, I developed a full-blown migraine. I could hardly wait to get off this learning curve to a time when running errands and traversing the city would seem routine.

The next week, my kind neighbor invited me along to the Xiang Yang "gift market." This vast outdoor market housed several hundred vendors selling designer knock-off clothing, watches, handbags, shoes, video games, jewelry, and etc. Thank goodness I hadn't ventured down into this maze of stalls on my own. I would have been lost in minutes and freaking out about the vendors barking out at and even grabbing at potential customers. "Look! Look! Watch, lady? Louis Vuitton! What you want, be-yoo-ti-ful lady? I got!" These hawkers generated such an annoying clamor Eden and I found it difficult to carry on a conversation. I made a mental note to ask Eden's in-home Mandarin teacher how to tell them "No," "be quiet," and "don't touch me!" at our upcoming lesson.

One of the main benefits of coming to the Xiang Yang with a veteran shopper like Eden was developing relationships with trustworthy vendors who sold good quality merchandise and who would take back anything that broke or didn't work. My new friend had already established guanxi, and therefore, pricing with some of the shops we'd visit. Translation: no haggling!

Eden's first stop was at her handheld games guy. He sold to her at 35RMB per game (about $4.50). Was that the best price a white westerner could get? I didn't know, but $4.50 remained a far cry from US pricing. So, I excitedly piggybacked on her deal, buying both Alexis and Anders each two games as Chanukah gifts. Then we moved on. As we passed dozens of stalls selling handbags and accessories, I stopped to pick up a great Gucci look-alike wallet for 50RMB (about $6). Next stop, Eden's evening bag lady. I could hardly believe it when we scored bags as pretty as the ones I'd seen at Nordstrom's for only 100RMB each!

After this, Eden phoned her driver, as our next stop, Ka De Klub, wasn't close. When we arrived, I learned that this shop sold legitimate, full-priced Chinese videos from its front room. But like so many places in China, it had a "secret back room," where they sold American CDs and DVDs for amazing prices. The clerk recognized Eden and knew what she wanted. He moved part of the wall to let us into the covert shopping area. Here, I saw hundreds of titles to pick from. They even had boxed sets of popular TV series. Eden had negotiated a price of 10RMB a disc (about $1.25 at the time)—a fairly standard price among most vendors at the time. I couldn't resist buying a bunch of DVDs for the kids, plus a couple of TV series for Planet and me. It felt a little sinister, but on the other hand, Chinese TV consisted of several channels of horrible state-approved Beijing Opera, CNN International, BBC International, a ridiculous Chinese children's channel, and sometimes Da Shan (a Canadian guy) giving Mandarin lessons. In other words, state-approved TV left MUCH to be desired. In addition, very few American or Western movies were shown in the handful of Shanghai's movie theaters. Before long, we all felt so starved for American movies, TV, and music, purchasing copies grew irresistible. I doubt film-industry billionaires suffered much from our clandestine purchases, as had I been in the US, I wouldn't have bought CDs or DVDs at all. They didn't need my money as much as local Chinese families did, either.

Our whirlwind shopping day ended there. Though I'd had another great, interesting day, I returned to Pudong with another migraine.

A few days later when my phone rang, I heard Noelle Hamburger's alto tone come across the line. Anders had already bonded with and adored hanging out with her two sons closest to his age, so I assumed she had decided to try me out.

"Can you go into Puxi shopping this morning? I have my driver, and there's a specific Louis Vuitton copy bag that Sarah wants."

"I'd love to, but I'm going to the SEA event. Please call me again, though. I'd love to do something with you another time," I replied, sincerely.

I definitely thought it would be good to become friends with the mom of Anders' favorite friends. I was glad she called and sincerely hoped she would make plans with me another time. But that's not how things turned out. Although we remained on friendly terms the entire time we lived in Shanghai, Noelle never asked me to do anything again. I thought I had been polite and encouraging when I told her I had other plans. Did she quickly find other friends who suited her better, or was she the kind of person who took one "no" as definitive? Developing a circle of friends certainly proved both mysterious and challenging.

After a few weeks of working out at MegaFit, I arrived at a "try it out" phase with two ladies. One was a Vietnamese-American named Linh and the other was an American from North Carolina named Carter. Over time, Linh and I began to chat before and after classes. She was one of those thoughtful people who, when they go to get a piece of equipment, also bring back one for the person next to them. One day, she asked me if I wanted to have lunch with her and a few other ladies.

"My friend's husband is opening a Vietnamese restaurant, and he needs people to come try the place," she explained. "You should join us."

"That would be great!" I replied, excited to get to know Linh and her friends.

On the designated day, about ten of us met at the new restaurant. Linh's friend, Thuy, played the gracious hostess role perfectly. She had ordered for us in advance a sampling of all the most popular dishes, but also some things that weren't even on the menu. What a treat! We all ooh'd and ahh'd as we devoured the delicious dishes. For me, the standout item was the minced shrimp kebobs fried onto stalks of fragrant lemongrass. Apparently, it wasn't on the menu because it took so long to make. I hoped I'd find it on a menu someday, some-where in the world.

Over lunch, I sat next to Linh, happily getting to know her. It hadn't occurred to me that she had a unique life story. I listened, spellbound, as she detailed her harrowing escape as one of the Vietnamese "boat people" we regularly heard about on the US evening news in the late 1970s and early 1980s. After all she endured, teenaged Linh and her sister came to live with an uncle in America, not knowing a word of English or what to expect. The difficulties people in other countries endure never cease to amaze me. I felt proud to call such a brave woman my friend, and we remained in each other's lives throughout our stays in China.

My other megafriend, Carter, lived in Jin Qiao's Jade Court apartments. Carter and I met for lunch once or twice a month, working our way through the variety of restaurants in the Jade Leisure Center. Unfortunately, our friendship didn't last long. Midway through the school year, her husband's company suddenly decided that they *didn't* need a "China guy." Through the grapevine I learned that American and European companies often excitedly sent someone over to China in the rush to capitalize on the next great business opportunity. When things went wrong with getting into the market or not selling enough product (which often happened for a variety of reasons), the representative ended up either called home or fired. Only a few months into my China experience, already, a member of my friend circle had packed her bags and exited through the revolving door.

The Kid Zone

Fortunately, there seemed to be an abundance of boys Anders' age in our compound, and he had the best luck of anyone in our family at developing a friend group. Anders' circle quickly included Quinn McDonough, an Australian boy whose mother served as the school nurse; Ricky Hall from Canada; and of course, Wesley and Wyatt Hamburger. Eventually, when the O'Brian's arrived, it expanded to include Kyle. Though he attended the British school, Eden Oberlander's son, Pierce, and Anders were remained friends. And somehow, my son also befriended Jens—a Norwegian boy who went to SCIS. Anders loved that Jens' father drove the boys around the compound in the sidecar of his stylish vintage motorcycle replica. The bonus was that Anders learned to like eating salmon from Jens' family!

As with any elementary school group, however, drama didn't take a break just because we'd landed in Asia. Only a few weeks after arriving at The Pearl, Anders joined a water fight with most of the boys from our street—the very young Australian boys who all had Celtic names, the older Australian boys from the end of the street, and Pierce. Not having anything better to do, Alexis and Priscilla had entered the battle. Was it the Americans against the Australians? I couldn't tell.

My kids had never had a water fight before, and my first instinct was to feel glad they were having normal, childhood fun abroad. Since we were still so new, I didn't know the Australian boys' wild streaks were no secret among the neighbors, rendering them not-so-popular with some of the mothers from more "reserved" nations. Clueless, I went into the house, thinking all was well. In reality, the seriousness of the attacks escalated, and the neighborhood veterans shifted their focus to giving the new kids (mine) a proper typhoon-style dousing. Priscilla charged out of her house with a bucket and dumped the entire contents onto Anders' head.

My son, unfazed, wouldn't be out done. He rushed into our house and grabbed his Tae Kwan Do *sahng je bong* (a long fat foam sabre, constructed for safe sparring) and his hand protectors (foam rubber boxing gloves, also safe). Anders raced back into the battle, popping Priscilla one in the back with the sahng je bong. She had to be more surprised than hurt, but by the Emmy-winning yowl she let rip, you'd have thought the world was ending. Unfortunately, today also happened to be Priscilla's birthday, which she had assumed made her untouchable and added insult to injury. So, the queen-of-the-day continued howling, while the younger set of Australians ran home to get their toy swords.

I heard the commotion and sped outside. I grew appropriately mortified when the kids told me what had just gone down. Eden emerged from her doorway as well. Priscilla ran into the Oberlanders' house, crying hysterically while we mothers managed to end the fight before the Australians could avenge their teammate. *Oh, great! Our first international incident.* Although Anders shouldn't have hit anyone with the foam sabre, he couldn't actually have hurt anyone with it. But the last thing I needed was a feud with my new neighbors or to have them spreading gossip about my family that would damage our reputations already.

"I think Anders needs to come over and apologize," Eden announced. Then she added, charitably, "It's a good thing I'm a good Christian person, so I'm the forgiving type. You all should still come over later for Priscilla's birthday party."

Whew! "Thank you. That's very kind. I'll walk Anders inside right now," I replied. Thankfully, here in the expat world people needed each other and were more willing to find ways to get along. Even though Priscilla had dished out as good as she got, my son was a trooper and did his best to smooth things over.

"I'm filled with Christian forgiveness! Let's just move on," Eden breathed in a sigh of relief. *Thank goodness!* "Please come by for cake after dinner. Really. I mean it." G_d bless Eden for helping move the situation forward in the name of friendship and international peace!

Later that evening the kids and I made our way across the blacktop to their house. We arrived to see Priscilla buzzing among the guests, enjoying her birthday-girl status. Priscilla regaled everyone with how her "awesome" father had promised to pick up a Birman kitten for her on his next trip to Amsterdam. For a moment, I wondered who jets off to Europe to pick up a pet? Oh, wait…I was now living in the exotic expat world. I was probably about to meet lots of people who did stuff like that!

Shortly after all the guests arrived, Eden assembled us in the family room. There, the group busted out the birthday song in Mandarin. Impressed, I envied these veterans and hoped my family and I would learn the language soon. When we left that evening, I felt relieved; the neighborhood lay peaceful once more.

August went less well for Alexis than it did for Anders and me. Quickly we learned that children mostly played with the kids in their own compounds because the long bus rides, traffic, and after-school activities made it difficult to get together with friends in other compounds, except on weekends. Even that could be challenging, given family schedule juggling. For that whole school year, Bianca was the only girl close to her age in the compound available. Unfortunately, Alexis often had to choose between playing with Bianca or playing alone. And when she got together with Bianca, trouble usually followed.

During the first few days of school, although Bianca had continually refused to sit with Alexis on the bus, despite any promises, the girl had charmed her into a playdate. The plan was for Alexis to go over to Bianca's house they finished their homework. After school, I got the kids settled in for homework. We had hardly been at the kitchen table for two minutes before the phone jingled. I answered.

"Can Alexis come over?"

I was surprised to hear Bianca's voice on the line. "Are you already done with your homework?"

"Yes."

"Really?" I replied in a motherly "I doubt it" tone.

"I didn't have any homework."

"OK. Well, Alexis will be over as soon as she's done with hers."

We settled back into math sheets, but about ten minutes later, the doorbell rang.

For a change, Xiao Ting raced to beat me to the door. I often forgot it was her job, and sometimes she got lazy and let me answer it.

On the other side of the door stood…who else…Bianca! This girl had some nerve.

"Sorry, Bianca. Alexis isn't done with homework."

"Oh, that's OK," she said, using an adult tone. "I was worried she wouldn't find my house. I came over to show her how to get there," she said, flashing her best toothy smile and tossing her blonde mane.

"Well, isn't that nice. Why don't you wait out in the yard? I'm sure she'll be done soon," I said, standing my ground.

Several times over the next forty minutes, Bianca slid open the door to ask if Alexis was ready yet. Each time, I tried to keep my cool despite my rising irritation. Finally, my kids were ready to play. Anders grabbed a bathing suit and headed over to the Hamburgers' pool. Bianca took Alexis' hand, and off they went to her house. I hoped all the kids would have a good time. After about an hour, however, Alexis came home.

"Mom, Bianca told me to go home," she explained, tears brimming in her enormous azure eyes.

"What happened?" *Why wasn't I surprised?* She said that she missed her sister and had to go see her. Right then. And that her sister was at another house."

Oh, the thing with Isabella again. *Grrr!*

"I'm sorry, Sweetie," I said, wrapping my arms around my sweet, friend-challenged girl. "That was rude. I wish she had told you she could only play for a little while today."

The next day after school, just as the kids were finishing their snack, the doorbell rang. On the stoop stood Bianca, a heavy brown bag in her hand.

"What's in the bag?" I asked.

"Candy," she smiled. "Can Alexis play?" What was up with the candy? "Yes, if you girls stay here," I answered. I wanted to keep my eye on them. I didn't trust this girl. "OK," she agreed, nodding her Gretel-blonde braids.

I sent the girls up to Alexis' room to play, and turned my attention to Mr. Zhou, who had just returned from the wet market with an entire fish. Thank goodness ayi knew how to clean and filet the thing!

I thought all was going well, until my daughter came down to the family room. "Mommy, my toilet doesn't work," she reported.

"What's wrong with it?"

"I don't know."

I followed her upstairs into her room. I looked at the toilet. Nothing appeared amiss.

"It doesn't flush," Bianca offered, matter-of-factly.

I gave the handle a push. No. It didn't. I rang The Pearl's management center, and five minutes later a blue-uniformed worker arrived along with the usual crisply-uniformed chaperone from the management office. It took the plumber less than a minute to discover the problem. He pulled not one but two Barbie doll heads out of the toilet!

"Alexis! What in the world is Barbie's head doing in the toilet!"

"Well, I've never liked Barbie very much…and Bianca and I were playing a game where…Barbie was evil…and had to be *killed*," she explained. I could hardly believe the words assaulting my ear passages. Was this *my* child? "What were you thinking?" I said to both girls. "Even if Barbie *was* evil, she didn't deserve to have her head pulled off and flushed down the toilet! You have more brains than that. Aside from that, you know nothing but paper goes in the toilet, especially here in China."

"I'm sorry, mom." Alexis said, truthfully. "Bianca said Barbie was evil and had to go to Poopville. And the only way to get there is through the toilet."

Poopville? Seriously? I understood exactly what had likely transpired. Alexis was afraid that if she didn't go along with Bianca, Bianca wouldn't be her friend. Her only friend here in the compound. *Oh, please G_d, let an SAS third-grade girl move into The Pearl SOON!*

I sent Bianca home and forbade the girls to play together for a week. My heart ached for my daughter. Now I knew for sure that any playdates with Bianca had to take place at our house and under close supervision. Later, Alexis admitted that in return for doing her homework, Bianca agreed to sit with her on the way home from school and give her candy. I should have known!

LEARNING CURVE

In September, it still felt like I had only covered a fraction of what I needed to learn to survive, and hopefully enjoy, Shanghai. In addition to navigating my shopping experiences, managing my household help, and making friends, I faced computer challenges, I needed to learn Mandarin, and I needed a Chinese name.

Plugged In

We had been weeks without email while waiting for our personal items to arrive from America, and I was anxious for my computer to arrive. Finally, the big day came. I pulled the machine out of the box, and, excited and unthinking, I pushed the plug into the wall socket.

Crrraackklle! Poof!

Oh, crap! OH, CRAP! I had completely forgotten to use the converter! My head spinning with panic, I pulled the plug out of the socket. Hoping against hope, I grabbed the converter, plugged in the machine, and prayed. No joyful whirring sound emerged. I had definitely fried the power source. For a few minutes, I feared I might implode. I had been cut off from the "real world" for what felt like years. Oh, who could I even ask for help? My heart beat wildly as I dialed Planet.

Luckily for me, Planet said that The Firm's computer guy knew of someone who could come over that afternoon. My heart pounded with hope. A few hours later, the doorbell rang. Xiao Ting actually answered, and when she opened the door, a young Chinese man explained his errand to her in Shanghainese. She turned and pointed to me.

"Please come," I motioned the man and my ayi to follow me upstairs. Once in the office, the repairman pulled a device out of his black bag. He plugged my computer into it, and it sprang to life. Beethoven's "Ode to Joy" began to play in my head! But as quickly as he brought my computer to life, the man unplugged the device, returning it to the dead. I watched in confusion as he began packing up to leave. "Wait!" I pointed to the power device, panicked. "For me?" I pointed to myself.

The computer guy explained something to Xiao Ting. As she translated, it amounted to my needing a new power source. He did not have one. I tried to buy the one he had with him. No, Madame. He'd have to order one, then come back in a few days to install it. *NO!* I couldn't believe I had been so foolish with something so important! Three weeks without a computer, and now what?

Next strategy: we had a global warranty on the computer. I asked about this via Xiao Ting. Surely this mishap was covered. No, Madame. And with that, the man made his way out the door.

I dialed my desktop's customer service number. We had purchased the most extensive warranty offered. This must be covered. The warranty representative confirmed that our policy *was* global, complete coverage worldwide...*except in China!* Oh, it just figured! A global policy that applies everywhere *but* in China! Unbelievable!

Thankfully, I only had to survive a few more days. With my communication device restored, I powered up and rejoined the world. Then, I learned some interesting things about using the internet while living in a communist country. Websites I had previously taken for granted—Google, Facebook, YouTube, and Wikipedia, for example—were banned. I guessed the Chinese might not care, since they had never used these sites, but for me, what a wake-up call! In addition, I learned through the grapevine that apparently, a small army of government clerks in Beijing actually read everyone's email and monitored internet use! Once, our internet went down for about two weeks. Planet and I were baffled. Finally, we gathered it was because the government was training new email readers. Imagine that! As a result of this monitoring, we were warned to be careful of what we looked up on the web or said in emails. Rumor held that if certain words appeared—such as Falun Gong—or foreigners made criticisms of communism or the government, they might suddenly find themselves without internet, or worse, facing a visit from one of Big Brother's agents. American freedom suddenly took on new meaning.

Mandarin Challenges

Now that I had my lifeline back, I could add learning Mandarin through a computer program to my repertoire. I'd always enjoyed learning languages. In fact, while earning my Ph.D., candidates had to pass reading exams in two foreign languages. So, I learned French and German. Everyone said Chinese was difficult, but I figured after my graduate school experience, I could handle it. And wasn't it easiest to learn a language by living in the country where it's spoken? I bucked up for the challenge.

One of the first things I did was ask my driver to give me lessons while we commuted. This was helpful, but of marginal value. He taught me numbers, how to say good morning/evening, goodbye, and please come get me at such and such a time. I also asked him to stop playing 1950s American music and play only Shanghainese radio stations so I could hear Mandarin. I tried watching Chinese TV. In addition, I asked Xiao Ting to teach me the names of foods and of the dishes we liked her to make.

Simple and useful as all this was, I found it nearly impossible to make the words stick in my head. I just couldn't relate. The sounds of Mandarin were so different from anything I'd heard or tried to learn before, and everything had to be said in the correct tone. As an expressive speaker to start with, having to blank my emotions in order to execute the correct tone just wasn't in my wheel house! Plus, I needed to hear every word and phrase multiple times.

Next, I tried using the popular computer software that Planet's company purchased for us. Although I made a real effort, I found little of the vocabulary useful. Realistically, how often do you use the words "triangle" or "square" in regular conversation unless you're teaching geometry? It seemed even less likely that "horse" would serve me well in conversation any time soon, nor did I expect to discuss hats. Though I could imagine "over" and "under" might occasionally come in handy, that was the extent of the software's usefulness. What I needed was common phrases and essential verbs.

Fortunately, Eden had kindly invited me to join her in-home Chinese class. Once a week a tutor came over to teach a small group of neighborhood ladies. What could be better than enjoying coffee and pastries with my neighbors while having individualized instruction?

Our teacher was a pleasant young man who called himself…of all things… Alvin! Where in the world did he come up with that name? I could only hope he had derived it from someone with higher status than the Disney chipmunk character! The good news was that not only was Alvin's English excellent and his instruction customized, you could hire him to come shopping with you, act as a tour guide, or translate anytime, anywhere! He must have been very successful, because the ladies remarked that our young teacher had plans to open a gift shop just outside The Pearl soon. I certainly admired the Chinese entrepreneurial spirit.

Unfortunately, the sessions with Alvin usually ended with me having heard more neighborhood gossip and chit chat than Mandarin. Yet, I found some value in learning how to ask a store clerk, "Is this a real antique or a copy?" "I want good quality." And "what day will this order be ready? I would like it Tuesday." Still, I felt overwhelmed. How would I ever be able to rattle off phrases and communicate like the legendary Da Shan? At this rate, it could take me years to learn to speak, I fretted. Learning to read Chinese characters seemed hopeless altogether. Without a doubt, I had to admit I'd finally met my linguistic match! Soon overwhelmed, I gave in to the fact that I probably wouldn't learn Mandarin until I overcame my mental block about being in the country in the first place.

Lost in Translation

While on the subject of language and translations, the expat crowd remained entertained by the multitude of mistranslations seen around the city. So much so that several websites even emerged to showcase these good-humored tidbits.

Out and about in Shanghai, I came across "lost in translation" situations regularly. I got a laugh from the cash machine sign that read, "please waiting." Someone had named their shoe store "Disney." The Dolar Store was not a take-off on the Dollar Store, it was a restaurant. The lotion brand on a China Southern flight was "ugly girl." Really? What a great way to ensure no one would use the product! I saw a bumper sticker that said, "No Kiss. Stop." Though it probably meant "no tailgating," it could also mean you should pull over if overcome by a sudden urge to make out! And my personal favorite, the Pudong restaurant sign that read, "Healthy Food Makes You Slobber." The Chinese equivalent of "finger lickin' good?" I got a kick out of it every time we drove by.

While the city had no shortage of items "lost in translation," let's be honest: the average Chinese person's English will probably always be exponentially better than my Mandarin. So, believe me, I'm not judging!

What's in a Name?

And speaking of translations, this bring us to the topic of names. In language classes around the world, students are asked either to use the translation of their English name, or if it doesn't exist, choose another language-appropriate name they like. Well, that remained true for both expatriates in China and Chinese people interacting with English speakers. Let the fun begin!

In Chinese, one way of translating a foreign name is to craft something that sounds like Chinese words. So, Alvin suggested I adopt the Chinese name 雪 Xui 美 Li (shway lee), because it sounds like Shelly. I thought the name seemed appropriate not only because it sounded similar enough to my English name, but because it means beautiful snow—I was born in January in Minnesnowta. Eventually, however, I decided it didn't really suit me. Cold snowy weather just didn't say enough about who I was or the identity I sought to establish while living in China. After another consultation with my Chinese teacher, my new Chinese name became Ai Wen (eye when). Ai 爱 means to love or enjoy. Wen 文 means literature, writing, language, or culture. The perfect name to suit my passion for reading, writing, editing, and teaching language arts.

Converting English names to Mandarin seemed a much more logical and simpler task than the multitude of methods the Chinese used to select English names. Perhaps it's because Chinese parents take names and their meanings much more seriously than Westerners, who often choose family names or names they simply like the sound of. Chinese parents name their children to reflect personalities or hopes and dreams. Their daughters should be like beautiful flowers or precious elements. Their sons should be as strong as dragons or powerful as tigers.

As it turns out, however, many Chinese names either don't translate or don't sound right to Western ears. *Wang Li, Chu Hua, Yu,* or *Xiao Hong* just won't go over in English as Beautiful, Chrysanthemum, Fish, and Rainbow. Sometimes the person selecting an English name truly just doesn't understand that the name they have chosen doesn't work, much to the amusement of Westerners. As with English-speakers trying to translate their own names into Mandarin, many Chinese names can use their sounds to derive their English names. Ling translates easily to Lynn, Li to Lee, Qi turns into Jade, and Jing Mi becomes Jimmy. Also popular, however, are girls' names reflecting nature. No wonder we met so many women called Lily, Daisy, and Rose. Fruit names were also very popular. Across China, you will encounter many a Cherry or Apple. Popular precious element names, like Jade and Pearl, also translate well.

Currently, however, deriving Western names from elements of popular culture or their own aspirations is growing in popularity. We met waiters named Gucci, Versace, and Mercedes, and store clerks with badges that read Gandalf, Frodo, and Batman. Does the pharmacy clerk Cinderella believe that one day her prince will come? Shanghai store clerks sported Yahoo, Sony, Toshiba, Panasonic, and Dell on their name badges—names that reflect successful international businesses and their own hopes for good fortune. Oreo's and Chocolate's favorite snacks seem obvious. In addition, Asian women have long had a passion for cute, sweet, cuddly animals and personalities. Hence, a plethora of women adopting Angel, Happy, Honey, Candy, Sunny, Jolly, Twinkle, Bambi, or Bunny. I would have expected to meet many more young ladies named Kitty, however, than I did. Sometimes, names went awry, however. Planet and I looked at each other, astonished, one evening as we noticed our waiter's English name: Beer! Cola, on the other hand, was likely named after her favorite drink or a translation of her Mandarin name. Tian—which in Mandarin can mean heaven or sky—made for some odd translations. We ran into more than one person who had called himself God, as well as one Heaven and a couple of Skys. What about the waiter who introduced himself as Alan, but whose name tag read "Anal?" And Planet's work assistant had a man's name—Wesley—which she mysteriously spelled Wresylie! Jessicase is out there, roaming the city with several men named Zero.

How did Milk and Bacon select their names? Were Blender and Microscope derived from these men's favorite job tools? Was Cactus studying to be a botanist? Who suggested the names Flower and Rabbit to young men? And why didn't someone tell Connie and Sunny (men) that these are usually women's names? Ditto for Wresylie and Oliver, both females. I don't think I want to know how Kinky earned his name, and I hope someone will have the heart to encourage Dipsy to change her name as well. I can certainly understand the aspirations of Harvard, Nikkei, Boss, Money, and Dollar; but what's up with the seemingly nefarious intentions of Evil, Devil, Hitler, and Monster?

We also had fun learning the Mandarin names for Western companies. Some names came from matching the English sound, some derived from the name's meaning, and others used a combination of sound and meaning. Starbucks, for example, translates as xīng bā kè. Xing (shing) literally means star, but bā kè (bah kuh) just replicates the English sound "bucks." McDonald's also got translated mostly by sound: 麦当劳 (Mài dāng láo). Mài means wheat, dāng means when, and láo is labor. Coca-Cola used both sound and meaning. Kě kǒu sounds close enough to Coca, and ke le resembles cola. So, kě kǒu ke le makes sense. Not only is it easy to say and remember, but the words translate wonderfully into something akin to "tasty fun" or "delicious happiness." The company's marketers could not have asked for better! I absolutely love Burger King's Chinese equivalent, 汉堡王 (Hàn bǎo wáng). In this case, both the sound and the meaning transform fairly well. 汉堡包 (Hàn bǎo bao) means hamburger, and wáng means king: hamburger king. Of course!

LIFE IS SOCIAL

Before we arrived, people in-the-know told us that life in Shanghai was very social. After only a few weeks in our new home, we understood what that meant. In a twist of fate, I suddenly found myself living out economist Thorstein Veblen's theories of conspicuous consumption and conspicuous leisure. In true leisure-class style, the Shanghai Tai Tais buzzed around the city lunching and shopping, twenty-first century testaments to their husbands' economic success. Most of the trailing spouse crowd had significantly more free time than in their home countries as a result of the perks of renting a home and having a driver and at least one household helper. The main activities of non-working spouses included deciding which SEA or AWCS (or insert the club name from any other home country) events to attend, lunching, shopping, volunteering, working out, or enjoying treatments at one of the multitude of spas. Some of the spouses were now free to tag along on business trips. People entertained at home and at restaurants.

During my first few boring weeks at The Pearl, with few people around, I never would have guessed how my life would change by September. Now, life wasn't a matter of figuring out what to do, it was about choosing from the plethora of competing opportunities. Obviously, the city had no shortage of social opportunities, but my new social life revolved primarily around four organizations—the SEA, the AWCS, the SAS PTSA, and MegaFit. On Wednesday afternoon, would I attend a fundraiser lunch for a charity or attend the SEA Indian sari fashion show? On Friday night, would we attend the American Chamber of Commerce Ball, join a fortieth birthday party at a swank restaurant, or enjoy the Bixby's I-Won-A-Chef party? What wonderful expat-people problems! Suddenly, the old saying that the longer people live in Asia, the less likely they are to ever want to return home, made perfect sense.

When invitations went out for the SEA and AWCS kick-off coffee mornings, Eden thoughtfully invited me to come along with her. We attended the AWCS coffee morning first, where about thirty women stood milling around the room, drinking hot beverages and signing up for Club memberships or paying their annual dues. Eden chatted with people she knew and politely introduced me. At times, I branched off and introduced myself to a few women who looked interesting. It took a great deal of energy. Within thirty minutes, my head started throbbing, so I sipped at my toasty oolong tea and walked over to grab an AWCS newsletter. I scanned the pages to get a feel for the group. Monthly coffees and lunches seemed its mainstays, but the group also organized tours, around-town events, and held a monthly book club. All of this sounded like a great start for me.

When Eden finished greeting her old friends, we moved on to the SEA's coffee morning. Again, we sipped our flavorful Chinese tea while working the room. The organization's beautiful, four-color, glossy magazine called the *Courier* immediately caught my eye. It would cost a fortune to produce this type of publication in the US, I thought, highly impressed. I thumbed through slick, enticing page after page. I spied articles on Chinese culture and history, book reviews, travel articles, human interest stories, and around town happenings. Each month the organization also offered lunches, cultural events, fund-raising formals, tours, and trips. I wondered how one became a contributor to this tome.

After the two coffee mornings, I returned to 110 The Pearl with a migraine again, but I considered the morning a big success. Thanks to Eden's generosity, clearly now between just the SEA and the AWCS, I could picture myself staying very busy and very happily distracted from the fact that I had left my dream life 7,000 miles away.

All the Tea in China

Within a week of joining, I attended my first SEA event, a traditional Chinese tea ceremony and lecture. When I arrived, I noted about twenty-five women gathered for the program. To my dismay, all of them seemed to know each other already as they gabbed busily away. Looking around the room, I recalled one of my regular nightmares, the one where in a panic I suddenly remember I have an exam. I arrive at school in the nick of time. I'm zipping through the hallways at top speed so I won't be late, but now I can't remember where my classroom is. Why don't I know where the classroom is? Because, as it now dawns on me, I have forgotten to attend the class all semester! Well, that's pretty much the feeling I had as I slid into my antique, carved wooden chair with the silk pillow top.

But as a newcomer, I knew what I had to do if no one talked to me. I waited and watched as the women around me yacked it up. When I found a lull in the conversation on either side, I started conversations with the ladies. They seemed mostly friendly and accommodating to me as a newcomer. Before I could exchange ming pian with anyone, however, the ceremony began. Watching the tea brewing ceremony itself seemed interesting, as was the theory behind what kind of glass each kind of tea required. Who knew? It amazed me that flower teas should be served in a brandy snifter. That way you can see the flower open and allow its fragrance to enhance the tea's flavor—how artistic! We also learned at what temperature and for how long to boil the various types of teas. It turns out that of course there is a proper way to store tea and a limit to how long you should keep it before it loses its flavor and special powers. I guessed that Chinese people never kept tea long enough for it to expire, though!

I also learned that originally, only the elite and the educated drank tea. They gathered in tea houses to conduct their lofty discussions and sometimes to hear storytellers or musical performances. Of course, just as with contemporary status symbols, because society's top echelons drank tea, everyone else wanted to drink it, too. Now, everyone drinks tea for both social reasons and for good health—it's considered a daily necessity. In addition, tea represents hospitality, and serving it to any type of guests remains the height of civility. At this point, I recalled going to Thailand to buy furniture in 1990, drinking endless rounds of the magical green liquid while negotiating. Now it made sense why. Here in China, tea shops wove through the landscape of every city and town, with endless varieties and qualities, prices running the gamut, from McDonald's cafe to the Ritz's high tea. I had noticed many people walking around in China carrying clear glass tumblers. Now I knew why: the clear jars allowed them to show off their tea leaves, like the designer labels on American jeans.

To me, the most interesting part of the program was the reasons for drinking the various types of teas. People discovered tea had medicinal properties around 500 BCE. Buddhist monks, for example, believed tea cleared their minds for meditation. More recently, modern science has shown that tea boosts brain power and mental alertness. Naturally all varieties (green, oolong, red, black, white, yellow, puerh, and flower) have numerous healing powers and health benefits, but green tea remains the most popular because people believe it the most healthful.

We also learned that it's crucial to brew tea it in the correct type of pot. Use a porcelain tea pot for green or white teas, as they require lower water temperatures. China's famous blue and white porcelain pots are best for black teas and puerhs because these leaves require hotter water for longer times. With flower tea, naturally a hostess should show off the opening process and the resulting foliage. So, of course these are properly brewed in a glass pot. All during the brewing discussion, a woman demonstrated how to prepare each type of tea and then passed around the brewed teas for us to sample. I found them all delicious and couldn't wait to get back to the supermarket to experiment with the different varieties.

With all this new, interesting information dancing around my brain, I dialed Mr. Zhou to pick me up. As we made our way back to The Pearl, I felt like I'd had a great introduction to the SEA and to Chinese culture. For once, I arrived home without a migraine—perhaps the tea worked its magic?

Chinese Opera School

Shortly after the tea event, I attended one of my favorite SEA events—a trip to the Shanghai Opera School, the City's version of a New York City performing arts school. The trip to the opera school took on additional significance for me because the information I gathered eventually developed into one of the first articles I contributed to the SEA's *Courier* magazine.

The SEA group began our tour in the dressing rooms, watching in wonder as the students stretched and put on their fabulously ornate costumes and magnificent headdresses. Coaches barked out last-minute directives, and make-up artists placed the final touches on their clients. About ten minutes later, a gong announced show time, and we filed into the auditorium.

The students presented scenes from five different operas to give us a taste of the variety of techniques that make up Chinese opera and to showcase their talent. The first story was of a young girl who rescues her village and then marries—oddly —the shortest of the village's attackers. This scene involved mostly vocalists, but also featured one troupe member doing a highly acrobatic dance with a spear. The second number was the Song Dynasty story of a rich hero who gives to the poor, much to the chagrin of his mother-in-law—a Chinese version of *Robin Hood*. This piece was followed by a scene illustrating the beauty and expectations of a young girl's life. The heroine tends her garden and her chickens, and later she takes up her embroidery. Interestingly, the piece involved almost no singing, relying instead on mime. The fourth scene also derived from a Song Dynasty opera. When a hero is banished, the governor who favored him sends a man to protect him in secret. While staying overnight at the same inn as the hero, the innkeeper thinks the protector is actually there to kill the hero. This scene was performed completely in mime and featured an inventive use of swords, acrobatics, and comedy, as the protector and the innkeeper crept around during the night. The grand finale showcased the entire acrobatic troop. About twenty boys danced with long poles, which eventually gave way to a complex series of aerial flips and spins. I never would have guessed that Chinese opera encompassed acrobatics and mime. I came away very impressed with the art form's richness and complexity and with the students' work ethic and remarkable talent.

In addition to the performance, we learned that the opera school's students ranged in age between twelve and fifteen. They came to the highly prestigious institute to study all aspects of traditional Chinese opera for seven years. Generally, they arrived from the countryside, with their tuition funded through a foundation. The students even earned a small salary. At the end, I felt surprised to discover the similarities between Chinese opera and Cirque-du-Soleil: music, dance, mime, and acrobatics. The difference, of course, was the splendid unmistakable costumes of traditional Chinese opera and the performers' unique make-up. While Cirque's performances can creatively take the audience anywhere in time and space—expect the unexpected—Shanghai Opera adheres to traditional stories—expect the expected. The Shanghai Opera School's young people seemed loaded with talent and devotion, and it was pure pleasure to have them introduce us to the infamous art form.

The American Women's Club of Shanghai

Though AWCS offered programming similar to the SEA's, for me the best part of my membership meant attending its book club. From my point of view, a good book club does for me what ecstasy does for clubbers—provides a blissed-out binge of words on pages and words voiced among fellow bibliophiles, making a good experience great. An international book club was like the ultimate frosting on a cake because it had the advantage of interesting, diverse perspectives of women who had lived abroad in one or more countries.

At my first book club meeting, about ten women assembled with their copies of *The Kite Runner*. As I took a seat on the hostess' couch, I felt fully aware of how privileged I was to have time to read, to have time to attend a book club meeting, and to enjoy this group's company. My stomach twittered in delight after realizing that *all* of the women had actually read the book as meaningful discussion flowed around the room. The conversation remained lively, as one of the ladies who had recently lived in the Middle East offered her unique insights. I found the talk about treatment of household help especially interesting, as this was my first experience having an ayi. I listened keenly as a woman from Mexico argued that while the main character's treatment as a servant seemed cruel, she had learned that there, and especially here in China, a lady-of-the-house who acts kind and friendly sets herself up for all kinds of problems. Societal roles were defined, and to keep order, needed to remain that way, she explained.

Some of the other ladies jumped in then, commenting that yes, indeed, they had experienced problems in Shanghai because they had empathized with their ayis and treated them too well. Someone chimed in that the hierarchy existed here in China—as well as in other parts of the world—for thousands of years. By being "American nice" and treating staff as equals, ayis see you as weak and easy to take advantage of. Numerous stories then unfolded about ayis stealing clothing and other household items or asking their Tai Tais to fund various expenses. I listened, spellbound.

I left that first meeting excited, enlightened, and weighted down with ming pians. On the car trip home, I scanned the list of novels for 2005-06.

BOOKS	AUTHORS
River Town	Peter Hessler
Cry, the Beloved Country	Alan Paton
The Kite Runner	Khaled Hosseini
Coastliners	Joanne Harris
Enemy Women	Paulette Jiles
The Good Women of China	Xinran
Reading Lolita in Tehran	Azar Nafisi
Sky Burial	Xinran
Women of the Silk	Gail Tsukiyama

I felt enthusiastic about both the book list and the opportunity to share productive, interesting discussions with this group. I felt relieved to discover another source of happiness in my crazy new life.

When I got home that afternoon, I ordered the books off Amazon, unsure of what would happen. Would the books by Xinran, the Japanese, or the Middle Eastern author be confiscated? Would the government assign extra "watchers" to me? I waited anxiously to find out.

Within a week, amazingly all my purchases arrived, apparently untouched by customs, and postmarked from Germany. Germany? Whatever the case, I felt very encouraged to know that even if the government planned to read all my emails, continue banning websites, and keep tabs on my book orders, so far so good! I'd keep ordering and hope for the best: I just had to remember that Big Brother was, for sure, watching.

Everything Old Is New

In addition to the SEA and AWCS events, the Shanghai Community Center offered programming. I've always been interested in alternative and folk medicine, so when Eden suggested signing up for a Traditional Chinese Medicine (TCM) class together, I thought it sounded like a great idea.

On the day of our first class, Eden's driver ferried us into Jin Qiao. There, in the living room of the Community Center, a Shanghainese woman named Dr. Yang gave us a general overview of contemporary TCM. As she explained, it's more of a long-term health plan, based on ancient Taoist theories. There are no quick fixes, as in Western medicine. For me, the day's big take-away was that walnuts will do the job if you're feeling low energy and want to clear and energize your mind.

At our second class, a Dr. Chu lectured on the practice's five essential elements. Each element relates to certain bodily organs corresponding to other body parts. For example, earth represents the spleen; fire, the heart; wood, the liver; water, the kidneys; and metal, the lungs. Each of these organs controls the functions of other elements of the body. The kidneys, for example, are responsible for your hearing and your bones. Improving your hearing, then, would require a kidney tonic. The lungs link to your large intestine, skin, nose, and throat. For clear, glowing skin, eat some almonds, suggested Dr. Chu.

Next, we covered how the TCM doctor determines what ails a patient and then creates a prescription. According to Dr. Chu, she starts by checking both the patient's pulse and her tongue in order to make a diagnosis and then recommends an herbal remedy. The pulse is connected to the heart function, so if the heart is beating too rapidly, a person might feel uncomfortably warm. In this case, the doctor would advise the patient to eat some "cooling" foods. If the patient's pulse is too slow, then her body is too cold, and she'll need "warming" foods or herbs to restore her body's balance.

When checking the tongue, the doctor looks to see whether the top of the tongue is clear or coated with a white film. Then she looks at the parts of the tongue that correspond to the five essential elements. The tip of your tongue, for example, tells the doctor what's going on with your heart. I found the information both fascinating and overwhelming.

Dr. Chu went on to discuss the differences between Western medicine and TCM. In the West, we tend to go to a doctor once we've already become sick. TCM involves long-range preventative measures. To maintain your heart health, for example—which promotes better sleep and improved strength—your TCM doctor might advise eating congee mixed with goji berries, peanuts, mung beans, red beans, bean sprouts, and certain herbs once daily. No wonder Chinese grocery stores were chock full of such interesting dried stuff!

Apparently, sometimes partnerships between Western medicine and TCM are beneficial. Take cancer, for instance. A Chinese person might be advised to ingest an herbal mixture to help prepare his body for cancer surgery for two to three months before the operation. He might then use acupuncture to try to diminish the negative effects of chemotherapy and use certain herbs—like ginseng—to speed the healing process. Although many people have had excellent results using TCM to treat serious illnesses, TCM does not work well for every type of severe condition. Though fascinating, I pondered how I might apply any of this in a meaningful way.

I looked forward to our third class, as it covered acupressure and acupuncture, which I wanted to try. The theory behind acupressure is that there are twelve meridians located along channels in your body. Your life force energy—or *chi*—flows along these routes, connecting to various organs. Blocked meridians create an imbalance or illness. Pressing on the point that corresponds to the area of trouble releases it and gets the *chi* flowing again. Do you have a headache? Just apply firm pressure on the space between your thumb and your first finger. I found this class worthwhile just to discover the spot on the foot that stops hunger pangs. Acupuncture is essentially the same, except it uses very thin, long needles to unblock the meridians.

Soon after this lecture, Planet and I got lucky when someone in his office hooked us up with Dr. Shao, the head of acupuncture at the esteemed Fudan University (basically China's Harvard). He made house calls, and his fee seemed reasonable. During my first treatment, Dr. Shao gently inserted the first needle into my hand. It caused a strange, tingling sensation. My third and fourth fingers began to feel stressed and numb. It wasn't painful, just uncomfortable, like my hand had a headache. Dr. Shao explained that he only planned to use four needles on me that day, as that would be enough for my first experience. After leaving the four needles in my hands for twenty minutes, I couldn't believe how clear my sinuses felt. I hadn't breathed this freely in years!

When he returned the next week, my sinuses had remained relatively clear. So Dr. Shao placed the needles needed for sinus maintenance, but added two more needles to create an energy boost. The procedure seemed to work too well. For the next few nights, I felt so wired I could hardly sleep. The third week I graduated to seven needles to keep my sinuses clear and my energy level high. This time, my energy remained strong during the day, but I slept well at night. Unfortunately, according to the good doctor, I still had a way to go toward the *twenty* needles required for weight loss treatment.

In the meantime, we had reached the final class in the TCM series: the long-awaited trip to the TCM hospital, pharmacy, and museum in the Yu Yuan garden complex. Dr. Chu met our group at the door outside the medical history museum to give us a short tour. There wasn't much to see, just some herbs and a lot of drawings. Unfortunately, all the explanations for the exhibits were written in Chinese, and translating them apparently wasn't part of Chu's agenda.

Fortunately, afterward we followed her upstairs to the third floor where we found doctors' offices. We assembled in a waiting room and she took us one-by-one into her office for our diagnoses. When it was my turn, the doctor looked at my tongue and then felt the pulse on both of my wrists. She concluded that I should improve my digestive system in order to have more energy. I said ok, but I really wanted something for my sinus troubles and some herbs to help me lose weight. Interestingly, she assured me that her remedy for digestive troubles would fix both of those problems, too. When I chatted with the other ladies back in the waiting room, I concluded that she probably gave us all the same diagnosis and possibly even the same prescription. Oh, well. It couldn't hurt, might help.

With prescriptions in hand, our group meandered down one floor to the fascinating compounding pharmacy. On one side of the room stood hundreds of drawers housed in sets of cabinets. It reminded me of the old library card catalogue system. Atop the cabinets stood dozens of the popular and infamous antique ginger jars. A number of people waited on the benches in front of the cabinets. On the opposite side lay the cashier's window, and just down from there, the two customer service windows. Behind them, I saw more cabinets with a multitude of drawers. A door behind the customer service agents stood open, revealing the actual pharmacists, pounding a bountiful harvest of herbs and flowers on long tables.

When my turn came, I handed my prescription to the customer service man. He pointed me toward the cashier. Oh, right. You always paid first in China. I gave the cashier the equivalent of only a few dollars. What a refreshing change from the high prices of medicine and the drama of trying to buy sinus medications (because of their role in illegal substances) in the US. With receipt in hand, I strolled back to the customer service side. The clerk thankfully spoke enough English to explain that I could either let the pharmacy boil down my herbal remedy into a jelly-like compound, which they'd place in individu-al-dose sealed plastic bags, or I could take it home in loose leaf form and boil the mixture myself for thirty minutes each time I required a dose. I opted to take the herb mix with me.

About fifteen minutes later, I made my way down to the first floor toward the door. The sights of the first floor distracted me, however. I spied an entire showcase the length of the back wall devoted solely to ginseng—the king of TCM remedies. The prices ranged from affordable-for-anyone to royal family only. I couldn't resist buying some reasonably priced ginseng root in hopes of strengthening my immune system for the winter and avoiding the flu. I thought I could just toss the ginseng into the pot with the herbal digestive brew, but apparently not. It could, however, be added to tea. Glad I asked.

When I arrived home that afternoon, I showed Xiao Ting the copy of my "prescription." She flashed me the thumbs up sign and announced *hen hao* (very good). She opened a packet. Inside I saw pieces of something that looked like tree bark, dried black discs, and something resembling barley. It seemed wise that I had no clue what I was about to ingest! Ayi poured the concoction into a pot of water and boiled it for thirty minutes. When I returned, the potion had morphed into something akin to thick, red cough syrup. After all the boiling, the substance only amounted to a teaspoon or two. Xiao Ting advised me to put the medicine into a cup of tea, but I opted to be brave and just chug it. While the flavor wasn't exactly bad—it tasted like strong, very tart cranberry juice, but more savory—I wouldn't have wanted to endure it through an entire cup of tea. Good decision! Between the TCM potion and Dr. Shao's treatments, my sinuses felt clearer than they had in years, and without the side effects Western medicines sometimes cause. I was quickly becoming a fan of TCM.

PTSA Days & Coffee Mornings

The final cornerstone of my Shanghai social life was the SAS PTSA and school coffee mornings. One lovely September morning, I anxiously rode out to Pudong Links for the year's first PTSA meeting. I was eager to get a feel for the school, learn how the parents could get involved, and meet some other parents. At the time, the school served about 350 students (about 150 families) in grades pre-K through tenth. As a result, I found it impressive that about fifty mothers showed up.

As an ice breaker, the PTSA president separated us into groups by how many languages we each spoke. The biggest group of course knew one to two, then three to five, and finally, five to seven. *Impressive!* In a way, I envied the women who had learned more than two languages, and I secretly wished that our overseas adventure would not end with China.

Once in groups, we eagerly discussed where we'd been raised and places we'd lived. We talked a bit about overseas moves and our first impressions of Shanghai. The best part was that everyone wanted to make friends, and I went home with several ming pian. One of the more memorable ladies I met that day was a tall, energetic lady from South Africa, about forty, with bright purple tips sprouting from her jet-black pixie haircut. I felt surprised that a woman her age would wear a hair style that in Ohio I'd have expected to see sported only by advertising copywriters and rebellious teenagers. Yet it reminded me how wide and interesting a world we inhabit, especially the microcosm that made up the Shanghai expat universe. I fell in love with the opportunities I now had on a daily basis to meet people from all over the world and enjoy their uniqueness, even something as simple as a trendy hairdoo.

After the brief get-to-know-you, we reassembled into one large group. Here, the PTSA president talked about the various projects for the year and encouraged us to join at least one committee. I signed up for Santa's Workshop and the Spring Gala. I looked forward to contributing and to getting to know more ladies.

My next opportunity to meet other SAS mothers and learn more about the school community was at grade-level coffees and compound coffees. Shortly after the PTSA coffee, I attended the second-grade event. A second-grade room mother who also served on the PTSA volunteered to host. Disappointingly, only about eight mothers showed up. We helped ourselves to coffee, tea, and cookies, and gathered around the dining room table. Then the meeting began. After only a few minutes, it grew clear that the agenda—welcoming new parents and getting to know the other second grade parents—had been high-jacked. The tone between our hostess—a charming Italian lady named Guilia, whose son became one of Anders' good friends—and one of the other mothers rapidly grew heated. The program rapidly devolved as the two of them nit-picked over various issues. After an hour, only two out of six agenda items had been covered, both without resolution. The meeting was clearly going nowhere, so, disappointed, I excused myself. I hoped the rest of the PTSA meetings would be more productive.

Fortunately, my next coffee morning went off without any drama. I looked forward to the session both for the topic—raising kids overseas—and to meeting more parents. When I arrived, women were busy serving themselves coffee and tea, loading their plates with pastries and fruit, and chatting. At 10:00 am, the PTSA president introduced herself, welcomed everyone to the new school year and to Shanghai, and then gave an overview of the day's topic. We began the session with an icebreaker that prompted us all to start thinking about the issue. She asked us to break into groups according to how many different countries we'd lived in.

"One to three in this corner, four to six in that corner, and more than six over here," she announced, matter-of-factly.

I searched the other women's faces. *Who else just got blown away by the fact that some of these families had already lived in not just more than one country, but more than six!* In awe, I kept an eye on how many ladies migrated to that part of the room while I made my way over to the largest group, the one-to-three countries. Not many, but still impressive. I noticed a surprisingly high number in the second largest group, four to six countries. I tried to imagine that lifestyle. Had I been missing something by not wanting to leave Shaker Heights?

In our breakout groups, we spent a few minutes interviewing the woman next to us and then presenting her to the group. Then we spent a few minutes discussing our own experiences raising kids overseas and how their lives might be affected by the number of countries we'd lived in. Wow, this was NOT something I ever imagined contemplating while dutifully undertaking crunches at Big Ben's gym or grocery shopping at Heinen's!

Soon, one of the assistant principals made his way to the front of the room. The President called everyone back to their seats and introduced him. Mr. Mundy began by saying that one of the elementary-level teachers had authored the book *Third Culture Kids*, his topic for today. Intrigued and impressed, I made a mental note to buy a copy. He defined a third culture kid (TCK) as a minor who has spent significant time in a non-home culture (their parents' home-country culture). As I already knew from meeting some of the kids in my compound, a home culture could seem challenging to define, especially when the parents each hailed from different countries or the kids had moved often.

Then, Mr. Mundy gave a brief history of expatriates in China. In the last century, expats arrived in the Middle Kingdom primarily as missionaries, with a few diplomats tossed in here and there. In the next phase, expats mostly served as military personnel or diplomats. When China reopened to the West in the late 1980s, expatriates primarily came to seek their fortunes in business. This turn of events gave rise to the TCK phenomenon.

Then he went on to describe some of the negative aspects of living as a TCK. One of the main issues is that kids may struggle with their identity because they feel like they belong both everywhere and nowhere. They may feel restless as adults, moving from place to place; or they might do the opposite, insisting on staying in one place the rest of their lives. Statistically, however, they are more likely to roam.

The assistant principal went on to say that TCKs may have never lived in their home country, or lived most of their lives away (like Eden's kids). So, when they repatriate, they feel out of synch with the culture of the country listed on their passport because it is actually new to them, and thus a reverse culture shock. TCKs may feel homesick for the foreign cultures they've lived in and tend to socialize only with other TCKs. Constantly moving may make kids feel insecure and powerless, which may result in depression and acting out (Bianca?). They may experience friendships differently, because their relationships are usually short-term. I could empathize with that, as I was now on a learning curve for the expat-friendship revolving door.

One last effect Mr. Mundy mentioned was that while TCK teens tend to be much more mature than their home-country counterparts, they tend to adapt to young adulthood more slowly. They are used to strong family bonds and spending much more time with family. The author also discovered that nearly one-hundred percent of TCKs earn college degrees, yet a high percentage of them move from school-to-school and take more than four years to graduate.

The good news was that TCKs tend to be in demand in workforces worldwide because they have learned three key skills: adaptability, flexibility, and tolerance. Apparently, the thought of an overseas assignment excites them, rather than floors them, and they tend to learn new languages easily and willingly. As adults, TCKs may even seek out jobs that offer them many travel opportunities or longer-term foreign assignments. Because they have friends all over the world, TCKs tend to see the world as truly multi-cultural, and they tend to be more tolerant and respectful of others. Other positive characteristics generated from being a TCK include independence, creativity, and a strong comfort level with risk taking They also tend to become good problem solvers and successful conflict mediators. According to the speaker, TCKs favor careers in education, the professions, or entrepreneurship as adults.

Given all the information I had just ingested, I hoped Alexis and Anders would benefit from our stint in China. I also thought back to the woman in my Ohio Rosh Chodesh group who had asked me to view expat life in China as a gift to my children. I suddenly felt grateful that I took this opportunity.

Shopping Is Socializing

What would September in Shanghai be without more shopping? In my shopping adventures, I both developed friendships and experienced cultural growth. This month, I learned about buying furniture, the Yu Yuan, and more about the fabric market.

Like a kid in a candy store, Planet had used our settling-in allowance to order a king-sized bed (for an eight-year-old?), a dresser and mirror, a desk, a chair, and two nightstands with two drawers each, for which he had paid about $2,000. He excitedly explained that he had been thinking ahead: our daughter would have this lovely French-style white wood ensemble to take with her when she moved into her first apartment. Since this event remained about fifteen years away, I thought the scenario unlikely. But my husband's plan was already in motion when the kids and I arrived, and now I had to schlepp out to Jisheng Wellborn furniture store in the hinterlands of Puxi's Gu Bei district to make the final payment.

I sat watching the traffic patterns, frighteningly similar to a Mario Brothers game, for a full seventy-five minutes. I couldn't say what worried me more: Mr. Zhou dodging disasters or the 7,000RMB that threatened to burst forth from my purse. Why was I carrying this huge wad of cash? Well, amazingly, the only places that accepted credit cards in China at this time were the big hotels. Consumers had to pay cash for everything, even an apartment! I heard tales of expats watching people depart banks with bulging pillowcases stuffed with cash for their major purchases. *Crazy!* Apparently, this was also why all businesses had bill counting devices. Thank goodness for these machines, or customers might have had to stand in line for hours while clerks counted and verified payments!

When we arrived, I walked into the marble building lobby clutching my handbag tightly to my body. The building's six floors displayed nearly every style of furniture, from over-the-top Versace to wicker. Finally, I reached Jisheng Wellborn's top-floor shop. I handed the clerk my receipt and my wad of cash. She piled the money into a bill counter, which began to whirr. A minute later, she removed the stash and put it back into the machine. Clerks always counted money a second time. All was well. She grabbed an English-speaking colleague, who explained that now they could complete my furniture order and would deliver it to my house in two weeks. Then she handed me a paid receipt, stamped in red. What a relief!

When the suite arrived, it filled up Alexis' empty bedroom very nicely. The quality seemed a little better and the prices a little lower than Pottery Barn Kid—a reasonable value. While I found the furniture attractive, I couldn't help thinking that we could simply have moved the guest room furniture in there. Seriously, what were we going to do with the suite back in the US, as she already had a high-quality bedroom set? I guessed this would just have to be Planet's problem, since this was his big idea.

My next shopping adventure came through Marilyn Bixby's generosity. Reg Bixby was one of Planet's major clients in Shanghai, and his corporate goals were one of the main reasons we were now trying to build a new life 7,000 miles from home. Reg's wife, Marilyn, was a good natured, petite Englishwoman with platinum blonde hair. She had one child who was Anders' age, who attended the British school. After weeks of exchanging emails, Marilyn and I had finally come up with an outing date. I waited excitedly for our date because she suggested we go to the Yu Yuan Gardens—a Shanghai must-see venue that I hadn't yet visited.

On the chosen day, I walked over to her house at 8:00 am, and we rode into Puxi with her husband. Their driver dropped Reg off at the beautiful old French Concession mansion that served as his firm's office. Then we went on to the Yu Yuan, an old warlord's mansion built around the 1500s. Streams of people wandered through remnants of the maze-like garden, visited the infamous tea house, sampled the legendary dumplings from the shop in the middle of the main thoroughfare, and strolled through the hundreds of little shops surrounding the property every day. Finally, I was seeing a place resembling what I had expected China to look like—taupe Shikumen-style one-story buildings with traditional, thick red-tile roofs, surrounded by elaborate gardens.

I soaked up the quintessential Chinese scenery as I followed my kind neighbor inside one of the larger buildings into a room where artists stood creating traditional silk wall hangings of poetry merged with nature scenes. This type of art interested neither of us, so we continued on to the next room. Here, artists labored intensely, hand-painting classical scenes with tiny brushes inside small snuff bottles. I couldn't imagine the skill and patience required to complete such a task! I decided that one of these bottles would make a nice anniversary gift for Planet. In fact, these would make excellent holiday gifts for various family members. I thought I might buy a few, depending on the price. I squeezed my hands together nervously. I wasn't well-versed in negotiating Chinese-style yet.

"How much do you want for this?" I asked the artist, pointing to a small yellow bottle with a lovely village scene on it.

"Two hundred eighty RMB," he replied.

That was about $40 US. It seemed way too much. Or was it? I didn't want to get screwed on my first outing! I expected Marilyn would step in to help me, but she didn't. So, the artist and I shot numbers back and forth a few times more times until the price reached about $15 US. I searched Marilyn's face. Was this a reasonable price? I had no idea. She gave me the "go ahead" side head nod.

I had no clue the bottles were standard, cheesy tourist fare, so, I bought three of them, thinking I had scored some unique, nice gifts. I walked away from the artist feeling pleased with my gifts, but less than happy with my bartering skills. Later, when I worked at the school's Santa's Workshop, I discovered the parent volunteers sold these perfume/snuff bottles for about $5 each! Clearly, as a newbie, I had a lot to learn! From there, Marilyn and I wandered through the rest of the small galleries, but nothing else caught my eye. We left the estate, strolling past the tea house and into the venue's shopping lanes. We browsed for a while, but at this point in my Tai Tai career, I quickly grew overwhelmed by the dizzying, endless array of merchandise and exhausted from negotiating.

After a couple hours, we were ready to move on to our lunch stop. Marilyn dialed her driver to bring us to the New Heights restaurant at Three on the Bund. "Three Bund," as the Old China Hands (someone who has lived in China long enough to know the ins and outs or has become an expert on Chinese language and culture) called it, housed four or five of Shanghai's best restaurants, several swanky designer boutiques, and some posh offices. New Heights occupied most of the building's top floor, and people flocked there as much for the photo opportunities (great views of the Bund from the terrace, especially when lit up at night) as for the fine food. We sat outside taking in the partly sunny, warm day and enjoying the superb view.

As I perused the menu, the variety of mostly international dishes, many of which appeared on menus across Asia as well as in Western Europe—proved a refreshing change from standard American fare. The restaurant's popular cold salad buffet looked ample and delicious, but the Hainan Chicken—very popular throughout Asia—caught my eye. In this dish, the meat is poached in spices and served on seasoned rice with hot chilies and cucumber. I thought I had to try it.

To my surprise, I also discovered that New Heights served iced tea. Since I had learned in my TCM class that the Chinese consider cold drinks very bad for the body and tea is the national beverage of choice, I couldn't imagine a drink more offensive than iced tea. But there it was, ice and all! Overall, Marilyn and I relaxed and enjoyed a wonderful lunch break.

Now I learned something else: in Shanghai, if you have the car, the time, and any money left, just keep shopping. So, with our stomachs satisfied and after a refreshing stop in a clean, posh bathroom, we decided to venture over to the Xiang Yang gift market. I suspected it earned the name "gift" market both as a way of getting around the place being technically illegal and the word "gift" being what you'd put on packages to get around nosy customs handlers. At times, international watchdogs would crack down, and suddenly the market would close or disappear, only to re-open a week or a month later. What a crazy world!

Some women love their shoes, but I'm a purse girl, and I couldn't wait to take a crack at them. For the first fifteen minutes or so, I poked, frustrated, through vendor stalls bursting with poor-quality junk. I had heard copy goods had quality levels, and now I understood what that meant. Finally, we located a stall where the purses looked like the real deal. Excited, I paid about 140RMB per bag (or about $17.25 each) for two Louis Vuittons that day. I wasn't sure whether this was a good price, and Marilyn seemed determined to let me make my own mistakes. Maybe the British considered stepping in impolite? I intended to give my purchases to family members back in the US as holiday gifts, so I thought they still made great presents at a great price.

Later, when I learned some Mandarin and had practiced shopping for a while, I discovered the real Tai Tai price. From then on, I never paid more than 70RMB (about $10 US) for handbags, except for the highest quality. Based on my recent shopping adventures, I began to develop a reality check that I called the "Target/Walmart/Kmart Test." Whenever I felt tempted to buy something, I would ask myself, "if I saw this item at an American discount store for this price, would I buy it?" If I could answer "yes," I purchased. This simple question helped me avoid buying absurd quantities of junk—a risk every expat and tourist runs. It also helped me walk away from less savvy deals.

Before long, we needed to head back to retrieve our children from the bus stop. I arrived back at The Pearl, tired but happy, and thankful to Marilyn for showing me around. Even better, I'd spent a day out and about without developing a migraine! As far as developing a friendship, Marilyn and I didn't become strongly attached, but we got along very well and spent time together about once a month.

Angela Templeton and I also gave friendship a try through a shopping day. Angela invited me and two of her church friends, Esther and Melissa, on a trip to the fabled Dong Jia Du. (Whatever the market's actual name, no one ever called it that. They simply always referred to it as the Dong Jia Du.) Angela's driver picked us up, and we ladies enjoyed getting to know each other during the forty-five-minute drive into Puxi. I learned that Esther and Melissa were members of Angela's church. Esther, also new this year, was a cheerful lady from the Midwest who had three kids at the Christian school in Jin Qiao. Melissa, still in her late 20s, had already spent several years in Taiwan, plus a couple years in Shanghai. She did not have any kids yet and was currently teaching both Chinese and English language lessons. I admired her fluency in Mandarin.

When we arrived at our destination, externally it appeared a ramshackle old cement structure, fronted by about a dozen small, simple vendor tents. From the outside, passersby would never guess a large, lively market lay bustling within. Inside, about three hundred 12x12 open front stores stood in a labyrinth on the tan cement floor. The tan cement walls displayed the cracks and stains of age. The stalls weren't organized by type, but seemingly by random. A leather vendor set up right next to the men's suit wools, ball gown taffeta neighbored with pajama flannels. As I examined the fabrics, I was disappointed; I thought they would be much higher quality. Later I learned that to obtain the finest Italian or English fabrics and work with the best tailors, you had to visit the chic European-style stores in the Maoming Lu area, near Xin Tian Di. The Dong Jia Du Lu was for the common folk and simpler items, not for Tai Pans (rich, successful business men). Nevertheless, this market became one of my favorite places to shop in Shanghai. I absolutely loved searching out various fabrics and getting whatever clothes I dreamed up made so inexpensively. It's one of the parts of Shanghai life I still miss most.

Strolling down the aisles, I noticed none of the aggressiveness I'd experienced at the Xiang Yang. Instead, these vendors cheerfully invited us to browse their stalls or happily thrust clothing toward us, gently calling *"shi shi kan"* (try it on). I found my stress melting away. I was actually having fun. Finally, my new acquaintances found a vendor they wanted to work with to purchase school clothes for their kids. Melissa chattered away in Mandarin with the seller, resulting in Angela and Ester paying only about $12 each for blouses and $6 a pair for shorts. They also ordered great-looking Chanel-style boucle jackets for themselves for about $18!

At one point, I had to go to the bathroom—a very undesirable situation, I was about to learn. Patrons could smell the briny stench from several aisles away. A cranky attendant sat outside, and you had to pay her some small change to go inside. Whenever I visited, I *never* knew how much to give her. I just randomly held out whatever coins were in my pocket. As a result, she always let me in, but sometimes she handed me a square of toilet paper, sometimes not. The smell, unfortunately, wasn't even the worst part of the bathroom experience. Inside the grimy, dimly lit toilet area, lay small square cubicles, like stalls, but with low walls and no doors. Patrons had to pee into a canal of water below, which connected to and ran past all the stalls. As river of various wastes streamed by beneath me, I wondered how many foreigners had managed to endure the smell as far as the doorway, but then passed out at the actual toilet scene. God forbid a lady wasn't a strong squatter—oh, the consequences!

I returned to my group, and after about two hours in the fabric market, we moved across the street to the well-known designers clothing store across the street. Since it reminded the Americans of TJ Maxx or Marshalls, we called it "Shanghai TJ's." It seemed to sell overstocks and samples of Western designer brands from Europe and the US at remarkable prices. There was no haggling, but the shop offered better prices than we could probably have negotiated for ourselves at the Xiang Yang. I scored some Armani, Burberry, and Chanel t-shirts for between 58RMB (about $7.50) and 78RMB (about $9.75)! More awesome gifts to check off my holiday and birthday shopping lists. This non-shopper was definitely growing converted, one adventure at a time!

Having worked up an appetite, Angela brought us to a favorite lunch spot next—a noodle venue near the Pudong Flower Market. Standing just outside the restaurant door, I looked through the large front picture window and watched the chefs cutting very long strands of fresh noodle dough and expertly stuffing dumplings with their *kuai zi* (chopsticks) at lightning speed. I was so excited to try a real, locals' Shanghainese noodle shop!

Already an Old Shanghai Hand, Angela ordered for us all. When the waiters streamed out carrying the delicious dishes to our table, I had no idea what most of them were. Yet, every one of the six noodle, meat, and vegetable dishes tasted absolutely delicious. When the bill came, I couldn't believe we had totally stuffed ourselves for only109RMB (about $15.75, no tipping required)! We even had left overs, which Angela gave to her patient driver. (Though I suspected the kind-hearted Angela had over-ordered intentionally.)

Latecomers

One day in late September, new faces appeared at the SAS bus stop. School started nearly a month ago, and I hadn't heard of the family's move-in through the grapevine. Hmm.

When the coach rolled up, and kids began to disembark, Anders' blonde curls appeared, a distressed expression on his face. A boy I didn't recognize followed closely behind.

"Mommy! He punched me!" my son shouted, wrapping himself around my legs.

When I looked to see where the offending boy had gone, I spied a tall, wiry, flame-red-haired child trying to hustle his mother away from the bus stop as quickly as possible.

"Excuse me," I said to the mother, whose hair matched her child's. "My son says your son punched him." I couldn't be sure what reaction I'd get, but I had to take the risk.

"Hey!" she turned to her wriggling offspring. "Did you punch this boy?"

Her son looked guiltily to the ground.

"Kyle! We've been here for less than a week! You have no idea who your friends are going to be! Do you think it's a good idea to start off by punching the guy who just might be your new best friend?"

Oh, excellent point! I liked this mom already!

"No," the boy shrugged.

"OK. Now say you're sorry and be more careful in the future," the woman commanded. Then she turned to me. "I'm so sorry. He should know better. I'm Meg O'Brien. We just arrived from Japan," she added, extending her hand.

I gave her my hand. "Shelly Aschkenase. We're new, too. We moved here from Shaker Heights, Ohio in August."

"Nice to meet you. I'm hosting the October coffee morning for the PTSA at my house. I hope you can come."

Wow! This wonder woman had been here less than a week, and she was already jumping into action at school? Clearly, I had much to learn from these scrappy expat ladies.

"I'm looking forward to it," I replied, sincerely.

"No hard feelings?"

"No hard feelings."

This exchange could have gone quite badly, but thankfully, this was expat life. I liked Meg immediately for both her parenting style and her ability to hit the ground running. She had just flown to the top of the list of women I hoped to enclose in my friend circle.

The SAS PTSA wisely asked parents to host coffee mornings in each compound so that they could get to know each other and develop a community. I planned to take advantage of the opportunity. So, on event day, I walked over to

Meg's. There, I learned that the O'Briens originated from Boston. Since Planet grew up in the Boston area, we just happened to have a DVD of the World Series 2004—the infamous year the Red Sox finally broke the legendary curse. I suddenly had a great friendship-building idea: I invited the O'Brien family to come over for dinner and watch the Sox's glorious comeback.

On the designated Sunday afternoon, I cooked up a big batch of chili, roasted hot dogs on the grill, filled bowls with salty snacks, and baked brownies—a typical American-style baseball feast. When Meg and her brood had settled into our family room, I fired up the DVD. After a few innings, we paused the ball game and moved to the kitchen dinette for a refreshment break. I had laid out our meal buffet-style and everything looked ready and plentiful. My family never put their wieners in buns, so I felt sure I had enough bread. But wouldn't you just know Murphy's Law would prevail! Today my kids decided that if the O'Brien kids liked their hot dogs in buns, then they would wrap theirs in white doughy goodness, too. And then the expanding group of bun eaters also had the nerve to eat more franks than anticipated. Now I faced not only a wiener shortage, but a bun crisis. In the meantime, my plentiful, savory chili remained completely ignored. This group didn't even have the decency to slather it on their wieners! My face and hands grew moist with anxiety. Ayi had the day off, so I couldn't send her to the compound quick shop. What could I do?

Meg must have seen the look of impending doom on my face. Mrs. Totally Organized stepped in and sent her teenaged daughter home to get buns from their house. Talk about embarrassing! I usually provide enough food for a small army when I have guests and end up with a ridiculous portion of leftovers, but somehow, I had completely misjudged this event. Did *today* really have to be the first time I messed up?

With the adults safely distracted by the bread emergency, Anders and Kyle concocted a plan to see who could eat more brownies while we weren't watching. The boys ate the *entire* batch quicker than a People's Square pickpocket! I had nothing to offer as a back-up. Now I had a dessert debacle, too! How had this happened to me, *twice* in one event? I chalked it up to the anxiety born of the Shanghai-life learning curve, but that didn't make me feel any better.

Though our boys developed a strong friendship, even the Red Sox's curse removal seemingly couldn't reverse the impending downhill trend I'd set with Meg that day. I didn't hear from her for a while after our family dinner. Was our potential friendship already as dead and dusty as a Ming Tomb?

Finally, Meg decided to give me one more chance. The kids had an upcoming half-day at school, and we made plans to take the kids to visit the Shanghai Museum of Science and Technology. I certainly hoped that my family and I would redeem ourselves on the outing. But the morning of the event, Meg called me to cancel. I wasn't surprised. Ever since our family dinner, I sensed that my "incompetence" had rendered me "not friend material." Though our boys remained best buddies until my family left China, Meg never made plans with me again. She remained cordial to me whenever we saw each other, but clearly, I wasn't cut out to be part of *her* circle.

Life's A Ball

It seems few Americans attend formal events any more, but in September 2005, Planet and I learned that formal balls actually formed an important part of the vast spectrum of Shanghai expat social life, even for regular people. A delightful throwback to a previous era, these grand affairs were thrown by embassies, charities, multi-national companies, and even schools. Most served as fund raisers. I thought formal galas seemed a refreshing change from the pervasive casualness of mainstream American life. "Prom for grown-ups." Nice!

Within weeks of our arrival, Tim and Trina, parents of the younger Australian boys on our street, invited us to join their table at the upcoming Australian Ball. (Clearly, the water fight fiasco hadn't even registered with them.) Their kindness gave us a chance to get to know them, meet more people, and figure out the Shanghai ball circuit.

"Do you have any magazines around?" Trina asked me one day as the Aussie Ball date approached.

"Um…not really."

"OK, well don't worry. I've got plenty," she assured me, reaching for a few. "Just look through these, then get whatever you want made at the fabric market. Or you can just call Mrs. Wong."

Get a dress made? From a magazine?

"Mrs. Wong?"

"She's the tailor everyone uses. She has so many customers at The Pearl, she actually comes here a couple times a week. I'll give you her ming pian."

"Wow. Thanks!" At the moment, I felt blown away by the fact that I, a simple housewife from Ohio, was not just attending a ball but getting an ensemble custom made for the occasion! Life in Shanghai really did seem like a completely alternate universe.

Trina also explained that the Aussie Ball had an intergalactic theme that year and someone from our table group would make masks for us to wear. Masks? How exactly did one craft a dress to go with an intergalactic mask? Oh, boy.

I opened a *People* and paged through until I saw some photos of movie stars wearing gowns. A delicious delirium crept through my brain: I could just pick a movie star gown, pick my fabric, and *voila*! I could get my glam on without spending thousands at a Beverly Hills or New York boutique! I was one up on Carol Brady again!

The next day, I phoned Mrs. Wong to set up an appointment. Then I ventured down to the fabric market. There, I chose gold material—hoping it suited the gala theme—and planned to have a tulle layer over the skirt portion.

A few days later the legendary seamstress arrived at my house with her young apprentice/niece in tow. Upstairs in my bedroom, Mrs. Wong looked at me, she looked at the fabric, and then she tsk tsk'ed.

"No. No, no, no." She shook her head.

Apparently, this fabric would not do. As I was still so new to China, I didn't know whether she was being honest based on her skills and training or whether I was being played into buying whatever she wanted to sell me. I listened carefully as she explained her superior idea. I held my breath as I asked her for the price. My eyes grew large as moon cakes when she told me that for approximately $20, I would have both the fabric and her custom dress-making service! Played or not, at that price I could live with the cost of my learning curve.

When I agreed, her niece whipped out a tape measure and carefully began making notes of my various body parts. The duo promised to finish my dress by the next week. I hoped Mrs. Wong's work would live up to her reputation.

When the frock arrived via courier (for free!), I rushed upstairs to try it on. I liked the lovely shade of the fabric, but not the stretchy texture. *Ugh.* I slipped it on. The dress fit perfectly, but it looked like a *costume*, not an elegant gown. *Oh, crap! Oh, crap!* There was no time to find another dress. I'd just have to pretend I intended my intergalactic ensemble to look this way. Thankfully, I thought, the Australians weren't stuffy; though I felt sure I wouldn't have been invited back to any British or French events after this couture fiasco.

As word buzzed around the city, I learned that people eagerly anticipated the Aussie Ball this year because it was being held at the Grand Hyatt Pudong in the remarkable, beautiful new Jin Mao tower. This jewel in the crown of the Lujiazui skyline received much media coverage as Shanghai's tallest building and one of the highest in the world. Towering over the River Promenade, it boasted eighty-eight floors—though the Chinese proudly said ninety-three, as they insisted on counting the spire. Like most other glorious skyscrapers, many of the Jin Mao's floors included stunning, upscale stores and offices. Notably, the five-star hotel guest rooms did not even start until the fifty-third floor, making the Grand Hyatt Shanghai the highest hotel in the world. That alone would make me avoid staying there, but I could appreciate other people's excitement about the outstanding views.

Thankfully for me, the ballrooms lay on the first two levels. At party time, Planet and I rode the escalator up into a foyer filled with glittery silver fake trees and scores of silver and gold balloons. The attractive, young Asian ladies hired to hostess made quite an impression on the guests, looking fantastic in their skintight silver-lame mini dresses and matching stiletto go-go boots. The hostesses encouraged us to step to the side, where a photographer would memorialize the event for us before we made our way inside. Gladly, we did. Entering the ballroom, I began to feel better about my dress. The Aussies proved their zest for life and partying by coming in style. Their interpretation of intergalactic did not disappoint, and I even wished that I had been more creative with my outfit. (Planet had played it safe by tossing on his standby—a tuxedo.) What a relief—my gown actually seemed to fit in!

Planet and I made our way across the room to discover an impressive buffet, consisting of every type of seafood, roasted meats, a plethora of vegetable side dishes, and some Asian favorites dominating the far side of the room. Even at a five-star venue I don't usually expect remarkable edibles, but kudos to the Grand Hyatt for their ability to maintain standards even for a crowd of several hundred.

Our tablemates consisted of Australians, Brits, a couple of Kiwis (New Zealanders), and several Americans. I found myself seated next to a British neighbor's husband. As we conversed, I quickly discovered that the man had little regard for political correctness nor was he reticent in his opinions. At one point, Rob was on a rampage about something or another, when his monologue suddenly veered into how he hated that Jews always had to tell you they're Jewish within five minutes of being introduced. *What?* OK, I do know one or two people like that, but this was just too much. Maybe I was tired of the way that some of the Brits seemed to believe they were the smartest, best, most civilized, and most superior people in the world. Maybe it was the copious amounts of excellent Australian wine. Suddenly couldn't resist. I laughed out loud, turned to Rob, and said,

"Well, I've been talking to you for over an hour now, so I guess I'd better hurry up and tell you that *I'm* Jewish!"

An expression of extreme embarrassment crossed his face. Clearly, as I have blonde hair and blue eyes, he never saw this one coming! He kept the conversation impeccably polite for the remainder of the evening.

Meanwhile, Planet and I devoured the scrumptious food while marveling at the live auction items featured in tonight's program brochure. Guests had the opportunity to bid on luxurious trips to exotic locales like Boracay, Philippines and Kota Kinabalu, Borneo. What were the live auction prizes at the last fundraiser we attended in the US? Tickets to a baseball game? A weekend at someone's rustic cabin in Wisconsin? Clearly, the Aschkenases were living large now!

After the silent and live auctions, the band fired up and people moved onto the dance floor. There, Planet and I puzzled over how a collection of the worst American and British music of the 1950s-70s tied into an intergalactic Australian theme. Before long, we deemed the tunes "undanceable" and returned to our table to chat up our neighbors. We called it a night relatively early and rang for Mr. Zhou to bring the car around. On the ride back to The Pearl, we called our first major Shanghai event a success (even my drama-laden dress) and looked forward to our next opportunity to step out in style.

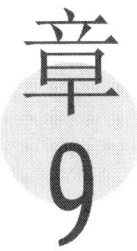

JEWISH SHANGHAI

China has long been Jew friendly. Recorded history reveals that the first Jews arrived during the Silk Road era (Song dynasty 960-1279), establishing a major community in Kaifeng. Descendants of these original settlers thrived, intermarried, and assimilated, successfully blending Chinese and Jewish traditions. Even today, Kaifeng remains notable for its large Chinese Jewish population. For more information about the history and culture of this fascinating group, pick up Xin Xu's *The Jews of Kaifeng* (2003).

Despite the Silk Road influx, China didn't receive notable waves of Jewish immigrants again until after the Nanjing Treaty in 1842, which opened the country's ports for business and ceded Hong Kong to the British. The first of three phases of Jewish immigration into Shanghai began in 1843 with the arrival of Sephardic Jewish businessmen from Baghdad and Bombay. Families like the Sassoons, Hardoons, and Kadoories amassed large fortunes in the thriving city. By 1932, nearly half of the Shanghai Stock Exchange's one hundred members were Sephardic Jews.

These families used their economic success to construct many of the city's landmark buildings, including The Peace Hotel, the Metropole Hotel, Grosvenor House, the Embankment Building, Hamilton House, and Cathay Mansions. They also donated funding for synagogues and other venues to support the expanding Jewish community. At one point, the population grew large enough to support seven synagogues! Of these, only two remain: Ohel Rachel and Ohel Moishe, though Ohel Moishe now serves only as a Jewish refugee museum.

Between 1920-1937, a second wave of immigrants arrived as Russian Jews fled pogroms and political issues. These families congregated in China's northeastern cities like Harbin, Tianjin, and Dalian. When the Japanese arrived in 1931, however, taking over Manchuria, the approximately 4,500 Russian Jews in that area retreated to Shanghai. There, the Russian Jews squeaked by as small business owners or entertainers. As a result of their ethnic and economic differences, however, the Ashkenazic (European Jews) Russians and the Sephardic Middle Eastern Jews rarely mixed.

The third influx of Jewish immigrants arrived between 1938 and 1952. During the dark days of Hitler's reign, China remained one of the world's few safe harbors for Jews fleeing persecution—the only world port that didn't require documentation, such as a visa. Approximately 20,000 Jewish refugees from Germany and Austria and about 2,000 Polish Jews escaped to Shanghai. All went well until the Japanese occupation. Pressured by their German allies, from December 1941 to 1945, the Japanese reluctantly interned all Jewish immigrants from the Allied countries. In an incredible twist of fate, German, Austrian, and Polish Jews who had fled the ghettoes of Europe, suddenly found themselves relocated to a ghetto in Hong Kou—a part of the city's International Settlement—while their counterparts from neutral countries remained free to live and work where they wanted.

When WWII drew to a close in 1945, approximately 24,000 Jews resided in Shanghai. They had developed a rich cultural life, with music, theatres, and coffee houses, and even published fifty newspapers in numerous languages. With the founding of the People's Republic of China in 1949, however, the golden era of respect and laissez-faire ended. Forced to leave by the new government, Jews relocated mainly to Israel, the United States, Canada, Australia, and Hong Kong.

After Mao's death, China re-opened to the West, and honoring their long tradition, the Country again welcomed Jews. In the late 1980s and early 1990s, Jews returned to the Middle Kingdom to seek their fortunes. The first Rabbi since the 1940s arrived in 1998 to lead the burgeoning community. By 2006, the Pudong side of the city had grown enough to have its own Rabbi. Though a far cry from the hey-day in the previous century, the Jewish population in the 2000s stood at approximately 2800.

I found the city's Jewish history fascinating. So, when I discovered that the SEA planned to hold a walking tour of the old Jewish ghetto, I immediately signed up. On the appointed day, a group of about fifteen people met at an ancient tea house in the Yu Yuan. As I sipped my chrysanthemum tea (from a see-through glass, of course), former foreign service officer and noted local expat historian Tess Johnston gave a short talk about both the history of the tea house and the Jewish ghetto area. Then we began to wander the old Jewish quarter. According to Tess, things went south for the Jews after 1937, when the Japanese took control of the city. The Japanese had no issues with the Jews at all, but their allies in Germany pressured them to ghettoize the Ashkenazic Jewish population. Although the group suffered the annoyance of limited movement and wartime deprivations, they understood their grievances paled in comparison to the treatment their families suffered back in Europe.

As we strolled, I noted that only tiny fragments of Hong Kou's Jewish ghetto remained. Many buildings had been torn down to make way for the skyscrapers that burst onto the landscape at breakneck pace. Shanghai seemed overly anxious to erase her past in the mad rush to create her future. Yet, the faint white outlines above the doors of two old buildings revealed that one had served as a Viennese pastry shop and the other, a tailor's shop. We strode past the meager apartments where Jews tried to survive the overcrowded, unpleasant conditions, and looked at the site of the cemetery—now a park. Then we moved inside the Ohel Moishe Synagogue, now a museum. I was surprised to discover that the congregation's first Rabbi was a Pole named Meyer Ashkenazi, who served from 1920-1949. It's such an unusual last name, that I immediately checked with my in-laws to see if we were related. Surprisingly, we weren't.

I came away from the hour-long tour contemplating the courageous, trailblazing people who had comprised Shanghai's Jewish community between 1843 and 1949. I felt grateful that the Chinese still hold great respect for scholarly, hard-working people who prosper and improve their communities, and I felt excited to play a role, in my own minute way, in establishing Shanghai's newest Jewish community.

Still curious after what I'd learned about Jewish life in the city, I ordered a copy of Ursula Bacon's *Shanghai Diary*. Through her, I learned more about WWII-era Shanghai. I also connected to the author because like me, young Ursula wasn't fond of the idea of moving to China. When she brooded over leaving her old life in Germany only to end up in the Hong Kou ghetto, her mother would say to her, "If you let the past live your life, the present will have no meaning, and the future is impossible." Excellent advice! Ursula's mother also reminded her that "after this time comes another." Yes, Shanghai would not be forever—for her, or me. These pearls of wisdom gave me some perspective. Had we remained in Shaker Heights, my family and I would never have had this amazing opportunity for personal growth. Perhaps change *was* good.

Shalom Shanghai Style

One of the places Planet and I eagerly anticipated making friends was the Shanghai Jewish community. In September 2005, Rabbi Goldberg planned a fall kick-off barbeque to welcome new Jewish expats and to honor the new Israeli ambassador to Shanghai. On the appointed day, Planet, the kids, and I happily endured the ninety-five-minute drive to the Rabbi's home in Puxi in order to make some Semitic connections.

Once there, I estimated about sixty guests had already arrived. Alexis and Anders immediately roamed off to the playroom, where some bigger kids were entertaining the smaller kids with a game. As Planet and I cruised through the various rooms, we quickly realized something unexpected: *all* the pods of people who stood talking were speaking either Hebrew or French! Planet read Hebrew well enough, but had never learned conversational Hebrew. Even though I had loved my high school and college French classes, my skills had grown rusty, and I only marginally understood the conversations.

While we stood looking at each other, perplexed, wondering if we would remain the dumb Americans for whom everyone had to stop and switch into English, some merciful soul introduced us to a charming, outgoing, also new-ly-arrived Israeli family. They wanted to practice their English, as their kids were enrolled at SAS. What a piece of luck! Their oldest child, daughter Siegal, was actually in Anders' class. As we parents exchanged ming pian, someone led another new family—obviously Americans—over to the English-speaking group we had just formed.

This family, the Neidermeyers, lived in Jin Qiao and had two boys attending SCIS. The older boy, Josh, was in third grade, like Alexis. The younger child, Jordan, just started kindergarten. The mother, Miriam—aka Mimi—was a tall, big-boned woman with very short platinum blonde hair, spiked up with black tips. She wore jeans, a black spaghetti-strap tank top, and a jeans jacket. A little on the chunky side, her ample cleavage threatened to drip out of her top with any wrong move. We exchanged the usual cocktail party banter: where are you from, how many kids, where do you live, what's the hubby do, and so on. The family had come to China because her husband, Don, had undertaken the challenge of negotiating supplies for a major automotive company. Mimi and I exchanged ming pian and agreed to call each other soon.

On the long trip back to Pudong, I lamented that we could never send the kids to Hebrew school, considering the ninety- to 120-minute drive each way—especially after enduring an hour bus ride to and from school. Would they be years behind and have to delay their B'nai Mitzvot when we returned to the US? Could we even find a private tutor here? Well, at least we had a Jewish community; therefore, I assumed all these issues would somehow resolve themselves.

Shortly after the barbeque, Michal Tzadaka, the Israeli mom, gave me a call. Anders' and Siegal's friendship had grown—in fact, later she became his first crush—and now with a half day of school for teacher-parent conferences coming up, Michal wanted to invite the kids and me over for lunch. At their house in Jin Qiao, Michal served us grilled hamburgers, salad, and cookies. Then the kids went outside to play on the gym equipment in the yard, leaving the moms time to talk. She gave me the details of her husband's excellent career as a tech company executive, and said she had found work as a lawyer. This seemed exciting as Shanghai didn't seem to have many lawyers at the time—nor many laws. Michal had found a niche for herself guiding Israelis—and other foreigners—attempting to do business in China. She also did the reverse—advocating for Chinese who wanted to invest in Israeli businesses. While the reality of her job made my head spin, I admired her courage and ingenuity. When she told me that she was pregnant and also starting classes to add an MBA to her credentials, my ears nearly burst into flames. Where did she get her boundless energy? This woman was smart, beautiful, successful, and brave!

As the Tzadakas intended to stay in China for their entire careers, they aggressively pursued Mandarin through regular lessons and daily drills. The children spoke Hebrew at home, English all day at school, and now they studied Mandarin on top of it all. *Wow!* These children would clearly, and easily, become citizens of the global village, empowered to take on any Millennial challenges. This family was doing the China experience right, and Michal definitely inspired me. Friend circle? Check!

At the same time, I also began to pursue my acquaintanceship with Mimi. For our first outing, we visited the fabric market. We had a good time exploring and dreaming up creative projects. We hit the Shanghai TJ's across the street, then ended our day by making plans for another adventure the following week. Somehow, however, I wasn't a bit surprised when Mimi called a few days later to cancel. I could smell it in the wind that she was the kind of woman who'd change her plans any time she got a better offer. Had I already moved down her "preferred friend list?" Or was she simply unafraid to reschedule me because she considered the friendship already secured?

Over time, Mimi still tended to include me in larger group plans, and I included her in mine. Very quickly, however, I learned that Mimi had one of those larger-than-life personalities; she practically vibrated with dramatic energy. The more I saw of her, the more her increasingly zany behavior made me wary. It seemed like wherever Mimi went, drama followed. A polite distance suited me just fine.

章
10

THE KIDS ARE ALRIGHT

Before we moved to Asia, I worried about how we would re-invent the activities the kids had enjoyed in kid-friendly Shaker Heights. Thankfully, we found a variety of sports in the compound and around the area to keep them happy and busy.

One of the first activities the kids tried was badminton. We found we could rent them racquets and a court at Megafit to keep them busy while Planet and I got in a workout. While playing one morning, the kids discovered Alexis' friend from school, Alice Liang, having a lesson. It hadn't occurred to us the gym offered lessons. So, we asked Alice to introduce us to her coach. He didn't speak English. Fortunately, Alice's mom saw us and came over to translate. She explained to Mr. Wu that we wanted lessons for the kids and helped us book a recurring day and time. She also informed us that Wu was some sort of retired national champion. This was one of the unusual but wonderful aspects of Shanghai. An abundance of retired Olympic and national champions seemed available to coach every sport at very reasonable prices. Excellent!

We also discovered that the kids could get tennis lessons on Sunday mornings at 9:00 am at The Pearl, so we gave that a try as well. The instructor was a talented young Australian man. But, the kids liked playing the actual game better than all the drills, however, so their fondness for that activity didn't last long.

On to the next sport. Ever since he was very small, Anders wanted to play hockey. What we discovered, though, was that he didn't actually want to do the *skating* part. Worse, the only available ice time was on Sundays at 6:00 am, an hour drive away! The good news was that roller hockey proved a popular sport local, and lucky for me, we had a team right in our compound. Hallelujah! It was a win-win: Anders got to play hockey without having to ice skate, and we didn't have endure more car sitting at ungodly hours for him to accomplish this.

The head roller hockey coach was a kind, young Korean man named Mr. Kim. He was accompanied by a young Scottish-Australian, one-armed assistant named Fergus. Coach Kim was naturally well connected in Shanghai's Korean community, so he found Korean roller hockey teams to come out to The Pearl once a month for tournaments. Amazingly, the tournaments were nearly as much fun as the pro hockey games you pay $300 a seat for in the US.

One of our neighbors, whose son played on the team, headed up a major multi-national soft drink company's Asian division. At each event, the soft drink company generously sponsored chairs, tables, drink coolers, sodas, and bottled water. The Pearl's restaurant set up a barbeque in one corner and served up low-priced grilled hot dogs and burgers. Best of all, though, the extremely hospitable, generous mothers of the Korean players set up several tables brimming with tasty Korean snacks to share. I found this a wonderful international gesture of friendship. Coaches Kim and Fergus also recruited The Pearl team's fathers to take turns serving as DJs and MCs for these afternoons. With the sports, the music, and the food, the event was always lively and enjoyed as much by the parents as by the kids.

The highlight of Anders' Pearl roller hockey team experience was when Coach Kim took the team to compete in Seoul, Korea! My son had a wonderful time, and I appreciated his having this unique opportunity. These kinds of priceless adventures made me glad that I decided to follow Planet to Asia.

Unlike her brother, Alexis wanted to ice skate, as she had been skating competitively in Shaker Heights since she was five years old. Finally, I found out where we could get her a lesson and booked her with a retired Olympian. On the appointed day, Mr. Zhou drove us to the enormous, well-known mall in Lu Jia Zui. We rode the elevator up to the eighth floor, where we found the rink. I paid the ice fee, and the attendant handed Alexis a pair of Pepto-Bismal pink gloves.

Immediately, as the instructor led my daughter into the center of the ice rink—not even marked off by safety cones—while a crowd of afternoon thrill seekers buzzed around the edges, I realized we had a problem. How in the world could she practice jumps and spins, or even concentrate on the lesson, for that matter, amidst the chaos? In addition, I noticed that several adult couples appeared to be on dates. The women purposely fell, tittering behind pink-gloved hands, so their boyfriends could feel manly scooping them back up. It seemed only a matter of time before one of the women launched into my unsuspecting child and took her out. Clearly, a skating lesson here was an exercise in ridiculousness, not to mention dangerous. As this was where and how she would also have to practice, sadly this was Alexis' first and last Chinese skating session.

Luckily for us, an organization called High-5 set up shop in Shanghai. They offered gymnastics in Jin Qiao on Saturday mornings; finally, Alexis had found a sport to replace skating. We discovered that High-5's soccer program took place at the same time as gymnastics, so we signed up Anders. Now, both kids had something fun to do, thankfully in the same place at the same time.

Probably every kid in China has to try the popular local activity, Kung Fu. So, my kids did, too. The classes were held at The Pearl, so the kids could walk to their lessons. Their teacher, Cherry, was one tough young lady, and definitely taught "Chinese style." She was demanding with the kids, all business, and rarely complimented her students. For a while, I questioned whether the word "good" even existed in her vocabulary. Her standard commentary fell more along the lines of a fierce, "next time do it better!" With praise a rare commodity, some of the kids couldn't tolerate her style and quit the class.

I didn't have a complete understanding of the class until one night when Alexis came home from class upset. She tearfully explained that when a classmate handed out candy as a birthday treat, Cherry had announced, matter-of-factly, *in front of the class*, "No! None for her! She needs to get slim!" Alexis was rightfully devastated. Imagine the fallout if a teacher said that to a child in the US! I consoled Alexis, explaining that she'd just received a cultural lesson—she'd had a "China moment." Cherry did not mean to hurt her feelings, the

Chinese are just very direct and factual. Cherry knew that athletes needed to be fit, and she simply wanted Alexis to be at her best to succeed in Kung Fu. I don't think Alexis understood, but fortunately she didn't want to quit. Kudus to my daughter for bravely sticking with the sport and the teacher.

Because Alexis liked gymnastics so much and Anders got so excited about trampolining at his friends' houses, Planet insisted—against my protests—on getting the kids a trampoline. I thought the device dangerous, and a headache I didn't need. I didn't want anyone else's kids getting hurt at our house, let alone Alexis and Anders. With no real EMT service and questionable hospital services, inviting danger into my home seemed idiotic. My solution was to hire someone to teach the kids not only how to have fun but how to be safe and responsible. Fortunately, I discovered that a young British woman gave trampolining lessons in The Pearl's community center. I got the kids onto her schedule, then privately I prayed for the contraption to blow away in the next typhoon!

When the Cub Scout troop formed in September, I was thrilled. Anders had wanted to be a member in the US for years, but we always seemed to have conflicts with the meeting dates or times. Here in Shanghai, we had the time, and the meetings would take place in our compound. Even better, Don Oberlander and Kevin Hamburger—his friends' dads—served as the second-grade boys' scout masters that year. From the Pinewood Derby to camping out, Anders not only learned some great lessons but found another source of friends. The Shanghai Scouts remains one of my son's best Asian experiences, and I'm not sure I can ever part with his rare, treasured uniform shirt.

Our Sponsored Child

For women expats, Shanghai presented an abundance of community service opportunities. I chose to donate my free time and skills to the SAS PTSA, substitute teaching, writing for the *Courier* and the AWCS newsletter, and chairing the AWCS book club. To get the rest of the family involved, Planet decided our family should sponsor a Chinese student through the Shanghai Sunrise (SS) organization. As a teacher, I loved the idea of helping a child get educated.

Planet, the kids, and I were exited to attend the annual "pairing" party—a kick-off event for sponsors to meet their SS child. From what we heard through the grapevine, the event was super exciting for the sponsored kids because often it was their first chance to travel into the big city. They also loved meeting their Western benefactors, visiting a posh hotel, and eating fancy snacks.

On party day, we wandered around the hotel ballroom, waiting for our child, Yuting. For nearly an hour, we watched other sponsors and kids come and go. Finally, we found the woman in charge and asked what had happened to Yuting. Within a few minutes, she realized that there had been a mix up. Our student had somehow received word that *we* were not coming today, so she stayed at home. Over the past few weeks I had grown so overwhelmed by the stress of trying to live in this crazy city and the demands of exapat life that this news became the straw that broke the camel's back. I actually burst into tears in front of my kids and everyone else in the room.

Quickly, I went to the ladies' room and composed myself.

When I returned to the family, I had a surprise. I saw a photographer for one of the local newspapers making a beeline towards my kids. A translator who just happened to be walking by explained that Alexis' huge blue eyes (rather than Anders' glorious head of blond curls, for a change) had attracted his attention! My daughter couldn't have been more delighted! He said the photographer wanted a photo of some Western kids with some of the SS kids.

The photographer grabbed a handy Chinese boy, posed him with my kids, and began snapping away. We understood that one of these photos would appear in a local paper, but we never figured out which one. At least she emailed us a copy of the photo from the paper.

Thankfully, this incident and one other item redeemed the day for me. Before we left, the organizer explained that we could arrange to meet Yuting another time. The organization would pay for her and one parent to travel to Shanghai, plus send along a translator to help us communicate. We all loved that idea.

So, one a sunny Saturday, we finally got to meet our Chinese child. We met at a major Puxi mall, which seemed like a good central location. Seven-year-old Yuting, who lived in a town about two hours away, arrived with her father and the SS translator. The young woman explained that our student's father, Mr. Chen, had been hurt in a motorcycle accident, leaving lingering ailments that prevented him from working—something about steel plates in his head and one leg amputated, though I certainly couldn't tell by the way he walked. I thought it seemed strange that under the communist system they wouldn't just re-assign him to another work detail.

Apparently, the family joined the SS program because they were unable to live on Mrs. Chen's salary, pay off Mr. Chen's medical bills, and send Yuting to school. (Again, a mystery. I thought the idea behind Communism was to provide for all that.) The Chen's situation, of course, started me thinking about how many parts of daily life most US citizens are privileged to take for granted. Planet and I felt thankful to know we could help this family by paying for Yuting's tuition and school supplies—which amounted to about $250 total. We also felt glad we could bankroll an exciting afternoon in the big city for this family. We knew it was a huge deal for country kids to have a chance to eat at an American fast food restaurant, so we planned to surprise Yuting and her family with lunch at McDonald's.

When we reached the plaza, however, I couldn't believe we couldn't find the golden arches anywhere! The translator didn't know where we could find one, either. But what was that? A Pizza Hut stood right in front of us! Hopefully it would do. Yuting had never heard of pizza. So, I hoped this food would still give her bragging rights among her friends.

Our group went inside, and a host led us to a table. Most Americans wouldn't recognize the menu. For starters, the featured pizza of the month was Ostrich! Crayfish pasta, anyone? The bill of fare also included local favorites like fried shrimp, fried chicken nuggets, Hungarian and Champs-Elysees fried rice, alcoholic beverages, soups, a salad bar, and a host of other Chinese-palate-oriented dishes and beverages. I thought the irony funny and imagined this paralleled the Americanized versions of *Chinese* food back home!

Yuting, Alexis, and Anders behaved shyly at first. As an ice breaker, Anders had thoughtfully brought our student a Beanie Baby rooster, as it was the "Year of the Rooster" in China. Alexis brought her an adorable plush star with a smiley face embroidered on it. I felt proud that my children had been so considerate and made such an effort to be kind to a new friend. I was also proud of them for trying their best to try to communicate with Yuting in their very rudimentary Mandarin. Yuting's English was about as extensive and Alexis' and Anders' Chinese, but by the time the waiter set pizza in front of us, all three kids were playing with the stuffed toys, giggling, and chatting like old friends in a creative mix of Chinglish and hand gestures. When our pizza arrived, we discovered that our student did not like this food at all. She had probably never tasted cheese, bread, or tomato sauce in her life, and she didn't care for the taste or the texture. Fortunately, four servings of the fried shrimp appetizer saved the day!

While we ate, it occurred to me that we probably spent on that one lunch what Yuting's mother earned in a month. No wonder Chinese thought Americans had endless money.

After lunch, we took the Chens to visit the swish new Shanghai Museum of Science and Technology. Though we spent about three hours there, we only made it through a couple of the rooms because—to Planet's and my delight—the kids spent so much time absorbing each exhibit. As a special treat, we took everyone to the Imax movie. My family loves any type of Imax movie, but today's movie was in Chinese without English subtitles. Oh, no! We couldn't follow the soundtrack at all. Interestingly, Alexis and Anders didn't seem to mind. As for Yuting, we enjoyed watching her reactions to this larger-than-life-sized film. Absolutely thrilled, she laughed and shouted through the whole thing as though the action was real and she was living it.

After the film, we wrapped up our outing. I hoped our afternoon together was one the Chen family would fondly remember. I knew we would.

章
11

GOLDEN MONTH, GOLDEN DAYS

Our second month in the Middle Kingdom had arrived as fast as a Chinese grandma knits a sock. We continued working on our friend circles, enjoying a variety of social adventures and forays into local culture, and integrating into the school community.

As popular as it was to explore Shanghai's varied and plentiful restaurant scene, dining in made for wonderful festive evenings as well. It was extremely easy to entertain because you could get all the help you needed so inexpensively. I once hired servers from The Pearl's restaurant, who cost an outrageous $3 an hour each! Between such plentiful extras and having an ayi to shop, cook, and clean, there was pretty much no excuse to skip entertaining at home. A Shanghai dinner party might consist of a simple barbeque with another couple or two, or it could be something as exotic as a multi-course chef-cooked affair. No matter what level, home parties made up part of the regular rotation in expat life.

One of the best home dinner parties during our time in China happened at the Bixbys' in early October. They had won chef David Laris' services in a silent auction at BISS, where their son attended elementary school. M on the Bund had been Shanghai's only international fine dining until Australian celebrity chef David Laris breezed in during 2003 to found his restaurant—Laris—in the recently, beautifully restored 1916 Neo-Renaissance building across the street at Three Bund. This newcomer superstar's menu pushed the boundaries of contemporary cuisine, with dishes served up amid the swank European/Asian interior of marble floors and half-circle couches stationed at round tables. What M was to European bistro favorites, Laris was to seafood. Laris also prided itself on its confectionary, located in a glass-walled room where diners could pass by for a peek enroute to the restrooms. Recently, the chef generously donated an in-home dinner for twelve to the BISS fundraiser, and lucky us, the Bixbys won the auction and included Planet and me in the event's headcount!

On Laris night, a group of Brits, Australians, and us lone Americans, gathered in the Bixby's large yard. There, we savored seven wonderful, absolutely sumptuous, trend-setting seafood courses—each of which included a perfectly paired wine—followed by an elegant dessert. As we relaxed and indulged outside in the warm, damp night air, the lights from the pool casting a bluish hue, I thought about what an amazing thing it was to indulge in world-class fine dining in someone's back yard. In addition, I felt glad that we were the only Americans; I found it refreshing to hear European and Australian perspectives on various topics for a change.

In contrast to this elegant affair, we also attended our first Pearl community dinner. Apparently, the management held a "welcome back" dinner each fall once all the families had returned. This year, about fifty neighbors came out to enjoy the international buffet dinner, small shopping bazaar, music, and dancing. Alexis and Anders ran joyfully toward the kids' tables, where our hosts had set up two craft stations. The kids painted ceramic Chinese opera masks at one table and tied together traditional Chinese dangling doodads at another. I sighed in relief, realizing that the kids already had a secure sense of belonging, as they flitted among food and activities and talked joyfully with all the other kids.

When Bianca arrived, she immediately claimed Alexis, pulling her here and there around the room. Fortunately, Miss Busybody seemed contained by the event space and on good behavior. She insisted that our families sit together for dinner, and I wasn't going to miss an opportunity to meet her parents. During the meal, I learned Mr. Hanson was a very nice, very patient man who was a potential client of Planet's. Over some reasonably tasty lasagna, I gathered from Bianca's mother that this was the sixth country her family had lived in, and her younger daughter's fourth. *Oh! That seemed to explain a few things about her behavior! An example of the downside of third-culture kids?*

At dessert time, a DJ materialized and blasted some great dance music. Everyone, kids and adults alike, slipped onto the dance floor at least once. My whole family had a good time, and Planet and I left the event feeling a bit more like part of the community.

Perhaps the month's best dining adventure, however, was the one that almost didn't happen. Encouraged by my experience at the SEA's Chinese tea event, I went to my first SEA monthly lunch outing. On event day, I had expected the journey into Puxi to take at least an hour. But an hour went by, and it was starting to seem like Zhou was…lost? As a man, a Shanghai native, a former cab driver, and now an expat chauffer, Zhou stood to lose big face if I even hinted at such a thing. So, I kept quiet, staring anxiously out the window. Finally, my driver gave in and pulled over. He whipped out his phone and made a call.

"Tai Tai, this is ah-no good," Zhou said, pointing his extraordinarily long, creepy pinky nail at the address in the *Courier* magazine I had showed him. "Is ah-no here."

I shot him a questioning stare. Did he mean the magazine printed the address incorrectly? What now?

Zhou picked up the phone again. He called what was probably directory assistance. A moment later his face looked like a boy's who'd received his first big truck for Christmas.

"I know! IIII knooow!" Zhou cried out, beaming.

"Thank you, Mr. Zhou," I smiled back. By finding the correct address, he got to play the hero and regain face. Within ten minutes, we arrived at the designated lunch spot, a lovely establishment called Mediterranean Style. The restaurant's charcoal-colored fence protected an attractive Asian-style courtyard, complete with a koi pond, a large faux-ancient rock, and manicured ornamental trees. Inside, I found modern Asian décor—dark wood, crisp lines, and chrome.

Because I had arrived late as a result of the misprint, I scrambled to find an open seat among the approximately sixty women packed into the room. I searched the crowd, but didn't spy a single familiar face. Feeling very self-conscious, I wandered from table to table, anxiously hunting down a seat. Engrossed in their conversations, no one bothered to politely point out an empty space. I couldn't blame the ladies, as many of them probably hadn't seen their old friends yet this year. Finally, I spied an empty chair. Relieved, I slid into place just in time for the first course.

For an appetizer, the organizers had chosen a traditional tomato and fresh mozzarella salad, with arugula and balsamic dressing. For a main, the staff served us fresh, tender sea bass in a tomato sauce, with grilled squash and risotto. A delicious ricotta cheesecake with fruit compote on the side made up the dessert. I noticed that the restaurant followed European tradition of serving coffee after the dessert. I marveled that for our gourmet three-course lunch with one beverage and a coffee, we paid 120 RMB (about $16)—and of course, in China there is no tipping. You could pay $16 just for an average-quality, somewhat small salad in America's large cities, not including a beverage, tax, and tip. Inexpensive gourmet lunches? Asia redeemed herself again!

The best part of this day, however, was the conversation with the ladies at my table, especially about the SEA's magazine, the *Courier*. The ladies discussed one of the articles in the recent issue and expressed how much they also liked the magazine. My radar buzzed like the Chinese government detecting a political dissident. From first sight at the opening coffee morning, I knew I wanted to be part of the impressive, beautiful publication, so I wondered aloud what one had to do to become a contributor. What a piece of luck: one of the ladies said she'd put me in touch with the editor, Benita Goodman! I thanked her and planned to call Benita as soon as possible. Thus, the lunch that almost wasn't led to a lucky last seat that created my inroad to writing for the magazine!

Soon, Benita and I talked, and she agreed to give me a try. Benita liked my ideas and my style, so she asked me to draft some articles on Chinese history and culture she'd wanted to include for a while but for which she lacked a writer. Hence, I wrote an article on Mah Jongg and another on bound-foot shoes. Before long, Benita had me submitting a book review and an article in *every* issue! My contributions grew until by my second year in Shanghai, I had become one of the magazine's main writers. I would have done the same research on my own, for my own pleasure, so I felt happy that I could share my findings with interested readers. I relished every minute I spent researching and writing articles, reading books to review, talking to staff at planning meetings, and occasionally editing other contributors' pieces.

One of the best moments of my Tai Tai life occurred one day when my family and I were having lunch at a popular French Concession pub. Another expat diner came over to talk to Planet and me. "You're the only reason I pick up the magazine. Your articles are always worth reading," he said. I smiled and emitted a contented sigh. The moral of this story is that when friendless in Shanghai, it pays to start conversations with people you don't know. You never know what happiness might result!

Friendship Round Two

In October, my outing with Angela served as both a friendship builder and a memorable community-service event. My neighbor went to an orphanage several times a month and always took along a group of ladies. The day I joined her, she gathered a group of about twelve. As we loaded into Angela's super-sized van, everyone chatted amiably. All the ladies seemed very nice, and I was enjoying myself. Suddenly, however, our hostess made what amounted to a public service announcement. She introduced me to the group, then mentioned that my religious thinking was liberal and that I agreed to read her religion's key book. I almost thought the group would break into applause. *Why had she done this! Oh, boy!*

Thankfully, one other non-member of that tribe accompanied us, and maybe she would deflect some of the attention now paid to me. Kandi Wells, newly arrived at The Pearl, was a tall, medium-boned lady with shoulder-length black hair. She had a very strong but pleasant personality, and she enjoyed leadership roles. As we talked that morning, I learned that she had moved to Shanghai from Saudi Arabia. I could hardly imagine life for an American woman—or any woman—there. She explained that her experience there "wasn't bad, but it was very boring." There was very little for women to do besides raise children. Kandi's husband worked in the oil drilling business, and they moved to a new country every few years. Kandi took her lifestyle in stride, which I admired. She wasted no time getting to know the Shanghai expat community and establishing her family. She seemed to know just what to do. Maybe that was a benefit of moving so often.

Immediately, ol' Kandi was taking The Pearl by storm. It seemed she was virtually everywhere, attending events and organizing, or re-organizing, everything in her path. I wondered when she found time to sleep. I would love to have even one-third of her energy and unflappability. Kandi seemed to have the best of intentions, but she was a force, too intense for some. (Surprise, surprise: she and Mimi quickly became best friends!) As a result, she wasn't everyone's cup of tea.

Take Eden, for example. Both ladies sold scrapbooking supplies from a US pyramid scheme company. Eden remained convinced that she alone complied with international law in operating her business; Kandi's operation wasn't legitimate. Kandi remained equally convinced that *she* was the one running her business properly. The Pearl community wasn't that big, so when both women held scrapbooking nights, the neighbors had to decide whose to attend. Eden had already spent a year selling her products to this group, and now it appeared the newcomer intended to take over. I'd started out with Eden's parties, but I also liked Kandi. I didn't intend to get caught in a turf war, and I wanted to remain friendly with both women. So, I simply avoided scrapbooking night at both households.

I liked that Kandi seemed interested in and open to trying everything, and she was a "doer." Thus, it wasn't surprising when she admitted she had actually visited the special religion church. From Kandi I learned that Angela's husband was the entire city's leader of their church and religion. Since the government remained officially atheist, they established many rules for expats wanting to practice their own religions. The special religion group could not get permission to actually construct a house of worship unless they agreed to allow a Chinese person to head the organization. This was standard practice in China. A Chinese leader for the group wasn't forthcoming, and as a result, over one hundred people per week trekked out to Pudong and packed into the Templetons' house for services and religious studies. In addition, Angela held a "holy book" study at 5:00 am on weekday mornings for girls. I tried to imagine getting up at 4:00 am in order to get to the Templetons' by 5:00 am and then shuffling off for an hour bus ride to school, a full day of school, and etc. Wow!

I thought visiting a church service was both kind and brave of Kandi. Although I was also curious and wanted to be friendly and neighborly, I would never go because I concluded I'd never get their "recruiters" off my back if I opened the door even a tiny crack. Given Angela's little announcement at the start of the van ride today, I already felt sorry I said I'd read their book. I wished Kandi luck with the potential fall-out if she chose not to join their church.

Chatting with Kandi made the hour-drive fly by. Soon we arrived at the boys' orphanage. There, I noticed all the children had some type of handicap. As we moved around the main room, most of the boys displayed various levels of mental retardation. Some had physical problems, and a couple of the babies were blind. They were all undersized because of the lack of attention, medical care, and nutrition. Apparently, the boys ended up here because their families either could not afford to treat their handicap or refused to accept a boy that wasn't perfect, since they could only have one child. Seeing these sweet little ones, I wanted to take them all home and improve their lives!

At the beginning of our visit, we worked with the babies. I held one baby, whose head was partly flat. He liked it when I sang to him, even if it was in English and he didn't understand me. Then I held a little blind one, whose limbs seemed shriveled from his inactive life in this place. He enjoyed when I tickled him, letting out the cutest, tiniest laugh. My third baby was a very charming little guy who seemed to have the Emmanuel Lewis (TV's *Webster*) disease. He stood laughing and entertaining himself in his crib. He was such a cute, cheerful little guy! After cuddling the babies, the older children and the teens assembled in the large multi-purpose room. They sang a couple of songs in Chinese for us. Then they loudly and proudly belted out the alphabet song in English. We danced with them a little, then helped pass around a snack of crackers and juice. With that, the visit drew to a close.

During the long van ride back to The Pearl, I burned with questions and ideas. If these children could have corrective surgery, would their families take them back? Had the ladies at Angela's church had considered raising money to pay for operations and other medical care for these kids? What happened to them when they reached adulthood? I told Angela I'd like to buy the place a multi-child buggy and a CD player.

She replied, sadly, "If you give a CD player to the orphanage, it will probably disappear. When you give them money, who knows? Maybe the employees use it to buy things for themselves."

Another lesson in Chinese ethics. She added that in the past, many times the toys her group brought disappeared. Still, her church group faithfully brought disposable diapers and formula every month, hoping these items actually found their way to the children and not into the employees' homes. Ditto for the money they donated toward medical care and food.

"I like your idea about the CD player," she continued, "but even if the staff didn't steal or sell it, they don't want to change anything in the daily routine. They're afraid they'll get into trouble with their bosses."

"Well, that just makes the situation seem even sadder," I replied. "I guess the best thing we can do to help is to keep coming to give the children a little attention." She nodded in agreement.

After this outing, I thought Kandi would make a nice addition to my friend circle, but I questioned whether Angela saw me as a friend or merely a religious recruit conquest. I'd have to wait and see.

About a week after the orphanage trip, I spied a small notice in The Pearl's monthly newsletter. An Israeli neighbor named Chava Peretz had constructed a Sukkah in her back yard for the Jewish holiday Sukkot. She invited the community to come by and learn about this tradition. This news was both unexpected and exciting. I don't know how many curious neighbors took up her generous offer that year, but the Aschkenase Family of Shaker Heights, Ohio did.

During the Jewish holiday Sukkot, the faithful remember when their ancestors wandered in the desert, surviving in temporary shelters. Jews are supposed to build a sukkah in their yard, decorate it, and eat all their meals in it. In the US, many people don't go to the trouble. So, I didn't want to miss an opportunity to meet a Jewish neighbor and for the kids to have the holiday experience. Eagerly, we headed over to the Peretz's after school one day.

"You're Jewish?…You're Jewish!" Chava exclaimed, hearing my last name when I introduced myself and my kids. She threw her arms around me in a big bear hug and then launched into rapid Hebrew.

"Whoa!" I stopped her. "I'm so sorry. I don't speak Hebrew."

Chava's expression grew perplexed. She had assumed that all the world's Jews spoke Hebrew. It united the race. It was a given. While that logic made perfect sense and may have rung true one hundred years ago, that ship had sailed. Especially in the US.

"No," I explained. "Most American Jews can *read*, if they've been Bar Mitzvah'd. But not many learn to speak. I'm afraid I'm just another dumb American," I grimaced.

"Oh, no," she said, truly disappointed. "I was so excited to finally find someone to talk Hebrew with. Speaking English all day is exhausting!"

"Sorry." I truly was. "I know."

She smiled. "Well, never mind. We will just talk in English, then. I need to practice anyway."

"Your English is excellent!" I encouraged her.

As we talked, I learned that Chava's family moved from Tel Aviv to Shanghai for her husband's high tech job. While Jordan worried that spending too many years in Shanghai would hinder his career progress, Chava worried about going back.

"Shanghai is the safest place in the world!" she informed me. "My only problem with being here is that the girls can speak Hebrew, but they won't learn how to read and write it. I'm not sure what I'm going to do about this, because they have to be able to write when we go back."

I knew many kids learned a first language from their parents, so they could understand and speak, but it never occurred to me they needed to learn to read and write. Definitely one of the things I loved most about living in Shanghai was how much I learned every day. My visit to Chava's today already proved no exception.

Chava stood at average height and had short, black curly hair. She came across as a very warm and kind person, so it seemed natural that she worked as a psychologist back in Israel. Chava's two dark, curly-haired girls, Tal (7) and Esther (4), attended SCIS. They understood more English than they could yet speak. I could hardly imagine what it would feel like to start a school taught in English without knowing a word. Then I realized that at these tender ages the girls had to straddle *three* worlds—Israeli culture at home, Chinese culture all around, and an international-style culture presented in English at school. *Wow!* What a unique world I now inhabited.

My new Jewish friend had all kinds of craft supplies in her sukkah, and she put Alexis and Anders to work creating decorations to hang from the walls and roof beams. Although Tal and Esther listened more than they spoke, the craft event ran smoothly and the kids seemed to enjoy each other's company. The little girls eagerly watched to see what kinds of adornments their new American friends would make. With several years of American Hebrew school experience under her belt, Alexis immediately set out cutting colored paper, which she glued into a paper chain to stream from the ceiling. Then she created a drawing for the wall. Anders followed his older sister's lead. Chava's girls did not know about the common American tradition of making paper chains, and they danced around the hut excitedly as my children showed them the technique. A couple of merry hours later, the Peretzes' sukkah emitted a festive vibe.

The afternoon had been an unexpected, wonderful surprise for all of us. Despite the fact that I didn't speak Hebrew, it seemed clear that Chava and I would join each other's friend circles. Before the kids and I headed home for dinner, Chava and I agreed that we would get together again one day soon.

While Anders' friendships were still progressing very well, Alexis remained challenged. For lack of other opportunities, she still played with Bianca sometimes. One Saturday afternoon, I agreed to a playdate as long as the girls played at our house where I could watch them.

When Bianca arrived, the girls happily scurried up to Alexis' room. I remained downstairs working on my own tasks, but I kept my mom radar on. Soon, I went up to check on the girls. As I entered my daughter's bedroom, I noticed water on the floor outside her bathroom. I followed the damp little trail across the room. To my horror, the balcony door stood wide open. Alexis was not allowed to use her balcony without supervision, for obvious reasons. *Oh, crap!* As I stepped through the drapery sheers, I heard Bianca shouting "take that!" as a pot of water shot from Alexis' arm onto some boys standing below in my driveway.

"Girls! Why are you throwing water at them?" I shouted, my heart skipping a beat.

"They were calling us names," Alexis informed me.

"What were you doing on the balcony in the first place?" I demanded. "You know you can't go out there without an adult."

"We were just getting some air. It was hot in here," Bianca replied, flashing me her most innocent expression. When I didn't appear supportive, she added, pretending to be scandalized, "then the boys came down the path and started calling us names!"

If I had to wager a guess, Bianca probably dared Alexis to pour water on the boys, bribing her with candy or some other prize. I thanked G_d she hadn't dared her to jump!

"Well, first off, you girls aren't allowed on the balcony," I informed them. "And I don't care if they were calling you names, you shouldn't have been throwing water on them." This was really too much. Even though I knew Alexis would be sad, I added, "It's time for Bianca to go home now."

Bianca must have understood that I was mad and she'd crossed a line. Thankfully, she left without any backtalk.

Shortly after she left, the phone rang. I answered.

"Hello?"

"Hello."

"Yes?" I said.

The line remained silent for a short while.

"Hello," the voice said again, flatly.

I wasn't sure who it was. "Who do you want?"

Another uncomfortable pause. Then, "hello."

I said nothing. I heard nothing. I hung up, annoyed. Bianca. Who else would prank call me as retaliation for spoiling her fun and for sending her home? I prayed for other friends to come into my daughter's life—soon!

Fortunately, shortly after this incident, at last Alexis started talking about some of the girls in her class. She began to make comments about a Korean girl named Eun Ji and a very nice girl from Taiwan, Lily Li. Finally, by the end of October, Planet and I were thrilled to hear that Alexis had found a best friend: Sofia, from Madrid, Spain! Sofia had already been in Shanghai for a year, but she recently decided not only to expand her friend group, but to make Alexis her number one! Though it wasn't easy, I went out of my way to ensure the girls could get together on weekends.

The girls remained friends throughout our time in China. In fact, our families remained in contact even after both left Shanghai. In the summer of 2009, we performed a "kid exchange." Sofia came to spend three weeks in Chicago, and then Alexis went home with her to Madrid for three weeks. Definitely, one of the best gifts Shanghai gave my family was enduring international friendships.

Alexis also soon added a nice American girl named Ashley Jones to her circle. Ashley's father worked for a multinational soft drink company. Her mother, Sandee, seemed very nice, and I got to know her through mutual PTSA volunteer projects. As a result of Sophia and Ashley, we were finally seeing very little of Bianca!

School Fair Affairs

In mid-October, SAS's Puxi campus held its International Fair. As we were new, seeking to support the school, and looking for fun things for the kids to do on the weekends, we went. On Fair day, we left The Pearl about 10:00 am, and it took us a whopping two hours to get to the Hong Qiao campus. I certainly hoped the event would be worth the travel time.

At the fair, games stretched out as far as the eye could see. Apparently, each grade on both campuses had to run one to raise money for its class parties and/or charity. On the far side of the field, a climbing wall, a giant slide, and a bouncy castle attracted quite a crowd of younger kids. On the nearer side of the field, maybe seventy vendors—selling everything from oriental rugs to stationery—staffed the shopping venue. Inside the school, an international food court stood waiting. *Impressive!* When the kids had finished playing games, we headed inside for lunch. In a truly remarkable scene—akin to a miniature Disney Epcot—parents representing about twenty different countries had donned their national costumes and set up stations selling their country's traditional foods. I found the Korean hanbok and the Indian saris especially beautiful. We had a great time sampling our way around this global food court!

At the end of the afternoon, we trudged back to the Chrysler, full, tired, and happy. Fortunately, the return trip took only an hour and a half. I gave the kids many kudus for behaving so commendably today, enduring three and a half hours in the car. It seemed amazing how much of our Shanghai lives involved sitting in traffic, and once again I felt thankful for Mr. Zhou.

About two weeks later, it was the Pudong campus' turn to hold their version of the event—the annual "welcome back" barbeque. When we arrived, we found the sports fields and playground area bursting with games (again sponsored by each grade on both campuses), plus a couple of bouncy castles and inflatable slides. At one end of the field, about forty vendors stood offering their wares. Instead of an international food court, however, Pudong served up a BBQ meal.

After playing games and using the inflatables, our mouths watered in anticipation when we saw that the Brazilian restaurant from Jade Leisure Center in Jin Qiao was catering the meal. We made our way over to their venue for lunch. I'm not sure what logistical problems the caterers were having, but everyone stood waiting in two very long lines for their food. Eventually the restaurant ran out of some of the side dishes each plate was supposed to include. By the time we received our meals, disappointingly they consisted of only a hamburger and some salad. We joined some families we knew, and sat down to eat. They tipped us off that we had overlooked the performance part of the fair.

So, after eating, we skipped over to where the Quick Silver skateboarding company had set up ramps. In addition to letting the kids try skateboarding, their teams gave periodic, thrilling demonstrations. Moving on from there, we found a portable stage, an audience slowly gathering on the ground in front. The Pudong campus PTSA had hired a troop of very talented Chinese acrobatics, and these young performers kept us spellbound for nearly an hour.

Now tired and happy, we dialed Mr. Zhou. On the ride back to The Pearl, the kids chattered contentedly about all the things they'd seen and done and played with all the little prizes they had collected. I thought about how we'd had two such amazing weekends in one month. Thankfully, since August Shanghai hadn't proved dull.

Evolution

Leave it to the SEA to plan another stellar adventure in October, which remains one of my favorite events—Gang of One's hutong tour. Gang of One—aka Gang Weng Fang—was a Shanghai photographer, well-known and popular among the expat crowd for his stunning and thoughtful photos of Chinese life and his expat family portraits, shot in colorful hutongs with the families dressed in traditional Chinese clothing. Gang was on a mission, both in his work and his tours, to capture the fascinating transformation of modern China on film.

Our walking tour took place in the highly transitional neighborhood where our guide grew up. There shiny, glam modern buildings now exploded onto the landscape at breakneck pace, challenging the lovely old Shikumen-style buildings and shaky hovels. I felt very privileged and excited to view the City's evolution through a native photographer's eyes.

We started our walk facing a substantial pile of rubble that lay waiting to reveal its tale. At this time, Shanghai's efforts to become a world-class city as rapidly as possible made such piles inevitable. In fact, the city dwellers constantly joked around, saying, "don't blink because the building you're looking at might be gone. Don't blink, because a new skyscraper will appear." So, there we stood on a dump heap; old white plaster, red-tile-roofed dwellings on two sides; slick, modern mirrored skyscrapers towering above us on all sides. I shot several photos immediately, as I thought this scene perfectly captured the Shanghai of October 2005: simultaneously traditional and contemporary, experiencing growing pains.

As we strolled through the neighborhood, Gang pointed out certain details of the building exteriors. He also explained that the government insisted the people in these old houses move into the newly constructed high rises. A family with guanxi (in this case people with government connections or party members) would likely get a place with a better location and/or more space: a bedroom, a family room, a tiny private bath, and its own kitchenette. These families waited anxiously for the government to buy them out and move them into new, appealing high rises. But those without any guanxi and many of the elderly saw no benefit in moving. They insisted on remaining. These stubborn resistors were called "nail families" (as in nailed down to one place).

"Why isn't having a brand new, modern apartment, even if it has only two rooms and a better bathroom, exciting to the nail families?" I couldn't resist asking Gang.

"These families have lived together in this communal way, in this place, for generations. If they moved to a Pudong skyscraper, for example, it would be difficult, time consuming, and expensive for them to visit their friends and relatives," our guide explained. "The younger people, who didn't grow up the same way, have no problem to go. But the old people don't like it."

That made sense to me. I thought it showed how the Shanghainese made relationships a priority. We outsiders could certainly learn from that attitude.

What Gang shared next sent an excited chill up my spine: he had arranged for us to look inside several buildings and actually visit people's homes! As we walked, he explained that the building interiors had been divided up in ways the architect and original owner had never intended. Dozens of families had been crowded into the now much sub-divided spaces, like sardines into a can, each family occupying only *one room*. It brought new meaning to the idea of urban crowding. Gang explained that during the Cultural Revolution (1966-1976), Mao celebrated "common laborers" of all types and penalized anyone who had money or a white-collar job. People who owned businesses and factories became the enemy and had their property taken away. Overnight, the floor sweepers found themselves turned into bosses, while the business owners now cleaned up the floors or were sent into the countryside to work on farms. Farmers suddenly found themselves working as doctors without any training (they were expected to learn on the job)! Teachers were banished into the hinterlands to slop hogs and plant crops. Since hordes of country folk streamed into the cities to support Mao's new economic system, buildings like this one were divided up again and again in an attempt to house them all. Wealthy families who owned swanky mansions in the French Concession found themselves relegated to a single room, while whole families of strangers occupied the remaining rooms of their houses.

We entered an elegant, old white-stone town house. Inside, I saw tasteful, classic French-style black and white diamond-shaped tiles on the floor. An enormous crystal chandelier hung above the foyer. What a showplace this must have been during Shanghai's last heyday! The layers of grime on the floor and walls and the massive cobwebs stretching across the foyer corners left me baffled, however. I could easily have been staring at the set of the *Munsters* TV show. It costs nothing to wipe a floor or brush away a spiderweb. Didn't the denizens share the responsibility of keeping this place tidy? You know, Communism and all? It pained me to see a grand old mansion in such disrepair.

What Gang shared next, floored me. In these houses, six or more families shared the single kitchen! Each family set up their own small double-burner gas cooktop and brought food from the market or their room down to cook.

There was no refrigerator in sight, probably because they are so pricey for regular people to afford and because the electricity to run them is much more expensive in China than in other parts of the world. The residents were thus limited to foods that could be stir fried or boiled. The idea of a communal kitchen seemed quite practical, however.

In many buildings, Gang informed us, multiple families not only shared a kitchen, but a single miserable, tiny, putrid bathroom. The one we passed by was so small it truly was little more than a "water closet." Other families had no bathrooms onsite at all. Even in 2005, they still used a container. In the morning the "night soil" worker came to carry away the waste, which was then sold to farmers for fertilizer. *Wow!*

From the subdivided house, our guide led us into the city's *hutongs* (alleys). Everywhere, we came across groups of serious-looking older men and women playing *Mah Jongg*.

"Gambling is illegal," Gang remarked, "but people always play for money anyway."

I appreciated the man's raw honesty. But wasn't he worried about telling Westerners the truth? Couldn't he get reported?

As we strolled, we passed a second-hand shop and a meat market. Pink slabs of flesh dangled from the window and ceiling in the approximately eighty-five-degree heat and high humidity. Since most people had no refrigeration, they purchased meat daily and cooked it fresh at every meal. Another small shop displayed the largest variety of egg sizes and colors I'd ever seen. Along with the usual white and brown eggs I recognized, I saw tiny brown speckled ones, small green ones, and even some blue ones. I wondered if they all tasted different. For sure, the variety of foods available in Shanghai remained astonishing.

Next stop as we cruised down the hutongs, I spied...fitness equipment?

"What is this?" I asked Gang, perplexed.

"It's a gym for old people," he explained.

Apparently, the older people who wanted a little more activity than a morning of Tai Chi exercises in the park came here to use the equipment. I found it remarkable that seniors had the option of a free outdoor gym, *and* they actually exercised!

Then we passed a Traditional Chinese Medicine clinic. Inside, clients sat in chairs or lay on tables with acupuncture needles protruding from their bodies. One man had a smoking moxibustion concoction on his chest. It smelled like a weird, woody, menthol version of pot. Another man lay face-down on a bed with several small, clear cups attached to his back, the skin sucked nearly to the tops. It looked horrific, and I wondered whether this treatment was painful. Still so new to China, I didn't know this was cupping—a popular and beneficial therapy.

Finally, we came to our last stop. Gang steered us into a popular neighborhood restaurant where we sampled authentic *xiao long bao*—Shanghai's famous soup dumplings. On the jam-packed first floor, diners slurped away at the popular fare. The hostess led us to the second-floor dining room, where she seated our group at brown wooden picnic-style tables. The place offered absolutely nothing in the way of ambiance: white walls, battered linoleum floors, and mostly basic metal and plastic tables and chairs. Clearly the diners didn't come for the atmosphere! When our dumplings arrived from the kitchen, I immediately noticed the difference from the "pot stickers" served in American restaurants. Copious amounts of broth lay waiting, momentarily contained, inside.

"Do not make the mistake of trying to pick up a dumpling and eat it whole," Gang warned us. "Stab it first with your chopstick, like this," he demonstrated. "Drink the juice," he added, then paused for emphasis. "*Then* you can eat the dumpling."

Schooled, my tablemates looked at each other curiously. "OK, let's do this," someone said, signaling us to move forward.

Though the directions seemed quite simple, I still managed to spill the broth and drop my slippery dumpling repeatedly. The more experienced diners at my table got a laugh watching me look like an ignorant tourist, a hopeless Westerner. For good measure, I laughed along and threw out a "*bu hao!*" (no good). But very little about living in China had been easy so far, and I wasn't about to be defeated by a mere piece of stuffed pasta! Downing the second one went better. I stabbed, I slurped up the broth, and then wrangled the feisty little dough ball onto my chopsticks, triumphantly inhaling it. *Whew! One step closer to becoming an old China hand!*

Household and Department Store Pests

My next October adventure involved pests. As a native Minnesotan, I was no stranger to mosquito problems. Yet, in Shanghai the mosis left ultra-itchy, huge red welts. People also seemed slightly paranoid about malaria. Despite the small electronic bug zappers hanging throughout the house, I thought why not give my family a little extra protection at night?

Soon, Mr. Zhao and I made our way to Isetan, the Japanese department store. I asked him to come inside with me, as I didn't know where to look for what I wanted or how to ask for mosi tents in Chinese. My driver led me to the housewares department. There, near the bedding, we found the domes. A middle-aged female clerk with a Mao haircut, dressed in grey wool pants and a burgundy sweater, zipped over, staring me down as if I might damage something if she didn't keep her eagle eyes on the unpredictable waiguoren. *She reminded me of a pesky insect, herself!* I pointed to the tents and asked the woman for *er* (two). A poisonous look crept over her face. Then she burst out in a vicious laugh, blasting a barrage of malicious words—probably something about how the city had been infiltrated by this nightmare of foreigners too stupid to learn Mandarin—to Mr. Zhao. I found this Chinese troll's macabre delight in my mistake bizarre and rude. I had been polite and attempted to speak the language of my adopted country; therefore, I was officially *not* an ugly American *or* a stupid tourist.

"Tai Tai, *liang ge*," Zhou whispered, not wanting his Tai Tai to lose too much face.

"Oooohh! *Xie xie* (thanks)," I grimaced.

Oh, it just figured! Though I had learned all the numbers, I didn't yet know that when you're asking for two of something, you needed to use liang instead! While I stood both humiliated and appalled by the woman's behavior, I felt thankful that Mr. Zhao came to my rescue. He stepped in, and reverting to Shanghainese (a dialect which sounded like angry barking dogs), he and the sales monster completed the order.

In case I didn't feel irritated enough already, I was about to learn how shopping in a Chinese department store worked. After a shopper selected merchandise, the clerk wrote up the purchase on a sales slip. Then the buyer had to take the slip to the cashier's booth, to pay. After paying, the cashier stamped the ticket, which the shopper then brought back to show the clerk. Finally, the clerk handed the shopper the merchandise. The only process more annoying was having to negotiate a price with a vendor when you actually really needed something and were in a hurry.

Receipt in hand, I retrieved my merchandise, skipped American etiquette standards that required me to say "thanks" —since niceties were clearly lost on the witch of Isetan—and made a beeline for the car. I achieved the mosi domes for our beds, but clearly, I still had so much to learn about my host country's language! *Sigh.*

De-Stressing

Thankfully, my stressful days were easily and cheaply remedied in Shanghai. The city had no shortage of massage venues. Taipan-style shops abounded, including the place that eventually cropped up just outside the gate of our compound. One of my favorite spas, however, was an expat-oriented chain called Dragon Fly. They had a branch in Jade Leisure Center, and I could pop in after a workout at MegaFit. My favorite treatment, the Heaven and Earth, involved two therapists working at once. One tackled the head, neck, shoulders, and arms; while the other covered the feet and legs. I loved the waterfall feature at the back of the room, and the therapy coupled with the sound of rushing water nearly always put me to sleep. The whole ninety minutes of bliss cost only $25 (and no tipping!)!

When expats wanted a splurge, the plush spas at the major hotels provided incomparable pampering—but not inexpensively. One of Planet's and my favorites was the Banyan Tree at the Westin. After two months of managing my crazy Tai Tai life, I believed I had earned a sojourn to the Banyan Tree.

On spa day, I strode through the Westin's elegant marble lobby and glided up the escalators to the spa. There, two very attractive young Chinese ladies dressed in the tasteful, charming hotel uniform chi pao sat waiting at their desks. I sank into a silk-cushioned chair in front of one woman to check in. While we discussed my treatment plan, another young lady served me lemongrass ginger tea in a tallish black cup on a black saucer, adorned with a single purple and white orchid. Fortunately, Planet signed up for a membership, so I could take advantage of the monthly members' special. Today's special was a two-hour massage and facial combination for 1188RMB (about $143). Though well outside the Dragon Fly league, I could hardly complain about the price since it basically amounted to a buy-one-get-one-free by US standards.

Next, I learned that the Banyan Tree's treatments centered on the five essential elements—water, gold, wood, fire, and earth. Each element had special properties, which lent the treatment its smells and specific natural products. I opted for earth, which supposedly generates the state of optimum balance, regulates and nourishes the other elements, and represents late summer. Just what I needed! Then the customer service woman pressed a button, and my therapist—a young Thai woman—opened the mammoth, black Asian-style doors.

I stepped inside onto shiny black marble flooring, noticing the matching black marble walls and feeling like I'd entered another world. Indentations emerged every few feet with white candles lighting the way. At the far end of the hallway stood a single bonsai tree, showcased in its own little foyer. The hallway certainly had the five elements covered. The whole hallway seemed so simple, yet evoked so much symbolism. It set the mood perfectly, and I nearly floated forward in anticipation.

The therapist led me into a corridor decorated with red carpet, candles, and ginger jars. When we reached the treatment room, I saw a large jacuzzi bath with a beautiful bronze waterfall faucet, steam showers, an elegant bathroom, and a dressing room. The therapist handed me a cushy white robe. Small purple and white orchids lay artistically placed on the bathroom towels and the vanity.

The massage bed stood ready, ensconced in beautiful purple and gold silk covers and topped with matching silk pillows. How posh!

When I stood enveloped in my robe and slippers, the therapist led me over to a chair at the head of the massage table and poured me a tiny white cup of warm green tea. Then she poured hot water with herbs into a large golden bowl and placed my feet into the heavenly brew. A moment later, she added white rose petals to the foot bath. While my feet soaked, and stress started melting away, the young Thai lady brought out incense sticks. Each one had a scent corresponding to certain properties: to soothe anxiety and warm the spirit, to increase romantic feeling, to clear a troubled mind, or to increase energy and mental clarity. Oh, I definitely needed them all! But I chose the scent that would decrease my anxiety and warm my spirit. When the therapist lit the stick, a scent of freshly cut wood and warming spices filled the room.

After the foot soak, the therapist motioned me to lie down on my stomach and put my face in the little hole at the front of the table. When I looked down, I saw an attractive gold bowl filled with water, black Chinese writing around the edges and a red flower floating inside. Even the geometric pattern of the carpet in the treatment area added to the calming effect of my view. Asian new-age music at just the right volume perfected the scene. The Banyan Tree spa definitely paid noteworthy attention to detail.

Balinese massage turned out to be a vigorous treatment, rather like a sports massage or deep tissue massage, but with more stretching. At one point the therapist even slapped and pounded the bottoms of my feet. The surprises of this massage were not over, though. Asian masseuses in upscale spas are allowed to touch nearly everything. Before I knew it, her hands gripped my… breasts! Er…my *chest muscles*. Right. I felt slightly weirded out by this, but I tried to put it into an Asian cultural framework: there had to be a health benefit to doing it. It made sense to massage this major muscle group, and I guessed American modesty laws probably kept it from being part of routine massages at home. After the rigorous and very thorough massage, the therapist ushered me into the shower. When I emerged, she had set up my earth facial. Unlike a typical European-style facial, this procedure focused less on getting rid of stray chin hairs and random blackheads than on balancing the skin. The treatment involved mostly slathering my face with various delicious-smelling fruit and herb smoothies. The best part, however, was when the therapist gave me a wonderful neck, upper back, shoulders, and head massage while I lay with a masque on my face that smelled so good I had to restrain myself from tasting it. The masque-time massage usually isn't done in the US, sadly, not even during $150 facials. *It should be required at that price!* I was thrilled.

After the facial, the therapist pointed me back to the shower for another rinse. When I reappeared, she served me more of the wonderful lemongrass ginger tea and a plate of fruit. A small black teapot and a tiny black cup, stood before me on a woven bamboo tray, with more orchids placed strategically in one corner atop a hot towel. I sighed contentedly, feeling completely relaxed, contented, and pampered.

Over the years, I returned to the Banyan Tree as often as possible. Each time, I experienced wonderful therapies that I still recall fondly today. I hope someday I'll be lucky enough to return.

Golden Week and Rosh Hashanah Phuket Style

It seemed like school had hardly started and already the kids had a break for China's National Day. The holiday seemed similar to July 4 in the US, except the Chinese people of course celebrated their own country and their government. Colorful lanterns and other festive decorations appeared all over the city in a burst of red, as the Chinese Mid-Autumn Festival coincidentally also took place the same week that year (because of the lunar calendar). This Festival is the second most important Chinese holiday of the year. The moon is supposedly the brightest and the roundest at this time, which symbolizes family togetherness, so people are in a frenzy to get home for a visit. Then, they eat moon cakes (always round, of course) and go outside at night to appreciate and pay homage to the moon. Just like people give each other fruitcakes for Christmas, the Chinese give each other elaborate bean or lotus paste-filled moon cakes (and they taste equally bad!). Together, the holidays comprised "Golden Week," resulting in a country-wide week-long holiday.

It amazed me that although the expats had just returned from their summer holiday travels about six weeks ago, nearly everyone jetted off to exotic locales for the October break. For me, at this point, a break from the intensity of trying to settle into Shanghai expat life felt incredibly welcome. Planet and I had loved Thailand when we visited a decade prior. From Shanghai, it was easy to get there, we could stay for free using our timeshare system benefits. We thought the kids would enjoy it, so my family shuffled off to spend our first Golden Week in Phuket.

From the moment we boarded the Thai Airlines jumbo jet, I felt like I had started my vacation. The atmosphere onboard resembled a flying resort—calm, Zenlike, and decorated in soothing lavender—and I immediately understood why Thai is consistently rated one of the world's top airlines. The attractive, shiny-raven-haired hostesses stood smiling benevolently at the embarking passengers, their hair pulled back into perfect, slick knots and their dramatic yet tasteful make-up perfectly applied. These goodwill ambassadors stood draped in gorgeous silk suits consisting of a short jacket with a decorative sash adorned with a purple orchid at the top and floor-length skirts. The suits came in several different styles—probably to denote employee rank. While I appreciated how lovely and glamorous the flight attendants looked, I couldn't help thinking how exhausting it must be to actually serve passengers, running up and down the aisles the whole flight in floor-length skirts and pumps. As each passenger boarded the plane, the flight attendants smiled, put their hands together prayer-style, and welcomed them with a charming traditional bow.

A hostess guided us to our seats, where we put away our carry-ons and buckled up for the four-hour flight to Bankok. Spa-like music piped through the cabin. Within minutes, a flight attendant came by with "welcome gifts" for the kids. When was the last time you took kids on a plane and they received anything more than a winged pin? Here, the kid-friendly pouch contained a well-thought-out activity book that even included kid-sized tracing tools, a flower-shaped eraser, and a pencil sharpener. In the exciting bonus round that immediately followed, the flight attendants offered the kids hand-held gaming devices. Good behavior guarantees, locked and loaded! After lunch, I deemed it wise to visit the bathroom before landing. To my surprise, I discovered purple and white Thai orchids both strewn on the counter and placed carefully in a vase off to the side of the sink. There was even a little vial of herbal-scented perfume to spray just in case you did something in there that the orchids couldn't handle. Lavender-colored fabric hand towels lay on the counter. I loved all the remarkable attention to detail.

The outstanding Thai Air hospitality caused the hours between Shanghai and Bangkok to race by. In no time, we found ourselves deplaning in Bangkok and wandering over to the gate to wait for our one-hour flight to Phuket.

On arrival in Phuket, a JW Marriott driver met us and led us to a sturdy-looking Mercedes sedan. In keeping with the Thai pampering we'd received all day, the driver handed us ice-cold, lavender scented hand towels, folded into artsy little coiled figures and placed on a ceramic plate with—what else?—a purple and white Thai orchid. Feng shui in a car? Yes! While we rubbed those cool cloths across our hot weary faces, the driver broke out perfectly chilled water bottles for each of us. I could absolutely get used to Thai hospitality!

After a short drive, we arrived at the Marriott, where the resort's security detail stopped the car. Serious-looking men searched under the vehicle with long-handled mirrors and shone their flashlights into the trunk. *What did the security measures really mean? Was this all for show, or did tourists at this resort actually face some risk? How much risk?* Finally satisfied, the men waved our driver onwards, up the driveway and into the carport reception area. There, a lady in jodhpur pants and a little 1940s army-style hat welcomed us, placing orchid and white ginger leis around our necks. Before we had walked ten more steps, another beautiful lady in a stunning traditional Thai dress floated over to offer us welcome drinks. The fizzy lime drink, complete with a mint sprig, came served in hairy brown coconut shells. The kids were in a tizzy of delight.

At the check-in desk, a clerk stood waiting, arms outstretched to the kids with welcome gifts: a small, brightly colored stuffed turtle—the hotel mascot—and a big chocolate cookie topped with brightly colored sugar sprinkles. Alexis and Anders beamed in delight. Although the hotel management offered apologies that they were still repairing damages to the beach and buildings from 2004's devastating Tsunami, we saw no signs of destruction. The manager also commented tourism had remained sketchy as a result, though we didn't notice any lack of guests during our stay. I hoped our visit provided some small means of help for their economy.

I sighed contentedly as we padded down dense pathways accented with river stones and Thai symbols, through tropical jungle greenery, to our unit. There, we dropped off our luggage and quickly set out to investigate the rest of this gorgeous property. Our first discovery was an architecturally intricate, two-level adults-only pool. Heavy teak chairs with thick rust-colored cushions stood invitingly, adorned with precision-rolled azure blue towels, with— you guessed it—a purple and white orchid resting atop each one. Going left from the pool, we came upon a huge wooden door frame holding an electric blue door, about fifteen feet high, which lent an air of mystery to the stunning garden. As we passed under this elaborate architectural structure, we arrived at the kids' pool, though it appeared we had just walked onto a movie set. The pool resembled a natural pond, featuring a slide on one end that emerged from a small jungle-style stone Temple. Pillars and stone elephants and turtles rose from the water in neat rows to enhance the pool's exotic theme. The children's pool presented itself as the obvious choice for a base camp for the rest of the day. Even here in the family area, thick, extra-long towels lay spread on the substantial, overstuffed chair cushions, and another towel for après swim had been decoratively folded and carefully placed at the foot of each chair, an orchid gracing the top of each. How refreshing to skip the niggling American process of signing-out thin, worn towels at a pool shed and worrying about getting charged for any that disappeared while in our care before we schlepped back at day's end!

Charmed, we all settled in to enjoy some sunshine and relaxation. It didn't take long for pool attendants to notice newcomers. They buzzed over holding small black wooden trays containing glasses of iced water and offering cold-water spritzes for our humidity-steamed faces and bodies. At regular intervals, attendants navigated around the pool deck offering the guests slices of chilled melon. Our children happily commandeered the slide, and we found that we could even see the ocean from our poolside perches—so no need to actually make the effort to walk down to the beach! Within minutes, we discovered we had no reason or motivation whatsoever to leave our chairs at all. Bliss set in. "Land of Smiles?" Yes, indeed!

As evening fell, the pool attendants informed us that at 6:00 pm each night, the hotel provided a short but powerful show honoring the ancient god of fire and light—a fancy way of saying they'd ignite the torches in the main reflection pool. At show time, we watched, enthralled, as three women in white robes and elaborate masks swayed like wildflowers in a breeze, while a tribally decorated drummer in a white mask thumped out the storyline. Suddenly, two men in traditional Thai-style shorts emerged, leaping through the water with their flame-topped bamboo poles, ceremoniously lighting each torch—which protruded from each majestic stone statue representing important mythological or historical characters. Now imagine this scene set against a majestic pink, purple, and orange sunset! We felt like we had just lived out an episode from the National Geographic Channel.

Over the next few days, Planet and I managed to de-stress into such a state of nirvana that we contemplated never moving from our well-provisioned poolside loungers. The kids had made some friends and now alternated between attending the resort's "Little Turtle" camp and playing in the pool with their new buddies. The kids' camp provided an impressive full-day itinerary of activities: computer games, X-box, PlayStation, a variety of crafts, face painting, snorkeling class, tennis class, Thai dancing, Thai boxing, movies, and baking cookies. Unbelievably, guests under twelve could attend camp *free*, with the hotel charging a fee only for a few of the more elaborate, high-quality craft projects.

One day, feeling a bit guilty, Planet and I tested the idea of actually removing our tushes from our chairs by strolling down to view the beach. As we approached, we noticed hotel security guards patrolling the stretch and a flag indicating the current swimming conditions. It was red today, so no swimming allowed. It had never occurred to us that we couldn't swim on vacation. I slid up to one of the security guards. "Do you think we'll be able to swim tomorrow," I asked.

"I don't think so, Madame," the man replied. "Maybe you swim after monsoon season."

Planet and I exchanged raised-eyebrow glances. Monsoon season? Again, something else not previously included in our frame of reference.

Later that week, I checked out the resort's Mandara spa. Mandara was definitely one of the most ambient spas I'd ever seen, with enchanting, feng shui décor and lush, tropical outdoor treatment rooms. I signed up for a Champissage—a head and face massage beneficial for people with sinus trouble and headaches.

After I checked in, my masseuse walked me down a flowering-plant-lined path past a remarkable series of portals. Massive slabs of carved wood adorned with gold knobs, about fifteen-feet high hung from the frames. Each jungle-temple-style door led to individual villas. Inside my treatment villa, glamorous tile gleamed on the floor. A table draped in bright Thai silk stood waiting. Then I saw the crowning glory: just outside my personal temple lay a small garden surrounded by an attractive grey stone wall. Inside the stone walls, a private outdoor shower waited. Paradise! In this memorable setting, I enjoyed an excellent massage, and I hoped to return to this spa soon.

I practically floated back to the condo, where I met up with Planet and the kids. While I had been deliriously floating in my own personal Shangri-La, he had decided we should partake of the resort's special dinner option. Guests could create a meal from the various menu selections, then the chef and his team would come to the guest's villa to prepare and serve dinner—room service extraordinaire! The kids watched, mesmerized, as the chef and his assistant prepared the food, cooking over a small grill on our balcony. The meal was outstanding, and we were glad we experienced a relaxed gourmet dinner in our own villa.

Finally, the day came when we managed to guilt ourselves into bypassing the pool chairs and the Little Turtle Camp in favor of a "four-in-one" tour. Our "Island Safari" included whitewater rafting, swimming in a waterfall and lagoon, touring an elephant camp, and ATV riding. When the tour company guides picked us up at the hotel, we had about an hour drive to the rafting launch, our first stop on this whirlwind day. At the rafting site, we suited up with helmets and dispatched our shoes onto the riverbank. The brochure had touted this as a family trip down a "lazy river, suitable for all ages." The rapids ranked a level two (pretty tame). Thus, we expected a relaxing morning as we set off down the murky, café-latte-colored river, gorgeous plush tropical foliage obscuring both banks. Just minutes into the excursion, however, we hit… whitewater?

This water was not "lazy" by any stretch of the imagination! In fact, the remainder of the thirty-minute trip involved me repeatedly flying onto the bottom of the boat and maneuvering to keep the kids from launching into the water. Midway through the ride, as we bravely battled the snarling swirls, our guide suddenly sailed feet-over-head off the right side of the raft. Still in mid freak-out that our guide was now in the water and no one was steering the raft, I happened to glance over at Planet. He clung to the handrails on the side of the boat, his body dangling over the side of the raft, butt first. He was taking the situation unexpectedly well. I, however, considered making a stink with the tour company for false advertising as I tugged Planet back into the rubber boat.

I looked up at the riverbanks. A number of locals stood, hanging out. Were they there to help rescue ejected rafters…because this occurred *regularly*? Expecting to earn a few bhat for their services? Or were they just there for the comic relief of watching foreigners go flying out of the rafts (again, because this occurred regularly?)? Mercifully the trip ended as scheduled thirty whitewater, white-knuckle minutes later.

"Let's go again," the kids shouted joyfully as we pulled up to the end point. *Oy!*

After rafting, the tour guide delivered us to a camp for lunch. A buffet had been set up under the trees in a clearing of picnic tables, consisting of a few of Thai curry dishes, tempura vegetables, rice, and fruit. While we enjoyed the lunch break, a rainstorm rolled in. Nonplussed, the guides urged us into a four-wheel-drive for our journey to the nature hike site. By the time we reached the stop, bolts of water poured from the sky, like G_d sending the flood down on Noah. The tour guide pretended nothing was amiss as he led us to the hiking trail. Soaked, we followed bravely. Fortunately, it wasn't far to the lagoon and main waterfall, and no one slipped in the rapidly thickening mud. Within an hour, however, the rainfall had rendered the lagoon's water level too high for us to safely swim. It was fine: some of us had already had our swim on the rafting trip!

On the walk back down the path to the jeep, I began to understand how roads suddenly washed away in this part of the world. Once, a friend's Filipino ayi had not returned from a visit to her family because the road out of the village had washed out. At the time, I thought that was a convenient excuse to stay longer; now I saw it was probably true. I felt relieved to see our vehicle and the road remained just as we'd left them.

Now we faced an hour's wet drive to the elephant camp. When we arrived, we saw scores of these majestic beasts waiting to serve the throngs of tourists. As the visitors were being assigned to their guides and animals, I grew uncomfortable when I noticed most of the handlers looked magnificently stoned. How well could they handle these five-ton creatures in their impaired state?

I crossed my fingers as Alexis and I climbed into the basket atop our elephant, and Planet and Anders boarded theirs. Fortunately, these gentle giants seemed peaceful as they sauntered down a shallow portion of the river. We bumped along, high above the ground, taking in the stunning scenery. Suddenly, I saw Planet's prize sunglasses fall to the riverbank. His elephant handler had noticed, too. This potential mishap now gave the young man a chance to show off his animal's skills and emerge a hero. In a moment, a long grey snout adeptly and gently picked up the errant glasses and handed them up to the guide straddling the beast's head. The kids laughed and clapped. As the guide handed the sunglasses back to Planet, I saw him examining his precious Revos for signs of beast snot. No elephant boogers, but he wiped the glasses on his shirt just in case, before popping them back onto his head. Everyone smiled approvingly. Soon, our guides steered the passive pachyderms off the river and through a small field.

Now, it was time for the elephant show! On our previous trip to Thailand, Planet and I had watched a demonstration of how elephants were used in place of machines for tasks that required strength—like lifting and pulling logs—or height, like picking bananas. This event had more of a circus vibe. Here, two baby elephants revealed the species' intellect and trainability. First, they trumpeted a greeting, and then played harmonicas. They stood up on hind legs, and then walked with their back legs on top of their front legs—elephant gymnastics. Next, one of them picked up a basketball and shot hoops. She even managed to get most of the balls into the basket. Then it was the other elephant's turn to give one member of the audience a "Thai massage." Anders felt quite disappointed when he wasn't chosen. A few moments later, I was glad! The animal picked up one foot and gently rubbed the volunteer dad's back in a circular motion. Next, she used her trunk as a suction cup and then patted him with it in a chopping motion. Finally, in a burst of humor, the animal pretended to give the dad a "happy ending" by pretending to massage his genital area with her foot! Every got a good laugh out of that one.

From the elephant program, the guides led us to a different area of the camp to learn how monkeys work the plantations picking coconuts and other fruits. Who would have guessed their bananas were harvested by chimpanzees? Of course, the kids loved the show simply because it involved animals in action. They laughed, thrilled, when a monkey handed *them* a banana, instead of the other way around.

After the animal events, our tour ended with the ATV ride—the event the kids had most anticipated. Although the rain deluge had abated, a drizzle had dripped continually since. I worried because I knew how easily people could get hurt on ATVs even in fair weather. Undaunted, Planet took first Anders and then Alexis around the looped track as fast as he dared in the slick sludge. Thankfully, the ATV portion of today's program only lasted thirty minutes, and my family remained safe.

Our Phuket vacation ended with an interesting twist. In a sea of straight black hair, elephants, and rice paddies, how could we create a meaningful Rosh Hashana (Jewish New Year) celebration? Well, I brought along one of my religious resource books and spent a day creating a Jeopardy-style game for the kids. Planet and I served as quizmasters, and correct answers earned points. The kids loved it! After the game, I presented my own elementary-school version of the service by reading to my family from my handy holiday service book. All went well. Definitely, there was something to be said for a do-it-yourself Rosh Hashana on a beach in Thailand. It caused my family to reflect more on the day's meaning than we may have in Ohio. Being away, we had to be more focused. Rosh Hashana 2005 was our most unusual high holiday, but also one of our best.

We returned to China by the time the next important Jewish high holiday—Yom Kippur—came around the next week. We debated whether spending hours in traffic to attend services in Puxi made sense. Planet and I would probably survive just fine, but we thought it seemed too much to ask of a seven- and eight-year-old to sit through three to four hours in the car plus a long service. Instead, Planet and I read our *Gates of Repentance* Yom Kippur section to each other and reflected. When the kids got home from school, we read them a condensed version of the service, then held a discussion about the holiday with them.

Mimi Neidermeyer kindly invited us to her house to break the fast. When we arrived, I counted about twenty people there. The families spent a couple of hours getting to know each other and enjoying the holiday together. We all had the unique shared experience of trying to be Jewish in Shanghai, which created an instant bond. This was certainly our most unusual Yom Kippur, yet it was one of the most memorable and enjoyable.

Waiting to Inhale

After our trip to Thailand, I now had first-hand experience with China's pollution anecdotes. Was Shanghai's pollution really as bad as its reputation? Without hesitation, yes. One of the main drawbacks to living at The Pearl, and in Shanghai in general, was the air pollution. Each day as I stepped out my front door, I never knew what type of foul odor would assault me. Planet and I jokingly began to call it "smell of the day," though joke it was not. On any given day, the world outside our front door might reek of *eau de* rotting garbage melted into plastic mixed with overtones of sewage or perhaps lawn fertilizer and wet dog. Who knew the world had manifested such a large variety of funky stenches or that they were all gathered here in Shanghai? I couldn't allow myself to consider the effects these aromas might have on our health.

In keeping with smell of the day, the sky remained suspect. No exaggeration, I can barely recall more than a few sunny days in the two and a half years I lived in that city. Most days it seemed impossible to tell whether the weather was just really cloudy or whether a noxious haze obscured a nice day.

Perhaps as a result of the odd aromas and the perma-gray sky, we lived with two unpleasant known side-effects: the Kleenex surprise and headaches.

After living in Shanghai for a few months, I discovered a sad truth about the City air: when I blew my nose, the mucus came out…black! What did this mean for my family's health? I certainly hoped the damage could be reversed once we returned to the US. Also, I noticed that on a daily basis, my head ached somewhere within a range of mild to migraine. When I mentioned this to a neighbor, she explained that breathing the city's contaminated air definitely caused issues.

"We try to go away as often as possible to 'recycle' our lungs," she informed me. "When we get back, we always have a headache for a week or so. We call it the Shanghai headache." *Astonishing!* Indeed, when we returned from Thailand, I experienced this troublesome and concerning malady. Now I knew what people were talking about.

Halloween

We rounded out the month with that excellent American tradition, Halloween. Thankfully, the school and the compounds celebrated. During the week before the holiday, I purchased pumpkins at the Pearl's weekly farmers market, and the kids were excited to get them carved after school. I downloaded a selection of pictures to choose from, hoping we'd have a stylish display on our front steps. Anders chose a scary face and Alexis chose a cat. I remembered to bring one of those pumpkin mini-saws from the US, so I pulled that out along with a small knife. We started with Alexis' cat. We carefully traced the design onto the vegetable's shiny orange surface and then attacked it with our fancy little tool. I nearly broke the saw attempting to maneuver it through the pumpkin's unyielding skin. I looked at Alexis, puzzled.

"Maybe we should try the knife. This seems to be a tough-guy pumpkin."

I tried the knife. What in the world was going on? Even sawing like a lumberjack, I managed to chop out only a small chunk. The sides had to be an inch thick! Where did The Pearl get these pumpkins? Forget Alexis' cat design; we'd be lucky to make the simplest of faces on this jack-o-lantern. Looking at the kids quizzically, and then, frowning, I tried Anders' pumpkin. Same problem. The sides were just too thick. We did our best to carve basic faces, with me working up a sweat and trying not to wind up in the ER in the process.

When the pumpkins began to rot only a few days later, I realized that The Pearl had ordered *pie* pumpkins, not carving ones! I hoped they'd last until trick-or-treating.

The school and the compound had both arranged celebrations for the kids, in addition to actual trick-or-treating. The Saturday night before Halloween, The Pearl held a kids' Halloween party. A committee of neighbors and some of the high school kids elaborately decorated the rec center. They even created a spooky house. Numerous games sprang to life on the lower level, and upstairs everyone enjoyed listening and dancing while a DJ spun tunes. We all had a wonderful time.

At school, I volunteered at Alexis' class party. When I arrived in the class-room, all the great costumes made it seem like many parents had taken advantage of the Dong Jia Du fabric market. One of the room moms wore a sexy black qipao-style witch dress, complete with a ragged hemline and orange spi-derweb accents. She added black fishnet stockings and a tall pointy hat that matched her dress. The outfit set off her slim figure perfectly, and she looked awesome. One of the art teachers made a perfect flower-power hippie. Most of the third-grade teachers hailed from Canada, so the entire team decided to come dressed as the Canadian Mounted Police. They even had toy broomstick ponies to pretend-ride around school. Clearly, I had to step up my game next year. Anders was so excited and proud to finally be a cub scout that he insisted on wearing his uniform as a costume. Who was I to argue with the concept of "I've already paid for it and I have it in hand?" Alexis had a closet full of beau-tiful, expensive skating costumes, so I encouraged her to wear one of those. She did, but we added a hip pink wig with shiny silver steaks to spice it up.

Everything was running so smoothly at the Grade 3 party that feeling unneeded, I stopped by Anders' classroom to see how things were going there. I had contributed the concept and the recipe for their caramel apple dipping and decorating, and I hoped the kids were enjoying it. The competent room mothers had everything under control there, and the kids were having a ball. During the parade, the kids' enthusiasm and delightful costumes warmed my heart as they marched excitedly through the halls and around the school's out-side perimeter. I enjoyed myself enormously and went home grateful I could share this day with my kids.

When trick-or-treat night arrived, The Pearl residents were ready. I left Xiao Ting home to hand out candy while I walked the kids around the complex. I thought that one hundred pieces of candy should suffice, but I was so wrong. Xiao Ting told me we ran out shortly after the first hour! In the meantime, my kids ran at top speed from house to house and made it through nearly the entire compound in two hours. I sat down on the couch, exhausted, while Alexis and Anders spent the next hour happily organizing their candy into piles. The sweets they received were definitely different than in the US. Here they received mainly bite-sized candies, and mostly the hard type, like a single Life-Savers mint or Jolly Ranchers. Other candies were Asian brands. Jellied fruit candies seemed popular, and Alexis even found one resembling an ear of corn. One family handed out cans of Coca-Cola—an interesting idea! Hi-Chews—the Chinese version of Starburst—made a very popular give away. My kids' favorite, however, was the White Rabbit vanilla taffy.

"Wooo! It makes you feel very *bouncy*, Mommy!" Alexis shouted, hopping around the room. I loved my girl's quick wit.

Overall, our first Halloween in Shanghai had been quite a hit.

章
12

NOVEMBER MISHMASH

We kicked off November with Alexis' ninth birthday party. The challenge was that Alexis insisted we keep her birthday party concept a surprise. Well, it certainly would be, as I had no clue how to give a child's birthday party in Shanghai! I asked my daughter to come up with three possibilities. That way, Planet and I could be sure she'd like anything we chose. Alexis would still be surprised, because she wouldn't know which of her three choices we'd selected, the day, or the time.

When we learned her preferences, Planet and I thought the MegaFit party idea seemed like a no-brainer. The package the Club created sounded great. The staff would lead the kids in what they branded a "mini-olympics" for an hour, followed by an hour of badminton and free play in the babysitting playground area. After all the running around, the snack bar staff would serve pizza, French fries, ice cream, and cake. Perfect!

Two weeks before the event, I received the list of games from the party coordinator, who instructed me to select five. The list read as follows:

1. Balloon volleyball
2. Music chair
3. Throw the snot-rag
4. Push-and-pull

5. Ping pong transportation
6. Rope-skipping
7. Looking for partner
8. Back running with hola [sic] hoop
9. Balloon transportation
10. Stick animal's tail

Hmm. Which of these would *you* choose?

Planet and I picked balloon volleyball (actual volleyball played with balloons?), push and pull (tug-of-war?), rope skipping (some type of game with a jump rope? It could be anything!), looking for partner (hide and seek?), back running with hola hoop (some type of three-legged or partner race?), and balloon transportation (egg on a spoon, but with a balloon on a badminton racquet?). We crossed our fingers, hoping that whatever these games were, we had chosen well.

We invited all five girls from Alexis' class at school, plus we let Anders bring his best buddy, Kyle O'Brien. Interestingly, two of the kids' siblings tagged along, so we thought it polite to include them in the fun. I wondered whether planning for extra kids was "a thing" around here, given the complexities of family scheduling and city logistics issues.

When everyone had arrived, the two MegaFit trainers led the kids into the gym and started balloon volleyball. In this game, the kids basically tried to use a balloon to play volleyball. It was as much fun to watch as it was for the kids playing. The kids then picked up badminton racquets for balloon badminton. Complete silliness! Next it was time for push-and-pull. Easy to guess, it was indeed tug of war, except that we played the parents and the two trainers against the kids. After this came "ping pong transportation." For this game the kids placed a ping pong ball on a paddle and raced each other down and back the length of the gym—pretty similar to the old egg and spoon game. It was really difficult to keep a ping pong ball on the slippery paddles, but they loved trying. We would not have guessed that rope-skipping was a team relay. Each participant had to run to the far side of the gym, jump rope for six counts, and then run back. The second to last event, "looking for partner" was an unexpected twist on an old standby. For this race, the kids had to determine who their partner would be. To start, the party leaders tossed scraps of paper with numbers written on them into the air. Each child grabbed a scrap of paper off the floor and was then partnered with whomever had the same number. The game was a timed three-legged race. As soon as the kids paired up, we tied their legs together, and each team tried to run as fast as possible down and back the length of the gym. We had such fun watching this event!

Our next game was "back running with hola hoop." This event had two parts as well. The group was divided into two teams. Each team's members had to first run backwards down and back the length of the gym. In the second set, each team's members had to run to the far end of the gym, hula hoop successfully for ten seconds, then run back to the start. Several crashes and tip-overs ensued as the kids tried to run backwards at top speed. In this game, it was hard to tell who was having more fun, the spectators or the kids. The penultimate event was "balloon transportation," which turned out to be the kids simply trying to run around the perimeter of the gym without dropping or popping a balloon placed between their legs. We ended the festivities with "stick animal's tail," which we thought was pin the tail on the donkey. It wasn't! The trainers explained the rules for…blind man's bluff? Had they written down the wrong name for game? It didn't matter; the kids had fun.

All of these games would have been enough for any third-grade party, but this was Shanghai. Now, the kids zipped over to the badminton courts. The MegaFit party leaders supervised and cheered the kids on as they hopped and hooted, gleefully whacking the shuttlecocks back and forth.

An hour later, the kids were more than ready for their pizza, ice cream, fries, and cake. Certainly not the healthiest fare, but definitely crowd-pleasing staples. We didn't know how MegaFit's management would interpret the concept of a birthday cake, giving Planet an excuse to order a very fancy birthday cake from the chef at the St. Regis. My husband had been to the hotel for a business meeting and left quite impressed with the food and the bakery.

"A fancy, gourmet European-style cake is a great idea for an *adult* party," I argued.

Planet refused to entertain the idea that kids wouldn't like the over-the-top pastry.

"These kids will eat any cake that's *chocolate*," he insisted. "It's the St. Regis. It will be delicious. You can't touch a cake like this for this price at home. Besides, maybe their parents will appreciate it."

I could see Planet's point, but I also understood kids. Kids aren't picky, and they're likely to consume a total of about three bites before they're off to the next activity.

Sure enough, at dessert time the kids avoided the elegant, decadent chocolate torte and downed very small portions of the MegaFit cake—the quality of which seemed somewhere between a US grocery store and a good bakery. Planet and I enjoyed a slice of the luxurious torte. It was indeed fantastic. Strangely, the other parents showed no interest in our gourmet dessert. Somehow, I restrained myself from saying "told you so" and got the majority of the fancy pastry wrapped up to put in the freezer at home. If only I'd had this outstanding back-up dessert last month during the O'Brien debacle!

As we tumbled into the Shang Hi-Ho Silver, tired and happy, I couldn't believe what an amazing time we'd all had. First birthday party in Shanghai, success! Check!

Chava's Mystery Day

Thankfully, my own social life was also going well. Chava made good on the plans we made in her Sukkah, and on a biting cold November day, my kind new friend thoughtfully arranged a "mystery tour" for me. She refused to give me any details at all about our journey, even after her driver, Mr. Su, eased the minivan onto the Yan An. About forty minutes later, we arrived at the River Promenade. Mr. Su left us off near a staircase leading up to the strip of restaurants along the river bank. I noticed the variety of establishments—the Paulaner Brauhaus, Dave's Italian Kitchen, a Starbucks, a Chinese place that looked like an old manor house, and even a…what?…an Ice Bar! From there, we had an excellent view across the water to the legendary Bund.

As we walked, we saw an attractive cluster of young Chinese people. One moment the girls were dressed in jeans, but in the blink of an eye, they popped on elaborate costumes over their street clothes. One girl slipped on a traditional, old-fashioned Chinese robe and grabbed a large, bamboo umbrella. The other girl dressed as a bride, complete with a traditional western-style white dress and veil. A young man with a camera started to film the girls talking, while a sound man dangled a microphone above their heads. Was this movie? A TV show? Add this to the list of things I loved about Shanghai: I never knew what unusual or amazing sights might unfold at any moment of any day. A word to the wise China traveler: always have a camera handy! We watched the filming for a few minutes, then walked to the end of the Promenade. There, a ferry floated next to a dock. We paid all of 3RMB to enjoy the five-minute ride to the Bund side of the Huang Pu. Before I could finish asking, "where are we going?" Chava's silver GL8 magically appeared at the Bund-side ferry terminal. It made me laugh. We had just done something so extravagantly non-Chinese: we paid to ride a ferry just for the fun of it. As we jumped into the van Chava announced, "Our next stop is the 225 building—junk-a-teria!"

"What is that?"

"You'll see!" my friend said mysteriously and enthusiastically.

For the next twenty minutes Mr. Su guided the minivan through the winding old city streets. He pulled over at a brick five story building across from the Starbucks and the dumpling shop bordering one edge of Yu Yuan Garden and bazaar. There, Chava led the way inside the junk-a-teria. We passed a plethora of small shops arranged in no particular order. Stalls hawked wrapping paper and bags, beads, yarn, hair accessories, wigs, socks, silk wine bottle bags, little tchotchkes for birthday party goody bags, and many similar small items. Clearly, this building was a great place to know, as they had nearly everything I would eventually need!

My friend knew that I liked to make jewelry, so she led the way to the fourth floor, where many of the jewelry suppliers had stalls. We had a great time browsing, and eventually I gathered a stash of swaroski crystals, lovely mother-of-pearl clasps, Chinese character clasps, and magnetic clasps. Delighted with my goods, I couldn't wait to create some new pieces.

Mission accomplished, Chava phoned Mr. Su, and we ended our adventure exhausted, but very satisfied. I felt thankful for all that I learned during my mystery day, but especially that I had a wonderful friend. In fact, Chava and I remained part of each other's core circles throughout our Shanghai years.

Carpets

During November, my primary shopping adventures centered on oriental rugs. While other expat women snapped up coffee tables, dining room sets, cabinets, and Chinese medicine cabinets at shops all over Shanghai and beyond, I found most of these items unenticing. I gave Chinese furniture and accessories my own simple purchase test: could I imagine the piece in my home in Shaker Heights? Would I walk into the room and believe the item added ambiance or interest, or only added a Chinese flavor? Given my "furniture test," rugs seemed a logical choice. I could readily imagine colorful Asian rugs on the wood floors in every room of my house back in the US. They would brighten up our rental home, and I knew we'd enjoy them in the US later. So, while others set off to purchase altar tables and Shanxi cabinets, I focused on carpets.

One chilly morning, Mr. Zhou and I ventured down to Puxi to a well-known, reputable gallery. The beauty and quality of the merchandise impressed me as I circled through the showrooms, but the New York City prices led me to believe these must be rare or antique pieces. Were they really worth what the vendor's asking price? He refused to budge at all on the prices. Hence, I left perplexed and rugless.

The next week, however, my luck improved. Fliers went up around The Pearl. A rug vendor would come show his wares at The Pearl this weekend. More notices followed. Another rug vendor would visit a week later. The rugs would come to me? I couldn't wait! On the morning of the first show, I found several rugs that appealed to me. The vendor said he would deliver them to my house so that I could try them out. Try in your own home before you buy? Great! About an hour later, a few young men arrived with five rugs, placing them around the house where I thought I might want them. Immediately the rugs made the house seem homier and more cheerful. But the more I kept looking at the rugs, the more I noticed that some of them seemed defective. They seemed…crooked. Crooked?

When the rug vendor stopped by on Monday to see what I wanted to buy, I asked him whether he knew the rugs were flawed.

"Madame, the weavers are nomads. The difference in the weave comes because the carpet is being handmade while the weaver moves from place to place on a camel. The imperfections make the rugs much more valuable," he assured me.

What? It sounded like marketing gimmickry, pure twaddle. Regardless of whether such imperfections made the rugs worth more, I knew looking at crooked runners would bother me. The man must have read the look of disbelief on my face, because suddenly the prices plummeted. Hmm. I planned to put the two small runners in my bedroom and master bath. Maybe at this price no one would notice the slight flaw, and I'd get over it. I also liked a large deep red rug with a blue and white geometric pattern. The salesman explained that geometric patterns were standard fare among the Hyde tribe, as their religion prevents them from imitating living forms. Suddenly buying rugs grew interesting. That one didn't look so askew, and I liked the price.

As I placed my three new carpets, I smiled. My rented house seemed much improved!

When the second vendor showed up, he had higher quality goods—and prices to match. He had some really unusual designs, however, and I couldn't resist taking some carpets home to try. When he came by the next day to see which ones I wanted to buy, he launched into a long-winded sales pitch. He spoke at length about what a devout Muslim he was and how he regularly spent two hours a day visiting sick people in hospitals. On and on, he prattled! I guessed this strategy was cultural. The Indian or Pakistani method of developing guanxi? I sighed as I listened. Buying things in Asia certainly took up a lot of time! The more he talked, the greater my desire to just get him out of my house. Maybe *that* was his strategy! Finally, I did the brash American thing and cut him off. I said I had business to attend to and had to cut the deal right this second or not at all.

We negotiated until I ended up with a beautiful, unusually long runner. It was the perfect size and color for all that wasted space in the front entry of the house and looked great there. I was also very excited about a highly unusual rug in yellow tones, featuring Persian people on horseback playing lutes, surrounded by flora and fauna. As the previous vendor had explained, the rug was remarkable because religious restrictions prevent most tribal nomads from representing humans in their art. *Then who made it? If only this rug could tell its story!* This carpet gave warmth and charm to the master bedroom, and I could imagine it adding that special something to some room in a house back in the US. I felt very satisfied with my purchases and relieved that I hadn't splurged in that pricey Puxi shop!

Back to Books

Book club, of course, also played a key role in my month. This month, we met at Jane Westfield's swanky Xujiahui apartment. A suburbanite all my life, I had no idea how spacious a city apartment could be. The jumbo picture windows in the living and dining rooms revealed a gorgeous view of the city hustle-bustling below. In the dining room, Jane had spread out a small feast of quiche, fruit salad, banana bread, and candied nuts on the table. The before-meeting chit chat centered around the fact that Jane was repatriating in January after five years in Shanghai. The concept of repatriating intrigued me. What did it feel like to be leaving after five years here? Moving here had nearly killed me, and it would probably take me the better part of this year to recover. Maybe it would take two years to even feel comfortable. I felt sure I would probably spontaneously combust if I had to return to the US in less than two years.

The conversation then turned to how each year spent in Shanghai had a different purpose and personality. The first year, the ladies agreed, revolved around adjusting, sampling the incredible smorgasbord of expat life, and shopping. The second year, people learned to focus in on what they really wanted to get out of their Shanghai experience. Some people, one woman remarked, were ready to leave after year two, but for most, it required three or four years to reach burn out. *Shanghai expat life had a saturation point?*

"What does that mean," I had to ask.

"By then, you get bored to death of shopping and lunching," one book lady explained.

Another club member added, "After year three, you're either ready to get a job or repatriate." What a fascinating education already, even before our book discussion had begun for the day! I soaked it all up.

"What about learning Mandarin? I feel like it's going to take me forever at the rate I'm going," I asked.

"If you're only going to be here a year or two, why bother?" someone answered. "Take as many tours and trips as you can, and just keep shopping!" Everyone laughed, but assented.

My brain swirled like the milk in my coffee with this tidbit.

When we had filled our plates and cups and settled into the living room, our group got down to business.

The women raved about the book we'd read. I, however, found the characters flat and only vaguely interesting. And had the author lost her thesaurus? She wrote, "she cackled" for at least half of the main character's utterances. At one point, I actually started counting, because the term appeared four or five times in the space of two pages. Where was her editor? In addition, there were several suspensions of disbelief that I would not have expected from a writer of this stature. I could hardly plod through to contrived and predictable ending. In my humble opinion, the novel garnered a C and belonged in the beach/airplane reading category. As the ladies gushed on, I decided to risk speaking up. My spine tingled. Would my opinion turn me into a pariah?

Waves of relief washed over me as my comments seemed welcome. This intelligent and worldly group actually *valued* a dissenting view! This was a for-real book club! In fact, one or two members who hadn't yet spoken said they had harbored similar thoughts. Sharing my contradictory opinion opened the door for a tangential discussion about importance of remaining open to everyone's diverse thoughts and views on our book choices and how that enriched our club meetings. What a relief! I had a new and deep appreciation for this rare group.

In Good Health

After our government physicals, luckily my family had remained healthy. Until the morning when Anders woke up with strep throat symptoms. I called for Mr. Zhou to drive us the Universal Health, the international health clinic provided by Planet's firm. When we arrived, we were assigned to see the doctor who came from Singapore. A few minutes after settling into the exam room, a medium-height, thin young man entered the room. Was that…fear…I read in his eyes? He seemed uncertain, his motions tentative, as he examined my son.

"So, is it strep?" I asked.

"Excuse me for just a moment, Madame," the doctor answered, to my surprise.

Now I played the nervous role while the unconfident young medic slunk off to the back room and looked up Anders' symptoms in a large medical volume. When he returned, he said, "I am not sure really what he has, but I will give your son antibiotics just the same," the look on his face revealing that even *he* didn't believe what he was telling me.

Had he really never come across a case of strep throat before? Well, at least he got the antibiotics part correct. Thankfully the Singapore doctor managed to get the dosage right and prescribed an American brand.

Why did this matter? Well, although Universal Health had an onsite pharmacy (big stress buster), they stocked brands from around the world, so it was a crapshoot whether you'd get medicines you were familiar with. This year's flu vaccine came from Italy, for example. In another instance, an American friend told me that she was unable to get her brand for a regular, monthly prescription medicine. Universal stocked only a British version. Having no other option, she tried it. But the effects were not quite the same, so she ended up having to find a way to import her brand on her own. Her situation clued me in to how such simple things could easily become so difficult here.

A few weeks later, Alexis caught a virus. This time we were assigned the Taiwan pediatrician. Fortunately, this doctor seemed to know what he was talking about, and we again received a prescription for a medicine we knew and understood. I left wondering, however, if there was some expat trick I had yet to learn in order to get the Taiwan doctor…or any doctor besides the Singapore one.

One day, I had a conversation with another mom about health care. I mentioned the experience we'd had with the Singapore doctor. She literally gasped.

"Avoid him at all costs! He *killed* someone last year!"

I looked at her in fright. "What happened?"

"Sheila Jones went on a fortieth birthday trip with her family," she explained. "After they got back, she got sick. She kept telling the doctor that she'd been in Africa. He kept insisting she had simply had malaria and not to worry. She got worse, but by the time they realized she actually had Dengue fever, it was too late! She DIED!"

I recalled the man's lack of confidence with Anders' strep throat. Now, I had just learned that even when the man felt secure in a diagnosis, he made mistakes! What to do?

Spa Experiments, Round Two

Fortunately, other healthcare concerns went much better in November. For starters, I tried the spa at MegaFit. The venue ranked second tier—somewhere in between the local footie places and the posh hotel spas—but it was convenient and reasonably priced. Two of the more memorable treatments included a series of facials and the spa slimming package.

I purchased the "four layer" facial package because a series of ten cost only about $35 each (no tipping), significantly less than in the US. The first two treatments went fine, but by my third visit, I found myself growing incredibly bored. I don't like to just lay flat with a mask on for twenty minutes in general, and the MegaFit facial mask dried like a papier mache lantern, leaving me also feeling claustrophobic. So, when I arrived for treatment four, I asked the desk clerk if I could try a different type of facial.

"No, Madame. Sorry."

"This other one *costs less*, though," I argued, assuming the Chinese penchant for practicality would prevail.

"No, Madame. You bought the *four-layer* facial series."

I ought to have known after my Blue Frog experience, there was no "having it your way." Even though the spa would theoretically save money if I chose a less expensive service, the clerk was afraid she would suffer a reprimand for varying from the set package. That would cause loss of face for her and her boss, and maybe even the whole salon. *Sigh.* I'd just have to suffer through six more sessions. Here, I learned, you literally got what you paid for!

I also gave the spa's slimming package a go. The package's series of ten sessions included a thirty-minute training session in the gym before each slimming treatment. At only 2,000RMB (about $285), the price was right.

The first session started with a trainer measuring my abdomen, hips, waist, and arms. He also weighed me. Next, we headed into the MegaFit gym for my thirty-minute training session. Having spent years working out with Big Ben, the sets he put me through proved annoyingly, significantly below my abilities. I felt sure I could have taught *him* a few things. When I got upstairs to the spa, I told them that I'd skip the personal trainer from now on and just stick to my body power class before the treatment sessions instead. The weight loss coach looked a little freaked out—as you already know, the Chinese hate deviations—but she agreed as long as I promised to attend my regular body pump class instead. I could hardly believe I'd won that battle!

The spa portion of the slimming session began with a sea salt body scrub. The therapist, Linda, laid me on a table and loofahed my body with the scrub. Next, she slathered my torso with sea protein/algae and then wrapped me up in plastic sheeting like a mummy. Then she left me to sweat it out *alone* for thirty whole minutes! No head massage while I lay there dying of excruciating boredom, praying to fall asleep!

When she determined my body had finished steaming, Linda returned and sent me to shower off. Next, she had me do about five minutes of abdominal front lifts. Then, she hooked up about twenty electrodes to my abs and my sides and cranked up a torture machine. The electrodes stimulated my muscles for another thirty minutes. (The next day, I felt like I'd done three hundred crunches!) Afterward, she strode over and gave me a vigorous ten-minute stomach massage. I left feeling like I'd actually accomplished something, yet I had trouble imagining myself mustering the patience to survive nine more treatments.

At my next session, Linda wrapped me in giant hospital bandages soaked in some sort of magical menthol-scented fluid. She motioned for me to lie on the table to absorb the potion into my pores. Knowing I would have to endure twenty minutes of deadly boredom, I took a risk and asked for a head massage. Linda looked frightened, but she obliged. About five minutes later, she stopped. I panicked. I told her I'd pay extra if she continued, but she shook her head and made a beeline out of the room.

When Linda returned, she unwound me and dried me off with a towel. Then she ran some sort of suction cup machine over my stomach for about fifteen minutes. After completing that task, she gave me another ten-minute turbo stomach massage. Session two complete.

After the treatment I spoke to the manager. She explained that even though I was willing to *pay* to have a head massage, I wasn't allowed to have one, because it wasn't part of the body slimming package. *Insert scream emoji here! Another China moment!*

When I arrived for my third session, Linda started me off with thirty minutes in the hot tub. I considered that a rip off and wondered when I'd get the seemingly helpful seaweed mud again. When the therapist returned after about ten minutes, she sprayed my body with a power hose. I don't think any of it did my fat cells any good, but it certainly helped relax me after my work out. After tenderizing my flesh, Linda set me up for thirty-minutes of the abs electrode machine. We finished, as usual, with the short but very vigorous abs massage. I left quite sore, but my abs now felt anything but flabby.

The remaining sessions continued in the same format, using various combinations of the different treatments. Since I found the seaweed wraps the most beneficial, I asked the manager whether I could have one at each session. If you guessed that the answer was "no," you're right. She explained that they tried to give clients the same therapist each time so she could look at my body and determine what I needed. What? A Chinese spa therapist making her own decisions? *Ha, ha, ha!* I doubted that. No, I felt pretty sure there was a set format for the ten sessions, regardless of the client.

The hot tub was clearly the cheapest option for the spa. It cost them nothing. And it did nothing for me! Hence, I decided to make a fuss to see what would happen. I adamantly refused to have any further hot tub sessions. The manager immediately gave in, and I received two more mud wraps!

Was all this time and turbulence worth the effort? Yes! When Linda measured me after session ten, my waist had shrunk by 4 cm (a little more than an inch), my abdomen got smaller by a whopping 7 cm (a little more than 2 inches), and I had lost four pounds. Linda practically fell over the door threshold in her haste to report this great success to her manager. Though I still didn't fit back into my fall clothes, at least I had made a good start and grown motivated to lose my "I don't want to move to China" weight. As a bonus benefit, Benita agreed to let me pen a *Courier* article about my spa slimming experiences.

Ayi Drama

Apparently, accomplishing the all the reasonably expected household tasks were pushing Xiao Ting to the brink. In November—when she'd only been with us for three months—she decided to take action. When I got home from the gym one day, Ayi pulled me aside and told me that she fell down our marble staircase. *Holy crap! My biggest fear about this house!* Horrified, I had no idea what a Chinese employee could reasonably expect an employer to do in this situation.

"I'm so sorry," I replied. "What can I do to help?"

This clearly wasn't the right response. She didn't answer, she just walked around looking pained the rest of the day.

Perplexed, I called Eden and told her what happened.

"Well, I think there's some type of ayi insurance policy you can get," she offered.

Hmm. It seemed unlikely in the land without laws, but maybe. Next, I rang Planet. He had no idea what to do and told me to keep asking around, especially about the insurance. Then I phoned my Australian neighbor.

"Why don't you let her go home early?" she suggested. Could that have been all she really wanted?

So, I sent Ayi home to rest for the afternoon. And then what? Was I supposed to take her to a doctor and pay the bill? Could she get the government to make us pay her? How much? *Oh, why hadn't we stayed in Shaker Heights, where our lives were happy and simple!*

The next day, Xiao Ting returned. Apparently, giving her the afternoon off was *not* all she wanted.

"Me fall," she reminded me, pointing to the marble staircase and climbing about halfway up. Since I was clearly a stupid foreigner, she decided to illuminate her point. Before I could respond, she proceeded to unzip her jeans and pull them down. She modeled the terrible, personal-pizza-sized black bruises dominating each outer thigh. Oddly, they looked like someone had taken an iron and run full speed into her, not like injuries from a marble staircase fall. And the two sides matched. Hmm…

I'd gotten nowhere finding out how to get ayi insurance or figuring out what to do. "Have you seen a doctor," I asked.

"No," she shook her head.

Not knowing what to do, I lamely offered her some Tiger Balm and told her to go home early again today.

After she left, in a panic I rang The Pearl management office. Surprisingly, the manager had no idea what I should do, either!

"Maybe send a fruit basket?" she suggested.

No, that couldn't be right. I was running out of people to ask. Then, I had an idea. Alvin! I paid him to get on the phone and ask Xiao Ting what she wanted me to do. I could hardly believe the answer. She wanted a few days off.

Really? This whole drama unfolded because she wanted a vacation? She'd already had two afternoons off! Well, I gave her two more days off, hoping this would solve the problem.

But when Xiao Ting returned, she spent the day limping around the house wearing a pained expression.

"Me get head picture," she griped.

She got her head x-rayed? What? Was I supposed to offer to pay for that? Now I started to feel both irked and suspicious. Why hadn't she mentioned her head before this? It would have made more sense than the identical iron-shaped thigh bruises.

"My husband say I can't work for you no more," she continued. "Too much work! And your house *toooo dangerous!*"

I could feel steam starting to waft from my ears, my right eyebrow lifting in irritation. She had it *good* in my household! She not only made nearly triple the average person's salary, she worked way fewer hours. She was even getting paid a higher rate for speaking English, through her language skills left much to be desired. Was this soap opera all the result of her thinking I should hire a cook? Did she really have the nerve to think she was over worked here, she could do better, or that I was actually stupid enough to pay her more?

"Well, I'm sorry to hear that," I said. "When is your last day?" I had some trouble conveying the concept of two-weeks' notice, but eventually I made myself understood.

I walked her over to the calendar. "When is your last day?"

"Me here two weeks. Help you train new ayi," she informed me.

My surly ayi had just fired herself! I wanted to skip around the room for joy! I strained to maintain a Chinese-style poker face.

"OK. Thank you," I replied calmly.

I made a beeline for my office, closed the door, and got on the horn to Kandi. She had a cheerful Filipino ayi, who spoke perfect English and played the role of job broker for the other Filipinos working as domestic help in Shanghai. This enterprising middle-aged lady not only worked as an ayi, she also ran a boarding house in Jin Qiao for newcomers looking for jobs or who lived out from their employers. *No more Chinese ayi antics for the Aschkenases!*

When I got the broker on the phone, she sounded pleased to hear from me. She had two ladies I could interview the very next day. The prospect of having a household helper who not only spoke excellent English but who was both competent and cheerful thrilled me.

The Filipino maids charged much more than the Chinese, however. Most of them expected 3500RMB a month (about $490), plus you had to pay for their Visas and one trip a year home to get the Visa renewed. That said, rumor held they were worth the money, especially if you wanted an English-speaking caretaker. After putting up with Xiao Ting, I felt more than ready to give the Filipinos a try.

I don't know what Ayi thought would happen, but you should have seen the incredulous look on her face when she answered the door the next morning and found three young Filipino girls standing there. (Apparently, the Filipinos always traveled in packs. When you asked for one, several more tagged along.) I sent the two friends into the yard to enjoy the garden, while I talked with the actual candidate. Xiao Ting hovered angrily, eavesdropping on the girl's perfect English and perfect answers to my questions.

"I am a good cook, Ma'am," the girl assured me. Like a Chinese ayi, she expected to do all the cleaning, run the household, babysit, everything…basically be a housewife. Like most of the Filipinos, she loved children and enjoyed being with them. *Don't let the door hit you on the way out, Xiao Ting!*

Although she said everything that I wanted to hear, it wasn't clear to me that this girl was "the one." She seemed so young. Knowing nothing about the Filipinos and having not interviewed household helpers before, I wanted to meet several others before I made a decision.

"I'll call and let you know soon," I assured her, as she and her friends piled into their taxi, giggling.

About an hour later, the next candidate arrived. Xiao Ting, realizing how badly she'd screwed up, knew she'd better get the door. She sized up the neatly dressed middle-aged woman standing there.

This second candidate had already worked for expat families in Shanghai for about five years. Her English was excellent and so was her experience. In fact, she most recently had worked for the SAS school nurse's family. Apparently, they had a cook and two ayis, thus they needed to cut back. I felt concerned that the woman had seven children back in her home country. That could spell trouble in any number of ways. I told her I'd let her know.

When this candidate left, Xiao Ting had abandoned any semblance of the Chinese poker face. She launched into a full tizzy.

"I bad ayi!" she told me. "Other ayi speak bery good Engrish. Cook. I no good for you!" she groused. "I *bad* ayi!"

Where was I supposed to go with this? Was she now trying to guilt me into keeping her in her own warped way? I found out that before us, she had worked for a two-career couple with no kids. She probably had nothing to do half the day but gossip with the other neighborhood ayis and watch Peking Opera on TV. They also had a cook, who shopped for the groceries and prepared all the meals. No wonder Xiao Ting acted so crabby—she actually had to *work* at my house. Well, no doubt she had earned this moment.

In the meantime, my neighbors put me onto another potential candidate. When the young lady came by around 2:00 pm. Xiao Ting knew her bluff had been called. Her mood now swung from self-deprecating pouting to launching a campaign to win her job back. She miraculously whipped out a pocket English dictionary.

"Me work bery hard speak Engrish," she announced, waving the book at me as she scurried to open the front door.

Oh, good grief! It was much too little, much too late.

The third candidate was a Chinese woman who had been working for an expat family at The Pearl for a couple years. She still worked for them, but part time, so she only wanted part-time work. I felt irritated that we'd both wasted our time, since I wanted full-time help. But Xiao Ting didn't have to know that. She just needed to know that this woman spoke English well, would do the job, and would work for a much lower salary.

Although at the end of the day I didn't want to hire any of these women, I felt really pleased that I'd been able to find three acceptable candidates within twenty-four hours of Xiao Ting accidentally firing herself.

The next morning ayi arrived with a new attitude. "I OK now!" she announced eagerly. "My husband say I can work for you *forever!*"

An overnight miracle? Um, no. What could I say?

"Oh, Xiao Ting. You told me you quit. So, sorry. I am already hiring a new ayi," I explained. "You said you would train her, remember?"

I thought flaming chopsticks might fly out of her eyes as she stomped off.

Desperate, later in the day she developed a new strategy. She walked over to where I sat reading on the family room couch.

"Me young. Strong," she assured me, holding up her arms like a body builder at a show.

I nodded and returned to my novel. But a little while later, Xiao Ting gave me the "young and strong" news again. This time, however, she reached out her arm. "You come. Come a-look."

Annoyed, but not wanting to be rude, I followed her. She led me to the ayi bathroom. Pointing to a used sanitary napkin in the trash, she once more insisted that she was fit enough to continue working here.

Oh! This was really too much! I couldn't take any more of her campaigning. How could I stop her and make it clear that she was finished at my house?

"I'm sorry, Xiao Ting. You quit. My house is too dangerous. Your husband is unhappy," I said looking serious, making direct eye contact. I pointed to the calendar. "You are still working here until this day. This day, *hao le* (finished)." Unfortunately, this only reassured ayi that she had another week to convince me!

That weekend, we gave Xiao Ting some extra work. She helped cook, serve, clean up, and babysat while Planet and I hosted a small home dinner party on Saturday night. She seemed happy to earn some time-and-a-half income. But on Monday morning, ayi returned as her usual grumpy self.

When I returned from MegaFit later that morning, I wandered into the kitchen, happily thinking this was one of the last few days I'd have to make my own lunch. Xiao Ting noticed my return and rolled up behind me.

"Satday, when I work late for you, my bike steal in bus stop," she complained. She actually looked a little angry and raised her voice, like somehow the bike robbery was my fault.

This did NOT sit well with me. Ayi was earning an absurd amount for how little work my household actually required. Here I was making my own lunch, for Heaven's sake! And now she expected me to feel guilty about her bike? If you've ever seen the average rusted out, falling apart Chinese bike, you'd know that a person would have to be quite desperate to steal one. And since stealing is rampant in China, anyone knows better than to leave a bike unlocked or unattended.

"Didn't you lock it?" I replied, growing more irritated by the minute.

"Yes, I lock. But still stole," she insisted. "I work late for you Satday."

"Well, I'm sorry to hear that," I said. I needed to get away from her for a few minutes to think about the situation before I imploded on the spot. I escaped upstairs with my sandwich. Now that she knew I wasn't keeping her, she was clearly fishing for money. Probably that's what the whole "accident" thing had been about. Outrageous! It seemed *insane* that an ayi would purposely injure herself just to wheedle some money. Well, this was the last straw. I wouldn't put up with her for even one more hour.

Seething, after lunch I marched straight into The Pearl's management office and grabbed one of the assistants.

"I am firing my ayi *right now*. I want you to come with me to my house, *now*, and make sure she understands that she is fired. *Effective immediately*. Tell her she needs to pack up her stuff and *get out*. *Right now*. I want you to stand there next to her so that she doesn't make a scene or steal anything," I explained as calmly but firmly as I could in my outraged state. I really hated the ugliness involved in this whole situation and the fact that I probably seemed like another insane Westerner to the office staff. But it was what it was.

The assistant, Julia, looked nervous. Clearly, there was no telling what an angry waiguoren was capable of. Fortunately, she understood and followed me. When we reached my house, I opened the front door and called for ayi. We found Xiao Ting in the kitchen making herself a cup of tea.

"Xiao Ting, you are done working at my house as of *right now*. You leave *now*," I said.

Julia, a pained look on her face, translated, just in case.

"Please go to your room and pack up your things. Leave *now*," I said, fearing the top of my head would blow off in my fury.

Xiao Ting, now hopping mad herself, started muttering to herself in both English and Shanghainese. While she packed up her belongings, Julia translated some of the rantings.

"She wants to know if you will allow her be able to work at The Pearl in the future."

What? I had the power to ban her from ever working at this compound again? Though Xiao Ting probably had earned an exile from this community, I thought that seemed a bit too harsh. It seemed unlikely that she would last long in someone else's household either, so why prevent her from trying?

"No, it's OK. She can still work here in the future," I responded.

When her few belongings were packed up, I handed Xiao Ting her pay for the month—even though it was two weeks from pay day and she'd had almost a week off because of her "accident"—plus 200RMB extra. I figured this more than covered the bike nonsense, too. Xiao Ting deserved none of this money, but that's how relieved I felt at being able to close this chapter in my Tai Tai life immediately. Then ayi stormed off, escorted out of the compound by Julia. *Woo hoo!*

My search for a new ayi continued. Eden advised me to call a British woman she knew who was working in Shanghai as a psychologist. Sarah's ayi, Florida, apparently functioned as another Filipino ayi broker. I was in luck. Florida had a "niece" who recently arrived in Shanghai. As I was learning, Asians called anyone in their network aunt, uncle, sister, etc., whether they were related by blood or not. Whether the woman was actually related didn't matter. Apparently, if you could call a woman "niece," in this world that even served as a satisfactory reference.

Sarah put Florida on the phone. She explained that the young lady, Pepsi, would come to interview this afternoon when she finished work. I crossed my fingers, hoping she'd be "the one." In the meantime, I had called one of the phone numbers I got off the bulletin board at Pines grocery store in Jin Qiao—another Filipina woman, named Josephina. She seemed very nice. She was able to come right over for an interview.

About an hour later, a tiny, petite, slim, attractive lady in her mid-thirties appeared at my door. She told me that she had eight children back in the Philippines! Her husband's farm was successful, but they could use the extra income. I soon learned how this information translated: moving to Shanghai often served as either birth control or a "Filipino divorce." Our conversation went well until she told me she was especially interested in working at The Pearl because she attended church at my neighbor's house. *Ding, ding, ding! Oh, a member of the special religion.*

I liked Josephina and seriously considered hiring her, but two red flags waved before me. With eight kids and a farmer husband, any number of dramas could distract her on a daily basis. Would she always be asking me to "donate" money for her kids' medical expenses and whatnot? While I liked that she belonged the special religion—normally, that would have made me want to hire her immediately because I knew she'd be pleasant, kind, and honest—I worried that once Angela Templeton learned that one of her church members was living in my Jewish household…well, I envisioned some very annoying and very awkward recruiting scenes might unfold. I thanked Josephina and told her I'd get back to her as soon as possible. Thankfully, I still had another candidate coming.

About 5:00 pm, Pepsi appeared on my doorstep accompanied, naturally, by two young friends. I sent the extras out to the garden and invited Pepsi into the living room. Pepsi was an attractive, petite woman in her early twenties. This cheerful girl seemed amazed to find herself in Shanghai and interviewing for a plum, well-paying job in a prestigious compound. Pepsi had received training on how to clean for Western households, and she assured me she had excellent cooking skills and would enjoy spending time with my kids. My heart ached when Pepsi shared she had a husband and two very young boys back in the Philippines. She had a college degree in the computer science, but, sadly, the country churned out significantly more professionals than it could ever hope to employ. Like so many of her countrymen, she did the only thing she could—sought work abroad in order to help support her family. She also explained that her ayi salary was more than double what she could make in her field back home. What a crazy world!

Pepsi and her little family lived with her husband's parents. When she called home, her husband—who helped out on the family farm—was usually drunk. When she showed me the pictures of her boys, about two and four years old, I fought back tears. I couldn't imagine how hard it must have been for her to move so far away from her two beautiful babies in order to support them. Aside from wanting to help with this hardship, I liked her. She was pretty, cheerful, young, strong, and I knew the kids would like her.

Like all the Filipinas, Pepsi hoped to earn the standard 3500RMB a month, plus Visa fees, and the one trip a year back home required to keep her Visa current—the standard package.

"I think that this deal is a little steep, considering you only have one month of part-time experience," I said, honestly.

"I understand, Ma'am," she nodded, humbly.

"I have a number of candidates, but I hope to make my decision in the next few days. I will let you know as soon as possible."

"Yes, Ma'am. Thank you very much," she said, shaking my hand warmly. Then, as quickly as they'd arrived, she and her friends zoomed off in their cab.

In bed that night, I phoned Planet, who was in Beijing on business for a few days. I explained why I liked both Josephina and Pepsi, but both had their issues. Planet understood my quandary. One of the things bothering me was that China offered no system of background checks and safeguards, as in the US. It was definitely unsettling to be interviewing and ultimately hiring a person to live with you, run your household, and babysit your children who you know nothing about except what others in the community can tell you.

"Sleep on it, and trust your instincts," my spouse advised.

I would, but I had another idea. I decided to give Sarah a call. I explained my concerns to her.

"Well," she explained in her British lilt, "the world is in some ways smaller in Asia. The people you hire are far more trustworthy in general than they might be other places in the world. Word of mouth here is as good as more formal means other places."

To illustrate her point, she told me she allowed Florida to bring ladies over from her village who stayed in her home while Florida trained them and helped them get jobs. I saw her point.

"Well, there does seem to be a strong sense of community among the Filipino ayis. I guess that counts for something."

"It definitely does. You'll see. It's going to be fine!" the psychologist/broker assured me.

Well, I decided to give Pepsi a try. I crossed my fingers and hoped for good luck. From my experiences this week, I had also learned that since ayi jobs paid very well, candidates remained plentiful. If she didn't work out, there were plenty of people waiting in line. I called Pepsi with the good news, and we agreed that she would start on Monday.

Later that evening, I was surprised when the phone rang. It was Pepsi's "aunt" Florida, calling to thank me for hiring her. I thought that was interesting and nice. Maybe Sarah was right.

On Monday morning, Mr. Zhou and I drove over to Jade Court to pick up my new ayi. Despite my concerns, I also felt really excited to have replaced the dour and crafty Xiao Ting with a good-natured, English-speaking helper. Since Pepsi would live in, I hoped she'd be pleasant to have around the house—which would be nice for me, and a stress buster, with Planet traveling for work so much. When we reached Sarah's apartment building, Florida and Pepsi stood waiting at the curb with two suitcases and a large shopping bag. There she stood with all of her worldly belongings in these three bags, coming to live and work at an American's house in Shanghai, thousands of miles and a world away from her home. What a brave young woman! What a different world.

I introduced myself and Mr. Zhao to the Filipinas. Then Zhou loaded Pepsi's belongings into the truck of the minivan, and we were off.

Once at the house, Mr. Zhou carried Pepsi's bags inside.

"This is the ayi room? It's for me?" She asked, excitedly.

"Yes," I nodded, smiling. "And this is your bathroom," I pointed to the full bath across the hall.

She seemed especially impressed with the cheerful, colorful linens I had put on the bed for her.

"Oh, thank you, Ma'am, for making the room so nice for me!" she said appreciatively, fingering the linens. I think she understood that her work environment could have been significantly harsher, and I hoped that these small kindnesses could comfort someone in her situation.

"You're welcome," I responded. "I hope you'll be comfortable here."

My new ayi immediately got the laundry started, then she sought me out to discuss dinner.

"Did you ever taste Adobo, Ma'am Shelly?" she asked me.

I already liked being respectfully addressed!

"Hmm. No. What is it?" I replied.

"It's a usual Filipino dish. It's with chicken and vegetables."

"Ok, let's try it!" I encouraged her.

When the kids got home from school that afternoon, they ran into the house anxious to meet their new ayi. This friendly, smiling young lady greeted them warmly in English and gave them each a big hug. She proved an instant hit! "Oh! They are so beautiful, Ma'am Shelly!" Pepsi smiled. She looked happy to be starting a life with my family.

"Do you want a snack?" she asked the kids.

"Yes, please!" they cho` ` ` "Yes, please!" they choroused.

As Pepsi moved back to the kitchen, I breathed a sigh of relief and tried not to jinx myself by getting too excited.

Later that afternoon, I noticed a wonderful smell coming from the kitchen. At 6:00 pm, we sat down to taste the adobo. After serving us, ayi showed off her proper training by making her way out of the room to do some ironing or another chore, leaving us to dine as a family. As an American, it felt a little strange. I knew I was supposed to keep a distance or suffer the consequences of being disrespected or taken advantage of, but I felt so sorry for this poor young mother, I couldn't help myself.

"Pepsi," I called out, "would you like to join us?"

With a big grin on her face, Pepsi trotted back to the dinette. "Oh, thank you, Ma'am!" Happily, she pulled up a chair and helped herself to a portion of the delicious chicken and rice. The kids beamed.

After the meal Pepsi asked politely, "Will there be anything more, Ma'am?"

"No. Thank you so much for the wonderful dinner," I smiled.

My new ayi shot a grateful, joyful grin my way and began cleaning up. What a refreshing contrast to Xiao Ting!

When she finished her kitchen responsibilities, Pepsi retreated to her tiny room. Although this constituted customary behavior on her part, I wondered whether she was glad to have some personal space or whether she felt lonely. I considered inviting her to watch a little TV with us, but knew that eating supper with us might have been boundary enough to cross for one day

The next morning, I heard the phone ringing. Pepsi picked up. I nearly fainted with delight when I heard her say, "Good morning. Aschkenase residence." In English! And she could take messages in English!

As the weeks went by, all seemed well. Pepsi and I had no trouble communicating about meals. She could read a cookbook and had just demonstrated her culinary competency. I didn't even have to demonstrate how to make recipes, and my lunch was waiting for me when I returned from the gym. She also communicated with the kids in perfect English, which thrilled them, and, missing her own children, she enjoyed spending time with mine. While I had originally groused about how much we had to pay her, now I understood the benefits. She never once grumbled about fulfilling any of her duties.

One day, Pepsi even got a chance to play hero. We received notice that The Pearl planned to cut off the water supply for a day. When I informed Pepsi, she instantly swung into action.

"OK. We fill the bathtubs and sinks now," she replied, knowingly.

I looked at her quizzically. "Why?"

Ayi explained that at her family compound in the Philippines, they had no running water. Ever. She had to walk into the town center and get water from the community pump. It made sense to her that we should stock up on water so we'd be able to flush the toilets, wash our hands, made tea, wash vegetables, etc.

"Oh, I'm so glad you know that!" I said. "But I don't understand how the toilet will work."

She led me into the bathroom.

"You just fill this part, like this." She demonstrated, opening the tank lid.

I couldn't believe I didn't know something so simple. Thanks to our new housekeeper's help, we managed throughout the day very nicely!

My mind reeled over this situation. Westerners can take so much for granted—running water, electric-pump toilets, heating and air conditioning, electricity, well-paying jobs in our fields, enough food, etc. So many people in the world lived with multiple daily challenges. They seemed to prioritize what they truly needed to survive and their relationships, which seemed a much healthier lifestyle than American consumerism. As a result of my Asian experience, I knew that I would definitely have a different perspective on life when I repatriated.

Shortly after the "honeymoon phase" of the relationship with Pepsi ended, however, some issues cropped up. She always got the laundry done and we enjoyed her cooking, but somehow, the house just didn't seem clean. Some days, she didn't manage to get the clean laundry ironed and put away. What was she doing all day? She had plenty of time to get everything done. We gave her weekends off—an unusual luxurious perk—yet sometimes when she returned early on Monday mornings, her eyes were completely bloodshot. She looked like she hadn't slept the entire weekend. Planet and I let it go, because we didn't know what else to do. We simply continued to gather data.

One day, when I arrived home from an SEA luncheon, Pepsi approached me, nervously.

"Ma'am," she said, "Today when I put away your underwear, I see money in de drawer."

"Uh, huh," I replied, nodding. I had a small emergency stash, as the compound ATM sometimes ran out of cash.

"But Ma'am, dere is American money in your drawer. You just going to leave it dere? You trusting me?" She continued, incredulous.

"Pepsi," I replied firmly, "If I can't trust you, then you shouldn't work for me."

She looked quite blown away. "Thank you, Ma'am, for trusting me," she responded humbly.

I imagined this would make me the topic of gossip in the Filipino community and beyond for some time: the crazy American lady who left money in a draw and insisted her ayi not steal it! Unbelievable!

Thanksgiving

At month's end, the weather had cooled off, but had remained pleasant—sweater weather, but not yet coat weather. For the first time in ages, I could see the sun, the air was faintly crisp, and "smell of the day" had come as a pleasant surprise—smoky, like a wood fire. The weather made me realize I needed to start thinking about Thanksgiving. Where would I find a turkey? Time to investigate.

I rang for Mr. Zhou to drive me into Jin Qiao. I started at Pines market. They had a few turkeys. I lifted one out of the cooler to check the price. $70 for an eighteen-pound bird! When I recovered from the shock, I remembered that turkeys are not native to China; they're imported. Well, that just threw a wrench into my holiday plans! I just couldn't bring myself to pay a small fortune to uphold tradition.

While I was pondering the situation, Mimi came to the rescue. She called to say that her friends Mandy and John Lansing had invited us to join them and the Neidermeyers for dinner at their compound clubhouse. *An excellent Plan B!*

On Thanksgiving day, it seemed very strange sending the kids off to school. Fortunately, they were too young to mind. They just wanted to see their friends.

That evening, Mr. Zhou drove our family to Mandy's house. The adults sipped wine and chatted for about a half hour before we all walked over to the clubhouse for dinner.

Once seated in the charming clubhouse dining room, we tucked into a delicious menu of American holiday favorites and enjoyed each other's company. I hadn't paid much attention to how much alcohol people had consumed, but eventually I noticed Mandy starting to slur her words. As the evening wore on, she began to make increasingly inappropriate or confusing remarks. We only spent about ninety minutes total in the dining room, but by the time we finished up, Mandy was so drunk she could hardly stand to walk back to her house. Mimi prattled excuses, saying what a rough week her friend had endured. I didn't know what to think. I wondered if this was her usual weekend behavior, or a rare incident. John and Mimi helped Mandy walk home, then put her into bed. No one knew what else to say, so we thanked our host, said goodnight to everyone, and rang for Mr. Zhou. It certainly was one of our more interesting holiday dinners. We learned that in Shanghai it was cheaper (and more reliable, given our shaky oven situation) to enjoy Thanksgiving dinner at a restaurant.

章
13

A DECEMBER TO REMEMBER

In December, the holidays and affiliated socializing continued, but at an accelerated pace. Naturally, all the women's clubs held holiday luncheons and bazaars, and everyone buzzed about their travel plans, either to see family in their home countries or to explore exotic destinations. I enjoyed more new shopping adventures, and I finally got a chance to work on a volunteer project at SAS.

Early in the month, Chava decided she wanted to buy a set of wine glasses: specifically, the popular kind with Chinese symbols for long life and prosperity etched on the sides. She knew of a business in Pudong where the public had permission to come in and buy overstocks. Mr. Su zipped us to the venue in only about thirty minutes. There, we walked up to the third floor of the concrete building and waited for a secretary to buzz the door open.

Once inside, a saleswoman showed us to a room filled with samples. We saw approximately one hundred different types of glasses and about two dozen styles of vases arrayed before us. Chava asked the sales girl for six glasses etched with the long-life character and six with the prosperity character. Yes, they were in stock. Everything *I* asked for, however, was *"mei you le"* (don't have it). The sales lady suggested I come back in a month or so and try again. At the moment, I was making do with only two, poor-quality wine glasses from the grocery store, hence I wasn't happy. I searched the vases and found a cute yellow and white one for Anders' room; the same one in green for Alexis' room; and a wonderful, large royal blue one with white dots on it for the kitchen table. To my relief, "*ke yi*" (can) emerged from sales lady's lips. Having both completed our selections, it was time to negotiate. I couldn't wait to observe Chava's amazing Israeli bargaining skills. I had no clue what might constitute a fair price for the glasses, but I prepared to enjoy watching her go for it.

As Chava and the clerk parried back and forth, however, my friend seemed to gain little ground. What was going on here? The saleslady remained steadfast on her price. Suddenly, Chava pulled out a fascinating new strategy I hadn't seen her use before.

"Well, I'm going to take a break now, while Shelly buys her vases," she announced.

After watching my bargaining guru get nowhere, I didn't know what to expect. Yet, within a few minutes I found myself surprised to get the kids' vases down to 25RMB each (about $3.75)! They'd probably cost more than that at Walmart. I could hardly believe I got the lovely blue vase for only 60RMB (about $7.50). Happily, I imagined filling my house with the inexpensive flowers from the Thursday farmers market now that I had vases and thought how cheerful this would make our borrowed house in our borrowed country. Now it was Chava's turn to try again. The battle remained fierce, neither side giving away any ground. Chava nearly walked away from the deal before she thought of one last angle. She asked to speak to the manager.

Then, my friend pressed on, putting the manager through all his paces. About fifteen minutes later, Chava emerged the victor. She managed to convince the showroom manager to sell the glasses for a rock-bottom $2 a stem! I marveled at her skill. That price was crazy! Those glasses would have been at least $20 a stem in the West, and maybe even more in Israel. The negotiating dance was exhausting, but clearly the results could be well worth the effort.

Why all the drama over prices? When you live in Shanghai and have to endure the daily negotiation dance, you piddle over very small amounts. It's a matter of pride, sure. But it's also because you set the standard for all the other expats. Nobody likes being overcharged or wants to ruin prices for her neighbors. I hoped I would benefit when I returned to buy glasses, as Chava's talent had now paved the way for me to get a decent price.

Victory finally achieved, we had worked up an appetite. We then grabbed lunch at Chava's favorite vegetarian restaurant. I'd never been to one, so I didn't know what to expect.

"You'll see," my friend explained, "you really can make seitan taste like *anything*."

When we took our seats at the restaurant, I saw the menu offered only seitan and rice concoctions, sauteed in every type of tantalizing Chinese sauce imaginable. I felt prepared to be impressed, and when the dishes arrived, I was.

While we forked the savory health food into our tired bodies, we discussed our unique neighbor, Angela. The saintly one had remained hot on Chava's trail lately, trying to get her to read their holy book and attend a service.

"Do you think there are special prizes she wins for recruiting a Jew?" Chava chuckled.

"Apparently. She also gave me a copy of their holy book and invited me to services," I agreed. "She does seem especially interested in discussing Judaism and keeps saying her religion is connected. Though, I don't get how."

"She told me that her religion teaches that the Jews are G_d's 'chosen people.' Jesus will return for her people when all the Jews return to Israel, because they are somehow derived from the Jews," Chava explained.

"Interesting. That's a new one. I think she said it's some weird thing about her group being one of the lost tribes of the ancient Jews or something."

"Something like that," my friend replied. "But finally I just said to her, 'why on earth do you think *everyone* has to be *your* religion?'"

With my American hyper-sensitivities to offending anyone, I could never have been so blunt. Yet, I found Chava's Israeli directness a refreshing change. "Good point. I guess in her mind, we are part of the same religion, we just don't know it. So, we need recruiting."

"Who knows? Who cares?" Chava said, waving her hand.

"How do we tell her that no one in her religion will probably EVER recruit a Jew…without hurting her feelings?"

"We don't," Chava insisted. "They don't care. They'll never back off. Oh, and by the way, it's illegal to do any religious recruiting here, you know," she continued.

"Yes, I know. I'm sure she's much more careful when trying to recruit the Chinese. We Westerners wouldn't bother to report her, but they might."

"Well, right now, she is very busy recruiting her ayi, who will probably convert just for the free trip to Hong Kong!" Chava chuckled. Since religious recruiting was illegal, the special religion had to fly potential converts to the nearest place of legal conversion. Although was Hong Kong officially part of China again, it was considered a Special Economic Region and played by its own rules.

Chava had no issue with Angela's religious promotion and pushiness. Instead, she found it mildly entertaining. But Angela's conversations and invitations made me contemplative. I had never been challenged to reflect this deeply on my faith before or called on to defend it. The result was that Angela's desire to fold me into her flock only served to strengthen my beliefs and to increase my satisfaction with my own faith.

"Right! But aside from their annoying recruiting habit, they do make great neighbors," I offered.

"Yes, all those committees and community family game nights," Chava countered, rolling her eyes.

I—Chava, not so much—really did appreciate that the special religion ladies had a passion for lighting up the world with their good deeds and good cheer. Every one of them undertook at least one volunteer service at school, from room parenting to some of the larger projects. They remained unfailingly the cheerful, reliable organizers and workhorses of the community. I'm sure I wasn't the only person thankful for the cornucopia of good deeds these spiritual wonder women performed. How did they manage, considering the wagonloads of children they were each raising? Angela, mother of eight and posterchild of goodness, somehow found time to volunteer at school, run a Bible study and a church out of her house, volunteer at an orphanage, serve as a Cub Scout leader, and undertake a plethora of other random good deeds. Just thinking about her life exhausted me!

Ironically, a few days later, a very large basket of holiday treats from the pricey City Shop arrived at my door. Inside lay a copy of the special religion's famous choir's latest holiday CD and a long, heartfelt letter from Angela. The letter expounded on the glories of the season and raved about how fulfilled the special religion made her and the entire Templeton family feel. It went on to exalt her religious beliefs and justify why other people should come to recognize that theirs was "the only true path" in life. *Good grief!* I wondered whether Chava received the same gift and letter.

First off, it felt strange to receive such a sizable gift from someone who was still more of a friendly neighborhood acquaintance than a good friend. Secondly, a Christmas CD is not an appropriate gift for a Jew. Having learned something about the special religion, I took no offense, as I knew she honestly meant to be kind and truly was ignorant. However, I began to agree with Chava: it seemed so presumptuous to insist that her religion, and any religion for that matter, was the *only* correct one and others must join it. Personally, I believed that since all religions are fundamentally about making people into their best selves and inspiring them to act ethically, it doesn't really matter which one is chosen, as long as it's the one that's motivating. *All* roads, therefore, lead to G_d. I respected Angela's passion for *her* beliefs, but this recruiting stuff really had to stop.

So, I decided to write Angela a note sharing my philosophy. I also suggested that when we got together we not discuss religion, as I feared someone's feeling might get hurt. *Enough already.*

Unfortunately, when Angela read my letter, she took it as further openness to joining the Special People. She assured me I could *never* hurt her feelings. *My plan backfired completely!* Undaunted, Angela also told me she planned to have a large wooden manger set custom made for Chava's family. *Oh, no!* Now I realized that Angela had probably never picked up a regular Bible and had no idea what Jews believed.

"No, I'm sorry," I explained to Angela. "Jews don't celebrate Christmas. We believe that Jesus was an influential Rabbi, but not actually G_d's chosen prophet. So, a manger wouldn't have any meaning for Chava's family. I think maybe a Noah's Ark would be more appreciated, if the shop has one." She seemed confused, but said she'd change her order. *Oy!*

I wondered whether the Templetons gave gifts to everyone they knew, or just focused on specific families. By now, Chava and her family had already left for the winter school break. How I wished I could call her and ask her what she thought about Angela's gift.

Xinran

This month, I anxiously awaited our AWCS book club meeting because *The Good Women of China* by Xinran had made quite an impression on me. I couldn't wait to hear the group members' thoughts. Xinran, a very popular radio host in China, was the first to expose the harsh realities and devastating tragedies of shocking numbers of Chinese women's lives. When women called her show to share their stories, Xinran provided advice. Naturally, the truths her callers vented didn't make her very popular with the government, which promptly canceled her show. What the government didn't realize was that she had evolved into a female folk hero—basically the Chinese version of Oprah. Chinese women raised such a storm of protest that they eventually had to put Xinran's show back on the air.

The Good Women of China consisted of an outstanding collection of appalling cultural revolution stories from radio show callers. In its pages, Xinran laid bare many ugly truths about women's lives in this vast, troubled country. I imagined that the book revealed what all those wise-looking Chinese grandmothers I saw on my bike rides, stationed in village doorways knitting at lightning speed with their chopsticks, would say to me if they dared. I found the stories astounding, and if I hadn't understood the concept of "eating bitter" (enduring hardship) before, I certainly had a clear, concrete picture in my mind now. No wonder Chinese women have traditionally had one of the highest suicide rates in the world! The club members agreed that Xinran's book served as a reminder of the many challenges women around the world still faced and the privileged lives we Tai Tais led.

My book club members enjoyed this read so much that toward the end of the year, we read another book by Xinran, *Sky Burial*. I devoured this true account of a young Chinese woman, doctor Shu Wen, in one sitting. Shu and her husband (also a doctor) had been married only a few months when he volunteered to serve Mao's army in a remote outpost in Tibet—not an assignment most people would seek out, unless determined to demonstrate their extreme patriotism and devotion to Mao's philosophies. Shortly after the young husband arrived in Tibet, Shu learned that he was dead. She decided that she couldn't live without knowing the exact particulars of his last hours. Perhaps he *wasn't* dead, the army simply somehow lost track of him. Apparently "losing" soldiers occurred quite often in 1950s Tibet territory. Hence, Xinran provided all the tantalizing details of Shu's dangerous and amazing journey. I would recommend the story to anyone who wants to learn more about life in Tibet, who likes stories about strong women, or who fancies a tragic and fascinating love story.

Santa's Workshop

One of the best things that happened in December was Santa's Workshop—a wonderful holiday shopping bazaar for the SAS students. The PTSA volunteers had spent the fall shopping, and now they could sell a huge selection of small gifts for everyone in the family at kid-friendly prices. The PTSA moms ensured no "junk" gifts infiltrated the stash. So, the gift tables stood filled with items like soccer balls, silk neck ties, jewelry, hand-painted glass bottles like I had recently bought at the Yu Garden, dolls, Swiss-Army-style knives, candles, hats and scarves, stuffed animals, holiday coffee mugs and plates, car accessories, pillows, gadgets for men and boys, small toys, photo frames, and much more. Best of all, nothing cost more than 50RMB (about $6.25 at that time)! I wished holiday shopping was always this cheap, convenient, and easy—for kids *and* adults!

The teachers helped the kids make out their lists and work out their budgets (a great use of "everyday math"), then brought their classes down to shop. PTSA volunteers helped the kids shop from their lists and worked as cashiers. From there, the young shoppers moved into a hallway where more volunteers wrapped the gifts for them for free. What a stress buster for both the parents and the kids! I found the whole project most impressive, and I felt happy to play a role in the kids' holiday cheer. During the event, I suspected that I had even more fun than the kids. It was such a joy to see their elated faces when they found just the right present and to witness their pride and delight in the neat, brightly wrapped packages they took home. For three days, fourteen of us moms wrapped gifts from 9:00 am until 2:00 pm. I wrapped more gifts than I've probably wrapped in my entire life, and laughed ironically thinking of how my own family's holiday gifts still waiting for me on the guest room bed. I could hardly bear to think about wrapping them! With sore fingers but a joyful heart,

I finished up my Santa's Workshop stint. I had a wonderful experience, and I couldn't wait to do it all again next year.

Party Time

What would a month in Shanghai be without parties, especially during the holidays? For starters, Planet's consulting firm invited us to a staff formal, held at the Grand Hyatt. After all the corporate cutbacks in the US, it felt refreshing to be invited to a celebration, especially a fancy affair that included spouses, again. I couldn't wait to enjoy a sumptuous five-course dinner and dancing to a live band, courtesy of The Firm.

Though my collection of formalwear had grown while in Shanghai, this event presented an interesting new twist. The firm had chosen *Chinese* formalwear as the evening's dress code. Well, it certainly seemed appropriate and like something every China expat should have as a wardrobe staple. Thus, off I went to the fabric market on a mission to get a "Chinese tuxedo" jacket made for Planet. Luckily, by this time I knew exactly which stall to visit. Once there, I couldn't decide between two patterns, as I thought both would look especially handsome on my husband. Then I remembered that infamous Shanghai shopping rule: the more you buy, the better the price. Why choose? I would simply negotiate for two jackets: one in each fabric! Surely Planet would get plenty of use out of two jackets while we lived in Asia, and maybe even afterward.

The vendor and I conducted our bartering dance until we agreed on a price of about $25 each. Mission accomplished! Ah, I so loved shopping Shanghai style! I already had a formal Chinese-style top that I bought in the US a year or two ago. I liked it a lot, but in the US, I never seemed to find the right occasion to wear it. Finally, I had the perfect opportunity. The jacket was a lovely gold and white patterned raw silk. I needed only a matching skirt. I recalled a vendor I had already developed some guanxi with carried plain raw silks. I negotiated with him for the cloth, then the tailoring. To my delight, I scored a custom-made raw silk mini-skirt for only 70RMB (about $10) total. I already had gold dress pumps, so with the skirt, my own ensemble was complete.

When Planet and I arrived at the swank hotel on event night, the rarity of the evening hit me: how often in my life would I stand in a room full of people from around the world wearing Chinese formalwear? Decked out in Chipaos and Mandarin jackets, the crowd looked absolutely great! Thankfully, the firm hired a photographer—coincidentally, Gang of One—to immortalize everyone in their rare finery. The picture from that holiday evening remained on our fireplace mantel for the duration of our life in Shanghai, reminding us that we were both insiders and outsiders in this amazing city of uncommon adventures.

With our Shanghai Jewish life going so well, I felt inspired to host a Christmas/Chanukah party. Planet and I invited two other families to come for dinner and then watch some American holiday movies: the *Rugrats Chanukah, Chevy Chase's National Lampoon Christmas Vacation,* and Planet's all-time favorite, *It's A Wonderful Life.* For dinner, I marinated a beef tenderloin and mashed potatoes. Chava brought over a wonderful Israeli eggplant casserole and some vegetable soup. Trixie Hall rounded out the meal with a salad and homemade pumpkin pie. I had also found the ingredients to bake my "death by chocolate" cake (the groceries were sometimes out of chocolate chips for months!) and stocked up on vanilla ice cream. A perfect feast!

Thankfully, having an ayi made entertaining so wonderfully stress free. What a treat to have already-paid-for help serving, bussing plates, and loading the dishwasher while we adults enjoyed another glass of wine and good conversation!

The adults' chatter turned to our upcoming winter holiday travel plans. The Halls—always such intrepid travelers—planned to take an extra week of vacation to tour Cambodia, Laos, and Myanmar. Chava, Jordan and the girls would journey to Ko Samui, Thailand. Then Chava said something interesting. My friend explained that they would have liked to visit several other places—like Borneo or certain Philippine islands—but their Israeli passports did not allow them to visit any Muslim countries. It had never occurred to me that other countries restricted their citizens' travel. This news made me realize how spoiled Americans are to travel nearly anywhere and everywhere.

The next weekend, we gathered at Trixie and Dan Hall's for another round of holiday cheer. Although not a fan of Asian antiques for my own home, I loved how the Halls had filled their home with treasures from their extensive travels all over Asia. A long, carved bench from Bali graced the foyer; a wonderful manuscript from Cambodia adorned the dining room wall; rugs from Singapore and

Tibet warmed the wood floors; and a Chinese hutch served as their TV cabinet. Somehow all the themes and messages and colors and textures played together harmoniously. While I loved how trendy and cool all this looked adorning an expat house in Asia, I also wondered whether they'd still want all these pieces if/ when they returned to Canada. I felt glad I'd stuck to rugs.

That evening, about twenty neighbors and friends showed up, and we shared drinks and appetizers for several pleasant hours. As everyone said goodnight, Trixie began handing out "party favors." She gifted each couple with a small, bowl-shaped green candle with a red ribbon tied around the top. As nice candles tend to be inexplicably expensive in the US, I grew curious about Trixie's ability to give everyone this parting gift. When I asked where she got them, she explained she'd found a factory. She said she'd gladly take me there, and I knew I'd look forward to that adventure!

Dream Trip to Bali

After years of dreaming about a trip to Bali, Indonesia, I finally found myself with tickets in hand for our winter break. A few people, mostly those at home in the US, asked us why we were going there, as a disco had been bombed in October and some consulates had posted warnings against traveling in Indonesia. Well, we were operating under the theory that hopefully the terrorists had already made their point (for now anyway). That also led us to assume that security would be at its highest level. We planned to lay low, mostly hanging out at the pool and the beach. We were unlikely to do much shopping and highly unlikely to visit a nightclub or a disco with children in tow. We believed our chance to visit this fabled land was now or possibly never.

Our journey got off to a stress-free start thanks to Singapore Airlines. As with Thai, Singapore's top-ranked customer service and painstaking attention to detail made travel an absolute pleasure (when was the last time you could say that!). The five-hour flight to Singapore went by in a flash, with everyone feeling relaxed and cheerful on arrival.

With a layover in Singapore's Changi airport, any traveler might wish for a longer delay. This airport, deservedly, often ranks as the world's best. It's hard to be bored with excellent duty-free shopping (everything from local handicrafts and souvenirs to big-name designer boutique items), purportedly the world's best massages from blind monks, and a multitude of enticing food options. As a result, time passed quickly, and soon we boarded our two-hour flight to Bali.

In Nusa Dua, Bali that evening, a hotel van driver wearing an exotic green batik sarong and a tropical floral shirt met us at the airport. During the approximately forty-minute ride to the hotel, I strained to take in the scenery on our drive through the evening dusk. Few people appeared out and about, and the restaurants and stores appeared empty. I noticed many police checkpoints along the roadway—both sad and comforting. Finally, we arrived at the guard station of a large gated compound serving several large, international resorts. The crisply uniformed guard on duty spoke to our van driver while another guard inspected the outside of the shuttle. He peered inside the van, his face etched in seriousness, and shone his flashlight onto each of our faces. Satisfied, he waved his arm, clearing our vehicle for entry. When our van pulled into the Grand Hyatt's driveway, more security guards came out for another inspection. One guy looked under the car with a long-handled security mirrors, then used his flashlight to scan inside the trunk. Finally, he gave the OK sign. *Could hotel security actually prevent anything from happening? Again, was all this really necessary, or just done to reassure tourists?*

As we stepped out of the van and walked up the steps toward the check-in desk, a clerk rushed over gushing friendly greetings and adorning us with deliciously fragrant Frangipani leis. The female staff wore wonderful long batik skirts paired with flowing, solid-colored tops and batik sashes. The men sported flowered or solid tops with short, batik sarong skirts. Colorful batik cloth wrapped each head. I thought they looked great and their clothing looked very comfortable.

We found ourselves standing in front of a stunning, carved teak gong, which the welcome lady encouraged us each to bang for good luck. We did! Then another attractive young lady dressed in a beautiful blue sarong strolled over and presented us with a tasty pineapple banana coconut welcome drink to sip while we checked in. Then a sarong-clad bellman escorted us to our room. Though we liked the ambiance of our room, we noticed the air conditioning wasn't cooling. Even with the air on full blast, we spent an uncomfortably warm night.

At sunrise, a high-energy choir of perky tropical birds decided to share their joy with us. No one could sleep through the warbles, so we showered, dressed, and ventured downstairs to check out the breakfast situation. Since Planet had Club Level status, the room included the breakfast buffet, which had the kids all excited. The lovely, exotic Club restaurant consisted of a series of connected open air gazebos situated on a bamboo platform, surrounded on three sides by koi ponds. At the entrance stood a charming Christmas tree carved entirely out of teak. Under the tree lay a series of charming, traditional hand-woven, hand-painted bamboo baskets the Balinese used for their Hindu offerings. What a wonderful sight to behold on Christmas morning. Who needed snow to feel festive!

At the buffet, we found an enticing array of exotic fruits, yogurt, cereals, cold meats, smoked fish, breads, and enticing European pastries. Of course, a variety of Asian-favorite juices, tea, and excellent Balinese coffee completed the picture. I felt like a princess, extremely grateful to enjoy this remarkable meal with my family in this fantastic setting. As we finished eating, the hostess encouraged the kids to feed the large koi fish with their leftover bread and pastries. Alexis and Anders never tired of this activity during the nine days we stayed there. After breakfast, we planned to camp poolside for the rest the day. There, Santa made his rounds. I felt bad for this poor man dressed in a traditional winter Santa suit in the eighty-degree tropical sun, but three cheers for Old Mr. Kringle as he good-naturedly presented gifts from his sack to all the kids he encountered. To their delight, Alexis received a Camp Nusa mug, and Anders got a Hyatt Bali key chain.

The Hyatt's spectacular pool resembled a lovely lagoon, with large rock formations, surrounded by flowers and greenery. The largest "rock" hid a slide and sported a charming Tiki hut at the top. An attendant monitored the top of the slide, giving kids the "go ahead" to launch themselves down into the water. The lounge chairs stood spread out in a two-tiered garden, so the parents could relax and enjoy the rainforest scenery while the kids wore themselves out in the pool. A band playing traditional Balinese instruments made their way around the pool area, working their way through many traditional Christmas tunes, as well as some Balinese music. Hearing "Good King Wenceslas" on a tinkly Balinese gamelon was definitely a fun first! From there, we strolled by the resort's kids' club, Camp Nusa. A charming teak hut, with floor-to-ceiling windows, served as the main building. Outside, in an enclosed yard, kids could play on a large, brightly colored play structure or tussle with the set of teak poles, adorned with brightly colored streamers. The activities included sailing, mini-golf, tennis, ping pong, and lessons in Balinese dance and language. We couldn't believe the resort only charged $18 per day per kid, including lunch!

After lunch, the hotel called to offer us a chance to upgrade out of our over-heated room. Because of Planet's frequent-traveler status, we marched our belongings into a regal-looking suite, where the air conditioning—huzzah!—blasted frostily.

That evening, we dined memorably at the hotel's main restaurant. The enormous buffet included a plethora of holiday favorites from around the world. They even had turkey! The restaurant had definitely gone all out on the desserts: Christmas pudding with vanilla-brandy sauce (England), red berries with cream (Scandinavia), cookies (Germany), brandied pears, exotic fruits in lime juice (Balinese), homemade ice cream, and more. While we got our holiday food coma on, an excellent jazz combo played traditional holiday tunes. As a wonderful surprise, a Balinese kids choir hustled in to serenade us part way through the meal. These thoughtful Hindu children had just given visiting strangers a lovely gift of both music and international camaraderie. I greatly appreciated the Hyatt Bali's efforts to create a special holiday meal for all their guests, and this dinner stands out as one of my family's most notable and enjoyable holiday meals ever.

The next day, the kids wanted to check out Camp Nusa, so Planet & I went exploring. After delivering the kids to camp, we squished through the beach's soft sand to the park we'd spied nearby. Attractive stone paths led us past numerous stone arches and monuments. We even found a stone temple with a secluded beach. A big sign stated no one could enter the temple without wearing proper dress. It also informed visitors that no woman having her period could enter. *Whoa!* We continued walking until we came across a path that led down to a fishing spot and a very energetic waterspout. Seven boys and one man stood patiently fishing there. Soon, the boys huddled into a group and began tittering among themselves. After much discussion, one of the boys finally shouted out, "give money." My smile evaporated. This scene had just morphed into an ugly tourist moment. Why couldn't they have just belted out "hi" or "welcome" or even just have flashed us the Richard Nixon two-fingered peace sign all Asian children seem for some inexplicable reason to know?

Overall, the kids had a ball at Hyatt camp and even made two new special friends. The friendship situation actually came with some surprising coincidences. Rebecca Park was not only in third grade like Alexis, but also attended SAS—on the Puxi campus, however. Her sister, Diana, was in second grade, like Anders. As I chatted with Mrs. Park poolside later that day, I found out that their family now occupied the room with the faulty air conditioning that we had just vacated! The kids played together at camp or in the pool for the remainder of the week and insisted on arranging a play date as soon as possible when we returned to Shanghai. Planet and I bonded with the parents, and we all remained friends for the duration of our stay in Asia.

Aside from holiday festiveness and making new friends, another highlight of the Bali trip was the volcano bike tour. On arrival, the guide led us into a slope-roofed hut overlooking a gorgeous lake and facing the inactive volcano. He motioned us to help ourselves to a cup of rich, strong Balinese coffee and delicious chocolate and banana crepes. *Crepes? What a nice surprise!*

Refreshed by another round of Asian hospitality, we selected bikes and started rolling downhill. We zipped past stunning, lush roadside flora, through charming villages, and past seemingly innumerable temples. When I asked the guide about the many temples, he explained that each family actually owns one, plus each village has at least one. *Wow!*

Along the route, the houses appeared unusually pretty, many made of white plaster and carved wood. Some had beautiful orange and taupe stone doorways and elaborately carved gates of wood or stone, others of brightly painted wood. Soon, we made a stop to actually visit a traditional Balinese home. Our guide explained that the Balinese traditionally live in family compounds, where several generations dwell together. Each generation has their own pavilion, with a separate kitchen area and a TV room on the porch. With the pavilions creating either a U-shape or a square, a portion of the resulting courtyard is devoted to honoring the family's ancestors. The key element in the ancestral area are the spirit houses established for each deceased family member. I noticed that in front of all the shops at the resort—and sometimes other places—people had left little trays woven from palm or banana leaves and filled with flowers, fruits, candy, bottled water, crackers, incense sticks, and such. Now I understood why. As we looked around, chickens and dogs ran excitedly through the yard, while pigs and cows stood peering out from stalls in the back yard. It seemed very pleasant to live a lifestyle that had survived, relatively unchanged, for centuries mostly outdoors, so close to and in harmony with nature and extended family (living and dead!).

After visiting this lovely family enclave, we pedaled onwards. Apparently, tourists-on-bikes day signaled an event in the towns we passed. Kids charged out of houses and stores busting out "hellos" with all the zeal they could muster. One village we christened the "high-five" village. There, all the kids bounced gleefully into the road, determined to slap us high-fives as we rode by. I laughed with pleasure. We bikers were having as much fun as the locals, equally fascinated by one another.

We made our lunch stop at a small café, where we enjoyed the tastiest tourist lunch I've ever eaten: pumpkin soup, stir-fried vegetables, curried pork, rice, stir fried noodles, and several more local dishes. Ice cream bars brought the day's excursion to a contented end, and we tumbled back into the van for the long ride back to the hotel.

The bike trip fueled my interest in Balinese culture and history, inspiring me to purchase two volumes on Bali and Indonesia from the resort gift shop. I plowed through them at the beach over the new few days.

Apparently, Bali's version of Hinduism arrived about 2000 years ago, successfully blended with native customs and Buddhist beliefs, and thus had survived pretty much unchanged since then. I did not know that Java lay only a mile away across the water and converted from Buddhism to Islam around 1500 years ago. The other Indonesian islands also converted. Bali, however, steadfastly clung to Hinduism and today still remains the only Hindu Indonesian island. Therein lies the long-standing feud between Bali and her Muslim neighbors. I also learned what issues lay behind the recent bombings. One terrorist group sought to convert this last hold-out island to Islam, another group struck because they believed Bali too sympathetic to American culture and capitalism, and the third group seemed motivated by jealousy over Bali's booming tourist trade. The Balinese, however, remained nonplussed. In fact, historically they have maintained a reputation for fiercely and successfully defending both their island and their religious beliefs.

I also learned that the major art forms included playing the gamelan, performing shadow puppet plays, and dancing. As I read about the gamelan, I learned that this was the music (a band made up of gongs, drums, and flutes) I heard in the hotel lobby. Balinese dance tells ancient stories, but unlike Western dance, the performers primarily use their hands and facial expressions to communicate. The costumes are elaborate affairs, complete with mountainous gold headdresses and copious gold jewelry. The puppet shows tell spiritual and mythological stories, using only the dolls' shadows. That explained why each night at the hotel, the small turn-down gift was a shadow puppet!

One of the elements of Balinese culture I found fascinating was their system of naming. All week, looking at all hotel employees' name tags, I noticed they seemed to have only a few names. Apparently, this was because Balinese children are named by their birth order. The firstborn sons are named *Wayan*, *Putu*, or *Gede*, meaning "eldest." A girl can also have any of these names or *Ni Luh*. Second born children are named *Made* or *Nengah*, meaning "middle," or *Kadek*, "little brother" or "little sister." Names for third children include *Nyoman* (pronounced like "Newman") or Komang, which mean "last." Why three is the ideal number of Balinese children, I never learned.

After a couple days of reading poolside, Planet and I decided to foray outside the resort again. The kids wanted to play with the Parks and other kids at Camp Nusa, so Planet and I hired a car and driver to go exploring. You wouldn't believe where we stopped first. Every husband has his bizarre quirks, and for mine, it was…laundry! Despite his generous airline luggage allowance, he adamantly refused to pack enough clothes for a two-week trip. What would a vacation be without Planet wasting half a day looking for a laundry and then having to return later to pick it up! So, naturally our first stop that day was a local laundry the concierge had recommended.

Soon, we were back in the car, rolling toward Kuta—the city recently bombed by terrorists. We saw security everywhere, and some of the local shopkeepers even searched our backpacks as we entered for a browse. As we walked through the town, it appeared quite touristy—like a bad version of Daytona Beach. Now I understood why the guidebooks advocated avoiding it. We strolled around for a few underwhelming hours, had lunch, picked up the laundry, and headed back to the resort.

As New Year's Eve approached, my reading about Balinese culture inspired me to score Planet and me tickets to the hotel's Balinese dance show and Indonesian dinner buffet. The kids wanted to join the Park girls at the special New Year's Eve kids' party at Camp Nusa.

That evening, we dropped the kids off at Camp Nusa and made our way over to the ballroom for our event. Sadly, neither the food nor the dancing seemed particularly interesting or notable. Maybe because we weren't used to the subtleties of the dance style, the dance moves quickly began to all look alike, and the performances grew boring. Only the elaborate costumes and getting to know our French tablemates who all worked for Carrefour kept us awake. While we tried to comprehend the subtleties of Balinese dance, we indulged in fresh, grilled lobster tail and the local specialty, roast suckling pig seasoned with spicy soy sauce and herbs. The homemade ice cream for dessert was also noteworthy.

Just before midnight, we picked up the kids, who whooped and hopped when they saw us. It didn't take us long to determine why. The staff had all dressed in pirate outfits and organized a fantastic evening of face painting, a pass the parcel game (with prizes, of course), several other popular games, and karaoke. The camp's dinner buffet pleased the young crowd with all manner of junk food favorites. Best of all, later in the evening, a troop of Balinese kids arrived to put on a variety show! The campers loved watching the performance as much as they enjoyed meeting the Balinese children. Planet and I were glad that the kids had just as cultural an evening and significantly more fun that night than we had.

On New Year's Day, we needed to change hotels. So, early in the afternoon, we hired a car to drive us to the Ritz in Jimbaran. Imagine my reaction when Planet announced that we'd be stopping off to find…another laundry! What! Twice, on one vacation! NO!

After another laundry delay, we finally pulled into the Ritz's Jimbaran property, where we endured the ubiquitous, requisite car-security drama. Finally, we checked in and took a stroll around the property. The site was outstanding, with the hotel perched high on a cliff. The resort offered magnificent ocean views from the stunning infinity pool and the inviting teak pavilions. It came as no surprise that a wedding pavilion stood on one end, and I spied a small dock leading out to a platform over the water where guests could enjoy a private, romantic dinner. The jungle-temple themed kids' pool was even more impressive than the Hyatt's.

During our stay, my favorite meal of the day at the Ritz remained breakfast. Set in an alluring pavilion surrounded by koi ponds, complete with a gamelon band gently tinkling background music, I could hardly believe the Ritz's breakfast buffet was even more extensive than at the Hyatt's: a fruit station, a pastry station, an omelet station, hot and cold samples of a multitude of dishes from all the restaurants, and a rice station. A chef even stood at the ready to griddle up Mickey Mouse-shaped pancakes! Here, I discovered a new favorite fruit—jack fruit. Each morning I looked forward to indulging in these delectable delights. You only live once.

My favorite restaurant on the property was Kisek, the beachfront fish place. On our first night at this resort, my family descended the narrow stone staircase to the small beach, finding ourselves under a thatched roof canopy, lit by tiki torches. A large fish tank stood at one end of the restaurant. As we squished through the sand toward our table, the surf crashed on the far side of the small dining area, the sun setting in a magnificent blaze of fuchsia, violet, and apricot hues. Within moments, our waiter came by to explain that we would each select our fish, then the chef would season and grill it any way we wanted. We'd never had fish *that* fresh before. I loved our waiter's, Pande's, style. To any and all requests, he charmingly responded with, "and why not?" I readily secured this magical family dinner in my memory banks forever.

After a wonderful meal, we wandered out to one of the large Bali beds in the resort's main square, with an outstanding view of the sea, where I read the kids their bedtime story. While browsing in the Hyatt's gift shop, I discovered a book titled *The Small Men: A Balinese Folk Tale* and couldn't resist purchasing it. The story involved a group of young local boys who lived in a village near Ubud. Together with their spunky monkey friend, they formed a band and learned to play traditional Balinese music. Reading the tale from a Bali bed under a brilliant seaside sunset seemed the perfect ending to a wonderful day.

One day, when the kids wanted to play at camp, Planet and I attempted a serious bike ride. We hired a guide through the hotel and soon rode off into

Jimbaran village. First stop, the fish market. Dozens of tanks filled with a big variety of fish species stood waiting to entice customers, as did anxious grill chefs. Our guide encouraged us to buy a fish and have it grilled right there on the spot. Had it been lunch time, we may have indulged; but at 10:00 am, it didn't exactly appeal to us.

We biked onwards. Soon, the guide had us pull over at the sundries market. As we entered, I noticed that vendors sold everything from plastic kitchen tubs to flowers. We appreciated that this place was clearly for the locals—no cheesy souvenirs, no pitiful maimed beggars outside, and no aggressive salespeople yelling at us or grabbing at us, like in Shanghai. The vendors were typical chill Balinese, naturally kind, and helpful. There, we picked up a few trinkets for the kids.

On the ride back to the hotel, the guide announced, "Sir and Madame, we will encounter some very big hills."

Planet and I looked at him, each of us knowing what the other would say.

"We don't mind," Planet began, "we like a challenge."

"Fine, Sir," the man replied. "But also, a rainstorm is coming. There is *very big* rain here," he continued.

While we certainly appreciated his attention to detail in taking care of us, steep inclines and rain had never stopped us before. In fact, Planet and I had to smile, as we actually seemed to attract rain storms when biking!

"I took the liberty of phoning the hotel to send a van for you," the guide confided.

My husband and I looked at each other. We weren't surprised that the average tourist would give up, but clearly our guide didn't know who he was dealing with.

"We're OK with both hills and rain. We'd like to keep going," Planet informed him.

"Very good, Sir," the guide nodded skeptically. And shortly we were wheeling along again.

All was well as we pedaled up the incline; we encountered nothing we couldn't manage. But then, suddenly, the heavens opened, unleashing a torrential downpour. The guide looked deeply concerned, as though he expected us to blame and scold him. He appeared confused when Planet and I looked at each other and began to laugh. We fully intended to finish the ride back to the Ritz, and to the guide's amazement, we did. About twenty minutes later, soaked and chuckling, we high-fived in the hotel motor court, leaving the guide shaking his head in wonder.

Our victory didn't last long, however. I reached into my pocket for my phone to check on the kids. *Oh, crap!* Because we left the resort in sunny and beautiful weather, not expecting rain, it never occurred to me to protect my essential communication device. My phone emerged from my pants pocket soaked, ruined. I chided myself for my ignorance. From this experience I learned to always plan for the unexpected by carrying my phone in a waterproof cover when I'm outside or near water—especially in Southern Asia!

Our trip to the beach also brought surprises. Strangely, the Ritz's sunning and swimming beach required a short van ride. When we arrived, we found the place small and secluded, with a river flowing down one side into the sea. The oceanfront was so limited there was nowhere to walk. After our experience in Thailand, we weren't too surprised to see a "no swimming" sign. Heavy rains had turned the water a disgusting shade of sewage brown, so even if we could have gone into the water, we wouldn't have. So far, this beach trip left everything to be desired.

Unflappable, Alexis amused herself by collecting various-sized pieces of driftwood. "Mommy, look! I'm making a drum set! How I loved my daughter's resiliency and flexibility! I, however, found the kinds of garbage washed up onto Asian shores and the sheer volume shocking. The number of sandals alone left my mind boggled. Near the Hyatt beach, one of the seaweed harvester ladies with a sense of humor had actually rigged up a tree made of bamboo pieces and hung all the stray shoes on it. More dismaying and more common, however, was the garbage: Styrofoam, bottles, wrappers, light bulbs, tires, etc. Even the Ritz, a world-class hotel chain, remained powerless to stop the debris that floated onto their beach daily. At least at the Hyatt, the security detail cleared up all the debris in the morning so we could walk on the beach. The Ritz's beach wasn't attractive to start with, and now all the rubbish made the situation seem hopeless. I hoped the world would find a garbage solution soon, and now I knew my family would find ways to do our part.

Although Planet and I enjoyed literally everything about our stay at the Ritz Bali (except the sadly small, polluted beach), one of the highlights remained the world-class spa. One of the main reasons for this was its unique "Aquatonic" center, featuring warmed, Indian Ocean sea water. At the Aquatonic center, visitors rotated through a series of twelve stations. They charged about $20 for two hours. When we started, I couldn't imagine anyone hanging out in a series of extravagant hot tubs for that long. I thought we'd be overheated and bored in thirty minutes.

At the Aquatonic's first station, we tried walking against a light current. Next, we moved to a stream-like pool where we walked over small, smooth rocks. The water temperature alternated between hot and cold zones. The more I walked, the better my feet and legs felt as my circulation ramped up. Then, we tried swimming against a strong current. The remainder of the stations allowed guests to frolic through pools where different types of massage jets pummeled different parts of the body in various ways. One of the hot tubs, made of beautiful painted Spanish tiles, offered a stunning view of the Indian Ocean. Suddenly, I noticed how quickly time was passing. Amazingly, we felt like we barely had enough time to enjoy each station before our two hours ended!

When we got out of the water, dried off, and dressed, attendants led us out to a charming patio, where they served us wonderful hot ginger-lemon brown-sugar tea to enhance our now improved circulation and health. As we sipped the drinks, I noticed spa attendants served every guest a special drink according to which treatment they had just completed or were about to receive.

During our stay, I also indulged in a few spa treatments. Unlike at MegaFit, during my facial I was thrilled to receive a hand and foot massage during the twenty-minute hydrating masque. After sipping my completion drink, I visited the relaxation room, which resembled a charming grotto, complete with sta-lagmites and a charming salt water pool. In addition, Planet and I both tried the "super slimming" package. During part one, the technician had me put on a funky full-body suit that felt like compression pantyhose. Then she used the legendary M6 machine to suction the "trouble" (fat) spots on my whole body. After about thirty minutes of being vacuumed, the therapist began wrapping my body in a seaweed compound. Once I was completely slathered in the briny mix, the mummification involved wrapping the cellophane blankets I had been lying on around me. While I lay for twenty minutes "baking," the technician gave me a thorough head massage. *Ahh! As it should be!* The last part of the treatment involved lubing up my entire body with a chilled, green "slimming gel." When Planet and I finished, our therapists led us out to the patio for the corresponding slimming beverage. I thought it would be something involving seaweed or maybe ginger (to warm the body), but it wasn't. The concoction just tasted like salty, mineralized water to me. I'm wasn't sure the slimming treatment helped me get rid of any of my holiday excess, but Planet assured me his clothes felt looser.

As our Indonesia trip drew to a close, we still wanted to buy a few souvenir items. Once again, we hired a car. This time, we tried our luck with a guy one of the waiters at the hotel recommended. We reasoned that it would be cheaper to hire a driver this way, and we might be more likely to discover local shopping places rather than tourist traps. We were so wrong.

As we set out for our shopping day, can you guess our first stop? Yes, laundry! Planet set a new record: THREE laundry trips in a single two-week vacation! Shoot me now!

From the laundry, we explained to our driver, Ketut, that we wanted to purchase Bali souvenirs in a place where he and his family would shop. After driving for about thirty minutes, he pulled into a parking lot of a ware-house-sized venue. All it lacked was tour bus parking and a sign proclaiming "Welcome Ketut and Friends!" Clearly, he received a kickback for bringing us there. Though Planet and I were annoyed, we decided to at least give the place a try.

We had to admit the store had nearly everything we wanted to buy; Ketut got that part right. The prices, however, seemed about ten times too high. We assumed this meant we could bargain. The first clerk I talked to refused to budge on the price. I tried another woman. No bargaining. *What?* Planet had no luck, either. Within ten minutes, we left in a huff. Ketut looked very surprised to see us back so soon.

Planet gave Ketut an earful about wasting our time and insisted he take us to a place where the locals shopped. Twenty minutes later we arrived at a place that was also probably owned by a friend or a brother-in-law. Still, we gave it a chance. Inside the large shop, I spied good quality batik fabric and appealing, high-quality t-shirts among the otherwise K-Martish items. The prices seemed on par with non-sale prices in the US—clearly tourist gouging. I immediately approached a clerk and asked whether the prices were set. I explained that unless they'd bargain with us, we'd be getting back into the car pronto. The woman seemed surprised, but agreed to work with us.

Happily, I browsed through the batiks, priced between $7 and $25. I chose three fabrics, envisioning trimming out bath towels and maybe having Mrs. Wang whip up skirts for Alexis and me. I called the saleswoman over and started negotiating. I worked arduously for twenty minutes and still hadn't quite gotten to half the starting price. Even at half price, I thought the fabric would cost the same on sale at home. Irritated to have wasted time, I gave up.

Alexis, however, insisted on buying a tacky sundress that we could probably have found on sale at Walmart for about $7. The starting price seemed ridiculous at $22. We could get it made back in China for about $6. But this was the souvenir Alexis just had to have, so I haggled with the saleswoman until we reached $11. Alexis loved the dress, so it was worth just paying the price to avoid wasting any more time. Anders, Planet, and I ended up with attractive, high-quality t-shirts. Since I had just scored a dress for $11, $14 for a t-shirt seemed ridiculous, but when would we ever be in Bali again? So, we paid the price and left with our souvenirs. Bali souvenirs mission accomplished.

Our winter break in Bali flew by much too quickly. Thinking back, it remains one of my favorite places I've ever been for its beauty, history, culture, people, and peaceful nature. I still regret not buying one of the legendary carved doors from the Ubud craftsmen. In fact, I wish I'd bought two of them: one to use as a door, and one to make into a unique, conversation-generating coffee table. This, of course, remains my excuse to return as soon as possible!

INTELLECTUAL PURSUITS & DRAMAS
LARGE AND SMALL

After our remarkable trip to Indonesia, the arrival of January meant settling back into our daily routines. Before we left for winter break, an acquaintance asked me if I'd like to join a small private group to which she belonged. I felt very flattered to receive an invitation, especially when she explained the criteria: to join, a member had to be a proven intellectual in some way (I guess she knew I held a PhD) and coordinate one scholarly, China-related event for the group per year. New members could join only through a current member's invitation. Delighted to add this kind of rare, unique experience to my China adventure, I gladly accepted. Then I went ahead and panicked about what cerebral program I could possibly dream up for this band of brainiacs. If I simply had to give a lecture on American Modernism or F. Scott Fitzgerald, no problem. Finding a China-related topic proved a much greater challenge, as I had no connections or guanxi yet. Fortunately for me, all the events for that year had already been planned. I had until next August to learn the group's tastes and dream up something.

Though all of our "intelligentsia group" meetings proved worthwhile, a few stood out. One of them was the film industry lecture, which involved trekking all the way out to a fancy French compound in Hong Qiao. Our hostess was an American, married to an Iranian who worked for a major multi-national company. The members cruised the table of tea and pastries while waiting for everyone to arrive. Naturally, I did the college first-year thing again, wandering around introducing myself to everyone. There, I met Ling Pan, who eventually presented her book *In Search of Old Shanghai* (1982) and *Old Shanghai: Gangsters in Paradise* (1985). I immediately ordered the gangster book and planned to draft a *Courier* article about the topic when I got a chance. Then, I met a PhD psychologist who was working and conducting researching in Shanghai. Another woman, Sally Jensen, had worked in the media in her pre-Tai Tai life, but found her niche here as the new managing editor of the SEA *Courier* magazine. She'd be taking over when Benita repatriated in June. Sally liked the articles I'd written thus far and wanted me to continue contributing. *Music to my ears!* I also met Betty Barr, who grew up in Shanghai during the WWII era, but left to attend Wellesley College. She later returned to live out her life in the Middle Kingdom. Neither of us could believe we'd just discovered a Wellesley sister at a club meeting in Shanghai! Later that year, Betty presented her interesting autobiography, *Shanghai Boy, Shanghai Girl* (2002) to the group. Betty's husband, George, came along, and the two could not have been more charming as they took turns telling their story. The pair were well known among the expat community and often turned up at events to give talks.

When our guest speaker arrived, we made our way into the large basement, where the house actually had a theatre room. Our presenter, Sue, came to the City as the managing director of a top multi-national entertainment company, for which she undertook the dubious task of getting government approval to import American movies to show in Chinese cinemas. She also faced the difficulties of producing and distributing movies for the Chinese market— restricted by tight, nearly impossible government guidelines. I felt truly privileged to sit in that room and learn first-hand the fascinating details of her job and the Chinese film industry.

As Sue explained, during the 1920s and 1930s, China's movie market consisted mainly of great romances. When Mao came to power in 1949, however, he decreed that film should only exist to promote the Communist party and its agenda. As a result, artistic talent no longer mattered, and acting as an art form died. Chinese film makers fled to Hong Kong with their treasures, yet even there, films lay rotting in vaults.

In the early 2000s, the industry started to revive, and interest in pre-Mao Chinese films grew. Surprisingly, a Malaysian company bought over 1,000 films of the hidden films and began to restore them. Sue commented that she could see the long-term value of rejuvenating the mainland's film industry, and she resolved to raise its status. As a result, she set up a joint venture between her company and the Chinese government. The group's objective was to make movies purely for entertainment, rather than films geared toward either government propaganda or developed with an eye toward industry awards. Getting the films into theaters remained very difficult, however, as Government rules and regulations represented a formidable foe. In 2006, though China produced 280 feature films, officials approved only seventy for release. In addition, theater owners preferred to show imported films because they attracted significantly more customers. Even so, annual box office sales totaled only the equivalent of one weekend in the US. Possibly, Sue noted, because the 40-60RMB (about $5.50-$8.50) price of admission for a movie seemed princely to the average Chinese person.

Sue remained unflappable. As a test market, her company released a movie in Chongqing, Sichuan. The soundtrack was recorded in the local dialect with Mandarin subtitles, and the admission price was set at only 3RBM. The project proved a huge success. As a result, the international film company produced a classic comedy for wider release. The chat rooms went wild—the Chinese people loved seeing a movie about themselves and their lives, rather than something foreign. In fact, that film remained in theaters for two months and grossed five times as much as expected.

One of the main challenges in Sue's job was predicting which films would be hits. So far, her company produced about thirty films a year. Of those, about twenty-five percent broke even, another one-quarter to one-fifth turned a profit, and the rest lost money. The market had a steep learning curve—both for the film companies and for the consumers. Lately, Sue had discovered that current Chinese culture sought lighthearted, fun films. Younger people had grown up with the internet, so they were not as movie-oriented as their elders. When they did see a film, they wanted frivolity.

Then fielding our questions, Sue reported that she did not envision Shanghai turning into another "Bollywood" or a "Hollywood East." She hoped Shanghai would keep only the best portions of what rendered Hollywood so successful and leave the rest. China, after all, represented a vastly different market. She added that she believed imported films would always have their place as long as Chinese people remained fascinated with American or Western culture, but it was time for them to revive their own film industry.

As she wrapped up her talk, our speaker ventured into the DVD situation. As many people know, China is famous for its pirated DVDs and CDs. To combat this situation, her company decided to release DVDs only ten days after the theatre release and charge only 15RMB for them. The pricing and the timing enabled and encouraged people to buy legitimate copies rather than pirated ones. The movie released in Sichuan, for example, sold a million copies this way, with no signs of a sales slowdown. Sue also told us something I didn't know about pirated DVDs: she explained that the same syndicates who owned the pirated media also own the drug and weapon cartels. Buying black market media, she informed us, served to fund drug and weapon deals. *Wow!*

When our esteemed guest finished, I applauded heartily with the rest of the group. This presentation had given me insights into doing business in China, into Chinese culture, and into the film industry. I left the event feeling both privileged and grateful to hold membership in this remarkable group.

Tibetan Trimmings

Another noteworthy event I attended in January was an SEA lecture on Tibetan design. Post-event, I came away with more than just factual knowledge. That afternoon I got acquainted with our hostess, Carly Weiss, a copper-tressed Jewish co-ed from Wisconsin who had arrived in Shanghai during the 1980s as an adventurous exchange student. Our hostess' story seemed at least as interesting as the lecture.

"Something about Asia just spoke to me," Carly explained. "Now, I can hardly believe that at twenty years old, I talked my way into a job as a trading house assistant in Hong Kong." She went on to explain that the government quickly discovered and deported her. Undaunted, she found her way back to China almost immediately. Parallel to the nine lives of the cats she rescued and adored, Carly re-invented her career many times, going from Oriental rug dealer, to gopher, to international business consultant, to animal rescue activist, to women's business promoter, and shop owner. Along this road less traveled, she married an Irish diplomat and remained in Asia permanently. She never looked back, and every new version of herself was always her best. Like Madonna, the woman had a gift for self-evolution.

In addition, this wonder woman was also wonderfully philanthropic. She talked briefly about how she had recently rented a small shop in order to help put Tibetan women to work. She bought their artsy-craftsy items, along with some Chinese greeting cards and tchotchkes, to stock the store. She hired a local Shanghainese woman to act as shopkeeper. I admired Carly's ability to simultaneously stimulate the Chinese economy and put food on tables in both China and Tibet. Amazingly, her philanthropic side didn't stop there. A lifelong animal lover, Carly had very recently managed to get city's first animal rescue up and running—the Shanghai Second Chance Animal Aid (SCAA).

I marveled at Carly's command of Mandarin, the remarkable Asian furniture, and the interesting artifacts adorning her charming old apartment as she played tour guide in her unique abode. I stood awed by the impressively carved, massive Chinese wedding bed—the magnificent centerpiece of her guest bedroom. I knew immediately I wasn't leaving Shanghai without one! When our guest speaker arrived, she led us back through Carly's apartment, discussing a chest, plant stands, gold sculptures, rugs, and Thankas (paintings by Tibetan monks). She explained that Tibetan decor remains highly influenced by Tibetan-style Buddhism. The furniture and art generally involved only five colors, representing the five feng shui elements. Blue symbolizes water; white represents metal; red equals the fire element; green denotes wood; and yellow signifies the earth. The designs painted on Tibetan pieces reflect Buddhist beliefs, Tantric symbolism, and nature. Some designs are intended to foster meditation, while others merely depict scenes from everyday life.

The furniture, rugs, and accent pieces also include key symbols. The conch horn sounds the Buddha's truth and represents power and authority, so in the home, it can drive out evil. The lotus plant represents the soul's path from the heavily weighted worries of the world to the lightness of enlightenment. The wheel represents the center of the world, with its eight spokes as the eight paths to enlightenment. The eight-sided parasol embodies the eightfold path to nirvana and symbolizes wisdom and compassion. The infinity knot shows how all elements of life are linked through cause and effect. As the knot has no beginning and no end, it denotes the infinite wisdom of the Buddha. Fish are a very common symbol of fertility, plenty, and joy, found in every type of Asian art. Pairs of fish show the Buddha's infinite energy. The victory banner illustrates the Buddha's triumph over temptation and wisdom's defeat of ignorance. Finally, the treasure vase symbolizes the Buddha's inexhaustible spirit.

You might recognize a few other common designs. The snow lion—Tibet's national emblem—symbolizes ultimate courage and victory. The Tibetan dragon is a shape shifter, who can become any size and who symbolizes heaven and the power of spring. The Garuda is a bird. He represents the fire element and is also the lord of the sky (it makes perfect sense that Bali's airport and the airline Garuda Indonesia are named for this creature). The ever-popular tiger embodies power, great strength, and extraordinary courage. The Garuda lion (winged lion) symbolizes the harmonious and triumphant bond between the earth and the heavens.

I appreciated that now I understood what I was looking at when viewing Tibetan décor! Then the speaker moved on to the Thankas. I'd never seen, or even heard of, one. Apparently, these religious wall hangings feature images of important Buddhist figures and philosophies, painted on cotton or silk, and serve as a key form of meditation for the artists. *Thank Ka* means "recorded message," thus the paintings teach—especially illiterate nomads—key Buddhist stories and help the viewer meditate. I came away with the impression that because monks had put so much positive energy into the pieces, the hangings were blessed and brought the owner good karma. I concluded I should probably buy one as soon as I had an opportunity.

Vaccines

This month's generally annoying thing about living in China involved shots. We needed to visit Universal Health to receive the third and final injection for a serial vaccine. By a stroke of good luck, we were assigned the Taiwan doctor. After hearing what we wanted, he simply responded, "ok," and sent us off.

Had I not been clear when I called to make the appointment?

"No, Madame. We have to order that vaccine." He explained.

"Order? How long will that take?"

"About one week. We get it from the UK. They are pretty good."

Though I guessed I should count my blessings that it wouldn't be a month, or a year (or that they could get it at all!), I nearly imploded at the inefficiency. We just wasted nearly two hours of our day, dragging ourselves to the clinic in afternoon rush hour, risking a traffic accident, just for the privilege of asking the doctor to *order* the shots! How irritating that the person answering the phone when we made the appointments couldn't have told me this or just ordered it! Now we had to spend another couple of hours schlepping all the way back to receive the injections. Why was it the simplest things could be so difficult here? On the bright side, at least we'd finally be done with all the shots required to live in this daily circus.

Our First Chinese New Year

Although it was our first Chinese New Year (CNY), the event actually marked our third new year's celebration for our first year in China! (We'd already had Jewish and international.) It seemed we had just returned from winter break in Australia, and now the kids had another week off for CNY, the most important holiday in the Chinese calendar.

Before school let out, however, the parents were treated to an impressive CNY holiday performance at SAS. The kids donned traditional Chinese clothing to present their special songs and dances. Interspersed among the numbers, talented Chinese child acrobats—hired for the occasion—performed incredible feats. The aspect of the show I remember most, though, was the poodles. Where in America could a school bring live animals on stage? Not only that, but each of the six dogs' coats had been dyed a different color! They jumped through hoops and performed all the circus-style doggy tricks that kids love. I had never attended a school event so entertaining and so memorable.

In the meantime, many people advised us to leave town and hurry up about it. Otherwise we'd never snag a flight with every Chinese citizen trying to get home to celebrate and every expat trying to clear out. Having already made two trips abroad that year, however, we opted to stay home and brave the "consequences." Could it really be that bad?

Well, during the first two nights, the fireworks really made an expat want to set pen to paper for the folks back home. Although we saw plenty of flashing lights from inside the house and startled to the accompanying blasts, we realized we'd have to go outside to truly appreciate the spectacle. From all possible directions shimmery brilliant colors exploded with bomb-volume bangs (fireworks were *much* louder than in the US, purportedly to scare away bad spirits). Multiply the sights and sounds of your July 4 fireworks display by about four, and you get the idea. At midnight, the intensity increased exponentially, as the dazzling explosions surrounded the house entirely. We could easily have been in the heat of battle in Iraq!

The kids reached saturation point within an hour or two and went to bed pretty much on time. Amazingly, they slept through all the commotion! When Planet and I decided to call it quits for the night, we slipped on our airplane sleep masks and popped in our ear plugs. Even so, we could still faintly hear the revelry that continued throughout the night. From what others told us, we could count ourselves lucky out in the hinterlands of Pudong. Apparently over in Puxi, the non-stop eruptions made it nearly impossible to sleep at all during the entire holiday week. Expat Puxi dwellers really hated that week!

Impressively, the hoopla continued throughout the next day and night, and we began to feel like we were literally living in a war zone. But with the fanfare reflecting life, hope, and joy, how could we mind? Thankfully, on day/night three, the celebratory fervor seemed to taper off to merely July 4-in-the-USA level. And fortunately, for the rest of the week, we experienced only sporadic outbursts. Now I understood why expats wanted to remove themselves to someplace quiet where they could think and sleep.

章
15

ANOTHER AYI BITES THE DUST, CHINESE SANTA, & ALL THE TEA IN CHINA

In December, while we prepared to leave Shanghai for our Bali vacation, I pondered what to do with Pepsi. The money in my dainties drawer remained untouched, so that seemed encouraging. Yet we'd be leaving Pepsi—ultimately still a stranger—alone in our house for two and a half weeks. There was so much she could do while we were away. She could invite a dozen friends to live here and party, or…well, who knew? I also considered giving her vacation time and asking her to vacate the house. But ultimately, Planet and I agreed it would better to have her housesit and continue working, since she'd been with us such a short time.

When we returned from our vacation, nothing seemed amiss, nothing was damaged, and nothing had been stolen. Yet I was annoyed when I looked around. It didn't seem like the house had been cleaned at all while we were away, though we had required *nothing* else of our ayi. What had she been doing? I sat Pepsi down and said I was disappointed. The house should have been spotless on our return, and we expected it to be obviously clean from now on. "Yes, Ma'am," she replied, head hanging. And life went on. Until…

In early February, when Pepsi had been with us just three months, Planet and I had to make a trip to the US Embassy to get a contract notarized. We took Pepsi along in case we needed to use her as one of our two required witnesses.

"Oh, we will be near the Western Union office. I need to send money to my family. Would you mind dropping me off there?" she asked.

I thought it extremely bold to ask such a favor—and somewhat inappropriate—since she was on duty. On the other hand, I also knew how much her family probably needed the money she sent home. They must be desperate for her to even consider asking.

"OK," I answered. "I will do you a favor, but only this one time." I didn't want to set a precedent or be taken advantage of.

When we finished up at the Embassy, we got into the car to return home. As we drove through Puxi, suddenly Pepsi called out, "Here! Stop right here!"

It seemed odd that she wanted to get out of the car in the middle of downtown, nowhere near the Western Union office.

"How long will you be?" Planet asked, thinking of all the work he had to do.

This seemed to occur to Pepsi only now. "Oh, yes. Sorry. You both have many things to do. I know where the subway is, and I can take a cab from there. I'll be back by dinner time," she replied anxiously.

I looked at Planet. This did not seem right. But our young housekeeper had already hopped out and was making a beeline for somewhere.

Back at home, at 4:34 pm I received a text from my errant ayi. She said she had gotten lost, but not to worry because she had called a friend, and he would bring her home. Lost? I didn't like the sound of this at all.

When 6:00 pm arrived, however, not only was dinner absent from the table, so was Pepsi. I called her cell phone. It was powered off. *Off?* I started to worry.

By 8:00 pm, she still hadn't returned, and I had grown every bit as angry as concerned. I called her phone again. Still powered off! My friends had warned me about "amah dramas" among the Filipinos, but these were simply annoying social intrigues and family complications, not ayis going missing!

As I seethed, about 9:30 pm the house phone rang. A Chinese man's voice came on the line, spewing Mandarin words as fast as my friend Bonnie's driver barreling her Audi down the highway.

"Whoa. Sorry. Can you tell me in English?"

"OK. Yes," he continued. "I found a girl sleeping by the subway. She was very cold and she looked sick. I find your name and phone number in her wallet. She is sleeping now."

None of this made any sense. Had this guy kidnapped and drugged her? Was he about to ask me to pay ransom?

"Well, wake her up. I want to talk to her," I demanded. What kind of trouble was Pepsi in? This guy had her wallet, too?

"No. No. I cannot."

I grew increasingly scandalized. "Of course, you can! Wake her up NOW!"

"I will have her call-a you when she wake up." And with that, the line went dead. I entered complete freak out mode. Where *was* my ayi? Who was this Chinese guy? What should I do?

About 10:00 pm, the house phone rang again. I picked up and heard Pepsi's voice on the other end.

"Ma'am Shelly, I wait and wait for my friend, but he never show up. Later he call me. He had a moped accident. This is why he didn't pick me up."

"OK, well you should have called me. I would have had Mr. Zhao pick you up," I replied firmly.

"I could not. I fainted. It was so cold sitting on de bench waiting. I didn't wear my coat. Just a fleece."

What? "I don't think you fainted because you were cold," I said, beginning to feel outraged.

"Maybe it's because I only had one hour of sleep on Saturday night."

No wonder she looked so weird when she came in on Sunday night and seemed so tired on Monday morning. I wasn't sure I wanted to know why she only got one hour of sleep.

"It's your responsibility to get enough sleep so you are fit for work," I responded, no longer masking my anger.

Strangely, she didn't apologize. "The man whose apartment I'm in will bring me home now."

Oh, I think not! "No. No, he will not bring you home now. You can stay somewhere else. You cannot come back to this house. I'm going to say good-night now. We will talk about this in the morning. I'll call you."

Planet and I agreed that Pepsi had broken our trust and that she had shown terribly poor judgment on several counts. She had obviously lied to us today about going to wire money. The entire situation was unacceptable.

"Let's have someone from The Pearl's security office call the guy back and find out what's really going on," Planet suggested wisely.

"Great idea!"

Planet picked up The Pearl hotline and got security on the phone. He explained what he wanted them to do. The security officer who called the Chinese man got the same bizarre story about finding Pepsi sleeping on a bench and her being cold. He also said the money she intended to wire had disappeared. *Gee, shocker!*

"Well, this sure seems like another classic case of 'no good deed goes unpunished,'" I said, annoyed.

Planet nodded in agreement. "I don't like that we were taken advantage of. Not at all."

"Nope. I'm going to call Sarah and see what she thinks about all this mess," I said.

I rang Sarah's mobile phone. When she picked up, I filled her in on what had transpired.

"You should forgive Pepsi. She's young. Use the experience to lay down the law with her," she advised. *What? Were we supposed to parent her?*

Sarah also said Florida had warned our young employee repeatedly over the past few months about her childish behavior and bad choices. What exactly did that mean? What *had* Pepsi been up to?

"While it would be nice to have a teachable moment, unfortunately my husband and I think the breach of trust is unacceptable."

"I understand completely that your trust has been shaken and that you want to fire her. She should probably be sent back to the Philippines, especially if she is running around with a man," she added.

When we finished, I filled Planet in on the conversation.

"Well, it sounds like they agree with our decision. There's nothing more we can do right now, so let's try to get some sleep."

But at 11:30 pm, we still felt keyed up and wide awake. Planet heard my mobile phone message alert. He looked at me as I rolled over to see who it was.

"It's Pepsi, asking if I'm awake," I told Planet. "I'm going to choose to ignore this."

In the wee hours of the morning, a longer text from Pepsi rolled in.

"I'm so sorry, Ma'am Shelly. I never intended for things to turn out this way. It is all because of my friend's motorcycle accident. I am so ashamed to tell you that he is my boyfriend. If only you know how lonely I was and how happy I was to meet him when I came here."

No wonder she had come in from the weekends looking like she hadn't slept a wink! I could only imagine how embarrassing and humiliating it was for her to admit she was an adulterer, but I was more concerned about her taking advantage of us and her generally poor judgment. Clearly, Pepsi was immature, but the worst part was that she had behaved badly and broken our trust. "I think if we take her back, we look like pushovers." I said.

"Not only that, but even if we forbid her to see her boyfriend, she's probably going to do it any way. She's already taken advantage of us once," Planet agreed. "The house probably isn't clean because she's texting him or talking to him on the phone all day."

"Maybe they've been having rendezvous here during the day while we're out. And I don't even want to think of what may have gone on in this house while we were on vacation!" I added.

"We have to let her go," Planet remarked. "No doubt about it."

"No argument here. It's just such a shame that she was foolish enough to ruin such a good opportunity. I feel bad for the dishonor and financial hardship she just brought on her family and the local Filipino community," I said, shaking my head.

About 8:30 am the next morning, Pepsi rang.

"Is there anything else you need to tell me?" I asked.

"No, Ma'am. I'm so very sorry," Pepsi replied through her tears.

"Unfortunately, you have broken our trust, so you are fired. Please come by here at 10:30 am to pick up your things."

"Yes, Ma'am," she responded, humbly. "But couldn't you just give me a punishment?"

What was this with punishments! Were household staff treated like teenagers in Asia? What would a "punishment" be, and would she even change her behavior as a result? Oh, this was too much!

"No. We cannot trust you anymore. We really can't give you another chance."

"OK. I understand. I'm very sorry."

When Pepsi arrived, she wept the entire time she packed. "I'm so ashamed," she said to me. "Do you hate me?"

"No. I'm just sad that you made such a big mistake. We all liked you, and you had a good opportunity here. I hope that you will learn from this and do better in the future."

"Yes, Ma'am. May I say goodbye to the kids, please?"

"Sure." I knew how sad the kids would be.

"Can you please tell Mr. Planet goodbye and thank you from me? I'm too ashamed to see him."

"Sure." I felt bad for her, but how could she have used such poor judgment with so much at stake?

Pepsi hugged me and the kids and said goodbye. Then, Planet came downstairs and pulled me aside. He insisted that we pay her for the few days she had worked this month. With impressive integrity, she refused to take the money. She looked so miserable, and thinking of her family, I shoved the RMB into her pocket while she, unaware, dejectedly eased all her belongings into the cab.

I shook my head. Ayi number two down. I hoped number three would be a charm!

Around 7:00 pm, my cell phone rang. "Ma'am Shelly, I don't want to bother you, but there's one more thing," Pepsi's voice came over the line.

Seriously? What now?

"Could you please not tell Florida about my boyfriend?" She seemed appropriately terror-stricken about the impending Filipino community scandal. But I could hardly believe my ears as she went on, "and could you please tell Florida and anyone else who asks that I am staying in your house for a month while I look for a new job?"

The nerve! Protect her reputation? No way! Where was she right now? At the Chinese boyfriend's?" You're asking me to lie for you! No! I can't and I won't do that," I answered, incredulous. My anger could have matched a bull facing a matador's red scarf. She couldn't have been more misguided, and I couldn't have been more relieved that I had just fired her!

"Please. Oh, please!" she begged.

"No. You've caused enough trouble. I'm going to say goodbye now. Good luck!" I hung up. *Unbelievable!*

The saga didn't even end there, though. That afternoon, Florida rang me.

"I'm so sorry for all the trouble Pepsi's caused," she began. "Is there any way you would reconsider firing her? Maybe give her a punishment?"

Again? I had no interest in parenting a twenty-six-year-old woman—who I was paying to be a responsible adult!

"No," I responded. "I can't have someone looking after my house and my children who I can't trust. She took advantage of us, and her judgment is just too poor."

"OK. I can understand that. Again, I'm so sorry she treated you that way. I would like to ask you a question, though."

"Yes?"

"What other things has she lied to you about?" her "aunt" asked.

I liked that the Shanghai Filipino community looked out for each other and policed each other, but I smelled a real four-alarm blaze brewing. It looked like Sarah and Florida planned to spend today gathering up all the evidence against this unfortunate young woman, determining whether to ship her back. Well, she had no one to blame but herself for that. I also now felt irritated that Florida and Sarah had sent someone with a questionable track record into my home. I guessed they hoped she'd straighten up when she got a good full-time job.

I saw no reason to hold back. I told Florida about Pepsi asking to come home on Monday mornings by 7:30 am instead of returning on Sunday nights, and how when she came back she looked like she'd either partied all weekend, not slept, or both. The house didn't seem particularly clean, and sometimes basic tasks weren't done. And, of course, I'd already explained that she was found in a Chinese man's apartment, robbed and unconscious, after going missing in the middle of the afternoon.

"OK, well thank you. And thank you for giving Pepsi a chance to work for you. I'm very sorry she didn't behave right."

"Well, these things happen. Thanks for your call. I wish you the best."

"Yes, Ma'am. Goodbye."

And with that, the Filipino ayi chapter of our lives mercifully closed. The kids remained quite upset that Pepsi was gone, but the situation created a teachable moment in their lives. We had several long talks about trust, making good decisions, and unpleasant consequences for wrong behaviors.

I didn't know our decision to fire Pepsi would soon become a blessing in disguise. About a year later, something went very wrong in the Filipino community's relationship with the Chinese government. According to the rumor mill, their representatives hadn't paid the appropriate monetary "respects." The government immediately conducted a raid, and Filipina domestic helpers were deported right and left. About half the household helpers at The Pearl suddenly disappeared. I also learned that the government's excuse (legitimate) was that some of the Filipino ayis moonlighted as prostitutes on the weekends and that many of them indulged in some party drug that they just couldn't get enough of. Some did both. It certainly made me wonder what Pepsi had gotten up to on her free weekends and glad she was gone sooner, rather than later!

Three's A Charm

I'd had enough "Amah drama," so I began interviewing Chinese ayis immediately. The first candidate was an older lady who spoke English well, but who didn't seem like she could handle an entire household. I had the impression she just wanted to babysit, so I wasn't keen on hiring her. The second candidate didn't speak English at all, so I had to hire Alvin as interpreter. It was worth the 100RMB I paid him for the approximately ninety minutes we talked.

Xiao Mei worked for a friend of a friend's family in Puxi who were relocating, and they highly recommended her. She stood about five-feet tall, medium build, with a pleasant face and cheerful disposition, her long dark hair neatly pulled into a ponytail. She hailed from Anhui province—an impoverished backwater. She and her husband had left their five-year-old daughter back home to be raised by her grandparents, while they earned an excellent living here in Shanghai. It was maybe not the most desirable way to get ahead in life, but very common in modern China. I imagined Xiao Mei and her spouse sending back not only enough money to support the Anhui household but to buy a restaurant or business through which they could improve the lives of extended family members and their community.

I also learned some unusual things during this interview. One was that Xiao Mei's current employer had taught her to cook American-style fried chicken—a pleasant surprise. The next item, less so. Though Alvin's translating, I learned that she wanted to know whether "comfort money" was part of this deal. *Comfort money?* Poor Alvin had to explain this delicate situation to me. Apparently, it was fairly common for the lady of the house to pay her ayi money to sleep with her husband during the "indisposed" portion of the month. *Oh, my!* No, I assured her, this would NOT be part of the deal in our home. I couldn't read from her traditional Chinese poker face whether this was a good or a bad thing. I guess some ayis counted on the extra pay.

As we exchanged information, I found that I liked her a lot and wanted to hire her. Alvin relayed this information. I was surprised to hear that Xiao Mei felt concerned about taking the job because she spoke no English. Somehow, my gut instinct said to hire her.

"Alvin, tell her not to worry about English. I'll give her 1800RMB a month and pay for her to have English lessons with you. When she speaks well enough, I'll bump her salary up to the 2200RMB she wants." Already 1800RMB a month was a princely sum, since she planned to live in. But I liked her and wanted to help her family.

Alvin relayed all this to the young woman. They spoke back and forth for a while. I gathered that she had some reason she really wanted or needed to make a certain amount, but in the end, I won. I had a good feeling about her. Excitedly, I gave her a tour of the house, hoping the size wouldn't intimidate her. When we arrived at the ayi room, suddenly Alvin was translating again.

Was this room just for her?

Yes.

Would she be allowed to use the heat?

What an odd question. Yes.

As Xiao Mei started to tear up, Alvin explained.

"In her last posting, she had to sleep on the floor in the children's room and get up with them all night. They also had no heat. She is *very, very* grateful."

Wow, I could hardly imagine treating someone whom I trusted with my children that way. Nor anyone at all!

When my new ayi saw that she also had her own bathroom, I thought she was going to faint from this embarrassment of riches. I felt glad that I could add some small comfort to her life as well as financial help. I crossed my fingers and hoped everything would go well between us.

On Monday, Mr. Zhao drove into Puxi to pick up Xiao Mei. He helped her move her things into the ayi room, and then she got right to work. When the kids arrived home after school, they couldn't wait to meet her. They liked our new ayi immediately. She was cheerful and pleasant to them, and she even offered to help the kids with their Chinese homework. What a bonus!

At dinner, we discovered we loved her cooking. Although we invited ayi to join us at the table, she always refused. Xiao Mei insisted on eating her own dinner in the kitchen, perched on her little stool. Months ago that would have really bothered me. Now, I understood this was part of the invisible hierarchy. Staying in the kitchen was what *she* felt comfortable with, and the relationship would work out better if I respected that. So I did.

Eventually Xiao Mei got fussy about a few things. It wasn't until after we left China that I found out why. She got snippy about getting to Puxi by a certain time on Saturday nights to meet up with her husband. We had to cut a deal. If Planet and I came back from our own night out too late, and she'd missed certain busses and connections, we'd have Mr. Zhao drive her to her husband's apartment. Also, a few months later, her English was coming along very nicely. Already, she had Alvin tell me that she felt she knew English enough to quit the lessons. She wanted to know if I could now pay her the full salary. Of course, I obliged.

Finally, when we were leaving Shanghai, I found out what was up with her salary and getting to Puxi on time obsession. Apparently since she and her husband were both only children, and they had a girl as their only child, the government would allow them to pay to have a second child—translation: to try for a boy! So, they needed the equivalent of about $10,000 to "buy" a second child. What a back story!

Thankfully, we enjoyed having Xiao Mei in our household. She kept the house spotless, she was an excellent cook, she was nice to the kids and they liked her, and she remained permanently cheerful. She gladly taught the kids and I Chinese, as well. Our third ayi *was* a charm!

Playing Chinese Santa

One of my favorite memories of Shanghai occurred in February 2006. On Sunday mornings, The Pearl's bike club assembled at Chastain Chenoweth's house at the frighteningly early hour of 7:00 am to explore Pudong. The group was started by a couple of *Guy Tais* (the male version of Tai Tais—men who had come to Shanghai to support their wives' careers and were taking a work hiatus themselves), including Chastain. Chastain's wife's job with a major soft drink company brought them to China. Suddenly finding himself with significant free time, starting a bike club seemed like one of many logical, fun things to do to stay busy.

Just outside The Pearl's fancy iron gates, a vastly different world emerged from the saddle of my new Giant mountain bike, a view of daily Chinese life that few Westerners would ever see. The maze of small back roads—some dirt, some paved—led into the won-ton-soup brown landscape. As we rolled by, I saw that some farms grew perfectly shaped, deliciously fresh-looking green heads of lettuce. Everywhere, the land lay dotted with clusters of boxy, taupe homes topped by quintessential red tile roofs. As we passed over a bridge into a village along a canal, I watched women cleaning their vegetables in the foul green-brown canal water. Once, I even saw a young lady washing her hair outside in a pink plastic tub filled with this murky slime water. *Would her hair glow in the dark?* One building caused me to hold my breath every time we passed. It may or may not have been a chicken processing business, but a large mound of chicken feathers permanently ornamented one side. The media reports of the bird flu era made me nervous to get too near it.

As we glided through small villages, I loved to see wise-looking grandmothers knitting with chopsticks in the doorways of their windowless one-room hovels, who still waved cheerfully despite enduring the hardships of no heat or running water. Heaven only knew what the families in these one-room cells went through to get to a bathroom, or what challenges that mission entailed. The children we encountered always surprised us. Some flashed the peace sign—the old first-two-fingers held in a V shape. Where did they learn that? Did Americans still know what that meant? Or did that hand signal now represent a V for victory, symbolizing how they probably grew up learning that China was the best and most powerful country in the world? Once, a group of boys pretended to shoot us with imaginary guns, complete with "pow, pow" sound effects. Would they have acted this way with Asian strangers, or was there some negativity toward Western foreigners we didn't know about? Other times youngsters simply chased after us, squealing in delight.

Thankfully, everywhere the villagers seemed to appreciate a sincere *"ni hao."* They appeared generally curious about and friendly to our group. How could they help wondering about these funny-looking invaders on princely priced, high tech bikes—fancier than most of them had ever seen before— dressed in outlandish clothing? The Chinese speakers among our group said the villagers often discussed our bikes, guessing how fast or light they were and always debating how much we might have paid for them. Regularly, when- ever we stopped for any reason, we attracted well-intentioned Pudongers who assumed we needed directions. It blew the locals' minds to learn that we were pedaling through the countryside just for fun. For them, bikes played the role of a car in the West—on it, you moved from point A to point B, nothing else. Regardless of what or who we encountered, I loved our forays into bustling Chinese daily life.

While all Pearl rides seemed memorable for one reason or another, the ride that stands out most for me took place during Chinese New Year. The group had targeted a few villages to ride through on an upcoming Sunday. Our plan was to play "Chinese Santa." We would surprise the residents by randomly handing out *hong bao* (red envelopes) to any youngsters we encountered. Hong bao are the packets of money that all Chinese children expect to receive in celebration of the holiday. We had ours stuffed with various Renminbi (RMB) denomina- tions. Most riders stuffed their hong bao with 10s (about $1.50) or 20s (about $3.00) for the smaller children. Other envelopes we stuffed with 50s (about $7.50) or 100s (about $12.00) for the older kids or anyone who appeared espe- cially needy. While those amounts might seem low—like McDonald's snack money to Americans—they actually stretched a long way for the locals.

Off we rode, pedaling vigorously in anticipation. When we reached the first village, we stopped as soon as we saw a group of children. To our surprise, they took off like startled rabbits. One of the bikers who spoke Mandarin called after them.

"We are friends," he explained. "We wish you a happy new year!" He stretched out his arm, a bright red and gold hong bao dangling from his fingers.

That got their attention! The children paused and looked back at us, still afraid, until one brave little boy crept toward us. Suddenly he sprang for- ward, snatched the red envelope, and sped back to his companions. The others gathered around him as he cautiously peered inside his red envelope. A loud squeal of excitement broke the silence as the boy pulled out a 20RMB note. A collective whoop of delight rang out from the rest of the little villagers. Several of us held out our red envelopes, beaming with good will. The children made their way guardedly toward us, but finally smiling.

"*Xie xie, ni*," (thank you) they called, as they grabbed the goods and ran nervously away as though we were on fire.

Well, this hadn't exactly been the victory we'd hoped for, but then again in the US many a kid cries on Santa's lap. Still, we felt happy that we'd managed to spread unexpected holiday cheer to at least a few families.

The group rolled on to the next village. Here, we spied a few sets of parents crossing a bridge with their children. I stopped near a mother with a baby about two years old. I smiled and held out an envelope to her lovely child. The baby's chubby cherry-cheeked face grew understandably puzzled, taking in this this alien-looking American lady with the bizarre hat. The mother smiled and slowly approached me. With a little coaxing, the mother got the baffled-looking child to take the envelope. The mother bowed her head in thanks. Success! I smiled and waved as the group rode on.

A very thin man with a sun bronzed face had been watching from the bottom of the bridge. He clearly knew an opportunity when he saw one. He actually pushed his son, who looked around seven years old, toward the bikers. The boy held back, but the man remained insistent, demanding he come forward, pushing him again. The son reluctantly retrieved an envelope from one of the guys, then charged back down to his parent. The father beamed, thumping his son on the back in approval. The father stared at our expensive machinery and clothing. Then he pointed at one of the riders in the front of our group who still held an envelope. He prodded his son to go get that envelope, too. But before the man could take advantage of the situation, the lead rider signaled the group, "let's roll," and we were off to our next destination, the red-faced villager staring after us, defeated, his cigarette dangling from his lips. I tried not to judge. What looked like greed from my perspective may have been practicality, opportunism, or even desperation, from his.

As we arrived at the third village, we encountered a small strip of stores. A stray dog roamed the dirt road, looking for scraps of anything consumable. A sienna-brown chicken bobbed along one side of the road on some urgent mission. Large and medium-sized metal sheets dangled from the curb into the road. China's roadways remained full of curiosities, and there was no telling what hazards an unsuspecting rider might encounter. I gazed in wonder at a shop with hundreds of noodles that stretched all the way from the roof nearly to the ground, drying. I never imagined that noodles started out so long! How did the chef make them that size? Why so long? That shop remains etched in my memory, the noodles were such a delightful surprise. We rode several more blocks before the area grew more residential. Though we hoped to find children to receive our remaining hong bao, our luck had run out, and our extraordinary ride ended. I couldn't wait for next year!

All the Tea in China

One chilly February evening, we waited anxiously for our special dinner guests. When Alexis and Anders were babies, Planet and I had a wonderful *au pair* named Katja from Germany. She wrote me that she, her boyfriend, and her uncle were touring China and hoped to see us in Shanghai. We haven't seen her in many years, and the trio served as our first official visitors in our new country.

Always wanting to play the perfect hostess, I decided that Katja, Robert, and Uncle Juergen should have authentic Shanghai dumplings for dinner. So, I rang Mr. Zhou to drive me to the wonderful noodle restaurant where I'd eaten with Angela. When I arrived, I asked for take away *jaozi* (dumplings). "No, no," the young man at the cash host stand wagged a finger at me.

"*Wei shen me*? (why?)" I grabbed a menu and pointed to what I wanted, just in case something got lost in translation.

"Mmmm…no," he shook his head. I knew he couldn't explain in English. No one would turn away business, so what was I missing here?

I went into the Chinese restaurant next door asking for take-out dumplings. The staff understood me, but the answer was again, no. This seemed nuts! I went to a third place just to see what would happen. Here, the young hostess spoke English well.

"Why won't anyone sell me take away jaozi?"

"They will not taste good. You must eat them in the restaurant when they are fresh and hot," she told me. "Sorry, Madame."

Well, no wonder the other restaurants thought I was another crazy waiguoren. I would not have guessed that Chinese chefs would care if wacky foreigners wanted to take their dumplings home and warm them up. Wasn't *selling* dumplings better than *not* selling dumplings? Apparently not. The lesson: don't mess with the integrity of the Shanghai jaozi!

By now I'd wasted an hour. I panicked over what I could serve my guests for dinner. Then I remembered that Katja had liked my spaghetti. I felt terrible that my poor former nanny and her traveling companions had to eat homemade Italian food in China! The fact that noodles originated in China provided me no consolation at all.

Fortunately, Katja forgave me, as she was very happy to see us all and hear about our lives. At the end of the evening, the three travelers and I confirmed our plans to meet up again for a shopping adventure.

Later that week, Mr. Zhou and I picked up the Germans, who were on a mission to buy Chinese tea and tea sets. So, I consulted my "Chinese Bible," the *Passport to Shanghai* reference guide that made expat life exponentially easier. The book had been compiled by one of the French clubs, the pages filled with recommendations for everything from restaurants to doctors, travel agents to home decorators. Book sale profits benefitted a local Chinese charity, so it served as a win-win for everyone. According to *Passport*, the city had a plethora of local teashops but one entry stood out: an actual wholesale tea market! Jackpot!

It took Mr. Zhou nearly an hour to navigate the Chrysler to Katja's hotel. Then it took us another thirty to forty-five minutes to reach our destination. The tea market area seemed like some type of commercial supply zone. We drove past dozens of carpet places, oodles of hardware suppliers, and endless door handle shops. Eventually even Mr. Zhou started to wonder when we might find the tea lane. In the end, he had to lose face by asking someone. Thankfully, we were close. Five minutes later we stopped before a mind-boggling scene: row after row, as far as the eye could see in all directions, hundreds of tiny tea shops.

We left the car, debating where to start. Robert, who had been working in Beijing for several months, had already learned a few useful tricks. He suggested that the shops in front probably got the most business and therefor would not give us the best prices. We agreed with his logic and kept walking. Finally, we picked a row and sauntered along until a particular tea set in a shop window caught Robert's eye. We went in to get a better look around the shop. We spoke very little Chinese among us, and the shop ladies spoke no English at all. Bring on another unique Shanghai shopping adventure!

Whatever we picked up and looked at, the two shop ladies wrote out prices for us in Chinese, as if we would eventually understand. We didn't. In the meantime, the women set water on to boil. Soon, the ladies served us the coveted green liquid. Clearly, no one on either team planned to let language get in the way. Tea was serious business!

Robert and I also understood that this transaction wasn't going to be quick. The shop ladies were more than pleased to have us try as many teas as it would take for us to hopefully buy at least their sales quota for the day.

Through Robert's limited Mandarin, our hand gestures, and facial expressions we communicated that we all wanted to buy some of the first tea they served us. Robert found a tea set he wanted, so he planned to negotiate all of his purchases as a package, using the rule that the more you buy, the better the price. Mission one accomplished, the ladies set about brewing a different type of green tea. We all liked the taste of that one, too. So, we added more tea to our growing piles of goods. Then, Uncle Juergen capitalized on the situation by adding a tea set to his small pile of goods. The shop ladies kept right on going, too. They brewed a third pot of Chinese elixir. I added a tin of that one to my stash as a holiday gift for my tea-loving dad.

Here in tea town, we were having a very different purchasing experience from the quick rushing in and out of American-style shopping and even from the Chinese gift market hustle. These shopkeepers understood the importance of developing relationships with customers. I think they would have stood there all day, brewing pot after pot of tea, if that's what it took. Clearly, our shopping today required a respect for this cultural difference.

Eventually, we made our final choices, and we needed to negotiate. We Westerners sat at the tea table looking at each other, wondering how we could reach an understanding. Maybe hold out an RMB bill that seemed suitable?

As we discussed how to communicate prices, one of the tea clerks suddenly produced a calculator from her pocket. Magically, she understood Western numbers!

Huzzah! We began the price dance. But suddenly, they stopped negotiating and did just what Chinese tea ladies who want to increase sales do: they served us *more* tea! This time they went for the irresistible impulse purchase. They brought out the flower teas! It worked. We all added some flower-tea balls to our growing inventory.

Once again, we agreed we wanted nothing more, but the shop ladies weren't hearing no. They insisted that we drink yet *another* round of tea. Though we were all about to float away at this point, we courteously took a few more sips. We continued to barter for only the items we had already chosen. Finally, both sides nodded in agreement. Though the final price seemed reasonable, we probably overpaid, because the shop ladies called us *pengyou* (friend) and allowed us to use their private bathroom—extremely necessary by that fourth cup of tea! At that point, we didn't care. We'd had a memorable, fun adventure.

With that, I dialed Mr. Zhou. Back at the Germans' hotel, we said our good-byes and wished each other well. I wondered in what part of the world Katja and I might see each other again and what kind of new adventures we might have together. It was a very pleasant thought to end the day with.

章
16

ENOUGH LUCK (GOOD & BAD) TO GO AROUND

March 2006 brought me good luck both intellectually and socially. For starters, I discovered the Shanghai Literary Festival (SHL). The SHL was the brainchild of Michelle Garnaut, an Australian chef who came to Asia seeking her fortune and established the City's first non-hotel, European-style fine dining restaurant in 1999—M on the Bund. People flocked to the restaurant to gobble up its delicious fare and enjoy the enticing rooftop patio overlooking the fabled Bund. The venue's Glamour Bar quickly developed into a gathering place for the city's expats and local movers and shakers. In addition, Garnaut sought to promote the arts in her establishment, quickly developing a cultured, elite community. Before long, M became the home of the SHL and the Shanghai Chamber Music Festival and Competition.

Extremely excited, I booked my ticket for the 2006 Shanghai Literary Festival. That year about twenty-five authors—many of whom had either won a prize or been nominated for one (like the Man Booker Prize or the National Book Award)—emerging authors, or simply those whose work would appeal to the expat crowd presented their work over the course of two or three weekends. That year, the biggest name I heard was Pankaj Mishra.

Mishra presented his perspective on the globalization of fiction. According to him, writing, and its sense of style, has always been a harbinger and recorder of change, yet American and European writing has not grown in centuries.

That is, until the September 11, 2001 disaster challenged Western writers' views and scope. Mishra had recently spent time asking various writers how the New York City trauma affected their work. Some stopped writing because their efforts seemed irrelevant and disconnected from this new reality. Others, like John Updike (*Terrorist* 2006) and Ian McEwan (*Saturday* 2005), felt challenged by 9/11 and so based their upcoming novels on this crisis. He went on to conclude that with this event, our awareness of the interdependence of nations, of how people's lives around the globe intersect and influence each other, heightened.

I also heard Beverly Jackson speak on how her passion for Chinese textiles led her to not only collect handmade embroidered shoes but to write a book about "lotus shoes" (shoes for bound-foot Chinese women). The concept intrigued me, prompting me to borrow a copy of Jackson's book from a textiles store in the Portman-Ritz complex and immediately draft a *Courier* article about bound-foot shoes.

Overall, the Literary Festival was one of the best events I've ever attended, and I looked forward to returning the next year.

The Virus

While my spring started off fabulously, my luck soon went south. A horrible virus ran rampant among the expat community, and finally, I, too, succumbed to the vicious malady. It was the sickest I'd ever been. For days, anything that entered my mouth, even a tiny sip of water, necessitated a mad dash to the toilet. I was glued to the bathroom so urgently and for so long that I couldn't figure out how I was going to manage the thirty-minute car ride to Jin Qiao to get help. Where was all this liquid in my body coming from, and how did it continue to spew violently forth for days? As seemed to always happen, Planet was away on business, and I had to fend for myself. Uncomprehending, ayi went about her business as usual. Finally, on day five, devil be damned, I willed myself into the Chrysler. I was so wrecked that any doctor would do. So of course, Murphy's Law, I ended up with…the Singapore doctor.

Lucky for me, I wasn't the first case of "the virus" he'd seen.

"You need an IV, Madame," he advised. That was obvious even to me.

He left the room to get the saline solution bag and needle. He jabbed the needle into my hand. Nope. Then into my arm. Uh, uh. Into my elbow crease. No dice. Finally, by about the sixth stab, we were in business. But he had the liquid dripping out so slowly, I had to question whether it was coming out at all. Two hours later, I lay still counting ceiling tiles. Only a bit more than three-quarters of the liquid had made it into my veins. My patience had run out. I called for a nurse and explained the problem. She grabbed the Singapore doctor. Timidly, he removed the IV and nodded at me. I made my escape, praying. By some miracle, the fluid actually remained in my body, and the virus seemed to have ended.

More Bianca Drama

Luck wasn't on my side in the kid department, either. Though Alexis had finally made friends in her class, arranging playdates remained challenging because of schedules, distances, and traffic. So, we still endured the occasional Bianca pop up. Early one Sunday morning—after a night of decadently filling our bodies with delectable dishes and fine Australian wine at a neighbor's party—our whole family was enjoying a rare chance to sleep in. In the middle of a wonderful shopping-for-great-stuff-at-less-than-Kmart-prices dream, I heard the phone ding-a-linging. I put on my glasses and looked over at the clock. Seven thirty. Oh, no! Who was hurt—or worse, dead—at home in the US? I picked up the receiver.

"Hello. Can I talk to Alexis?" came a young girl's voice, sugary sweet.

Oh, for the love of jiaozi, it could only be Bianca calling at this hour!

"Is this Bianca?"

"Yes." "Ok, it's only 7:30 am, and she's still asleep."

"Well, could you wake her up?"

What!

"No. She needs her sleep."

"Well, she needs to wake up. I was thinking that this is a good day to go to the amusement park."

"I see." *I had to be dreaming.*

"My dad can't take us because he's traveling," she urged persistently. "So, I was thinking that Alexis' dad should take us."

Insanity! Did her mother know what she was up to? And at what time?

"No, Alexis' dad can't take you today," I countered, firmly. Even if he could have and would have, her behavior alone generated a reason to give her a hard no!

"Are you *sure*? Well, then your driver can take us," she replied, apparently impressed by her own stroke of genius.

Well, while there were parents in Asia who would be cool with that, I, however, was *not*.

"No, we gave Mr. Zhou the day off today," I countered.

"Oh. Well, we can just take a cab then."

Wow! An even less safe and less appealing idea. At the moment, I felt more like I was speaking to a thirty-year-old con artist than a nine-year-old!

"NO. Alexis is *not* going with you to the amusement park today. She has tennis this morning, and then we're having some family time."

"Well, could you wake up Alexis. I want to talk to her." *Was she kidding?* The artful dodger here probably assumed she could get Alexis to manipulate us, since she'd had no luck with me.

"NO. At our house, we don't wake people up on a Sunday morning. Alexis needs her sleep. She'll call you later." In my irritation I couldn't resist adding, "Oh, and please don't call us before 9:00 am anymore. *Ever*."

Without waiting for her response, I hung up. But I couldn't go back to sleep because I found the call so disturbing. Was this the ugly downside of raising a third-culture kid?

Apparently, my denying Bianca what she wanted and telling her not to call early in the morning generated consequences. Later that day, when Alexis tried to log into her favorite computer game, Club Penguin, she found herself locked out. After some sleuthing, my kids figured out that Bianca had managed to get Alexis' password (perhaps another bribe?). Bianca logged in as my daughter and broke the game rules by abusing other penguins (players) with swear words and insults. This type of behavior, of course, caused monitors to step in and punish the offending penguin (Alexis') by kicking her off the website for a couple of days. My rule-loving, honest, sweet daughter cried and cried, mostly because she found it so hard to believe that anyone would do this to her, especially a friend. My daughter was learning some hard life lessons this year. I prayed for girls near her age to move into The Pearl soon!

Fortunately, I had much better luck in the friendship department that month. One day when I walked the kids to the bus stop at The Emerald clubhouse, I noticed a tall thin woman with white blonde hair sitting with a boy and a girl. A new neighbor? And no word on the grapevine?

"Hi, I'm Shelly Aschkenase," I said, walking up to introduce myself. "Are you new here?"

"Hi, I'm Bonnie Douglas. Yes, we just got here," the woman replied.

"Oh, you're American! Where are you from?" My ears trilled with excitement to hear an American accent.

"Ohio."

"What grade are your kids in?"

"My son is in sixth, and my daughter is in fifth."

I felt bad for them changing schools in March.

"Well, welcome. Here's my card. Let me know if you need anything."

I remembered how kind Marilyn, Eden, and Chava had been to me, so I immediately invited her out and did my best to help her adjust to the crazy expat life we lived. Bonnie had just moved into a house on the street right behind mine, and though our kids' ages didn't overlap, she and I bonded immediately. We had many adventures over the years, and we remained friends, even after my family repatriated to the US, occasionally visiting back and forth.

Canine Capers & the Language of Cats

Before we had any inkling that our family might move abroad, I promised the kids we could get a pet. Of course, they wanted a dog, so I looked into getting a Belgian Shephard that didn't make the cut at a police or service dog academy. I was still researching the idea when our move to China went through. Now, I couldn't have been more relieved that we hadn't arrived there with a canine—especially a big one. Bringing a pet along into the Middle Kingdom presented challenges. For starters, when a beloved furbie arrived, s/he had to spend a week (in the best case) or up to a month (the worst case) in quarantine. Once health certified, the pet parent had to figure out how to transport Fido home. Expats with drivers were lucky, as dogs were not allowed on busses or the subway. Rumor held that negotiating with a Chinese taxi driver to allow your dog into his vehicle was on par with selling ice to Eskimos.

After Rover's escape from quarantine and certification, next a family had to register him. Yes, the local police expected the same from both humans *and* their pets. Pets required yearly registration with the local police, who were delighted to take advantage of the opportunity to charge around 2000 RMB (about $290), more if they also provided vaccinations.

Had dog owners finally reached the good part, where they could relax and find a stick for Spot to retrieve? No. This was often the part where ayi quit and stormed out cursing. Many an expat experienced the unpleasant surprise that ayis did *not* like dogs (perhaps a legacy of old communist attitudes or perceived hygiene issues?) and many were afraid of them. And let's be honest for a moment here, many a canine could take down one these petite ladies before she could yell "*aaaiii oooooo!*" Some of my friends complained that when they finally found an ayi who accepted their dog, she demanded a higher salary for the "danger" and extra work load her job would entail.

You might think that once an expat had jumped all the government hurdles and found an ayi who made peace with Fluffy, all was well. Unfortunately, sometimes dogs—including expat pets—went missing. The reasons might surprise you.

For one thing, it's not an urban legend: dog appeared on the menu in some places. Beijing supposedly had over one hundred restaurants that either specialized in dog or served dog. So, it wasn't unreasonable to assume that a roaming canine might end up on someone's dinner table. According to Mimi's driver, the best ones were the big black ones (translation: Labradors). Clearly, eating dogs *was* a thing. Why? Partly, it may stem from antiquity, when ritual sacrifices featured dogs. It stands to reason that any food fit for the gods represents a rare delicacy for humans. As a result, dog meat eventually found its place in traditional Chinese medicine and Daoism. Dog is conventionally eaten during the summer for its cooling properties. Dog meat also supposedly supports liver functioning and serves as an aphrodisiac. Who knew? It's been joked about that the Chinese will eat anything that swims, flies, or has four legs—except a table—but there's truth in humor. Realistically, how can the country reasonably expect to feed a billion people adequately? Any edible food source, therefore, seems legitimate. To be fair, canine dishes still appeared on dinner tables in Germany and Switzerland through the 1900s, and plenty of Americans once survived on possums and squirrels. I was also surprised to learn that even now Americans can legally kill and eat a dog or a cat. They just can't sell the meat. *Oh, my.*

As a result, Shanghai expats were warned to watch their pets closely. Any dog not attached to a human was considered fair game. Opportunists had no qualms about selling an unattached canine or serving them up as a tasty, free meal.

When my friend Jennie's dog went missing from her yard one day, of course she suspected the worst. But the truth was a scenario no one imagined. The following day, Jennie received a ransom note—stereotypically composed of words cut from magazine pages—demanding 2000RMB (about $285)! The kidnapper stated where she should leave the money, and assured her Duke would be waiting, tied to a nearby tree. When she reported the dognapping to the Pudong police, she learned that while they *could* prosecute the thief (if found), they didn't waste their time looking for stolen dogs, because they were usually sold or eaten within hours. Jennie left, shocked, hoping poor Duke wasn't already marinating in a kitchen somewhere.

While still pondering whether to bother paying the ransom, Jennie got into the car to make a grocery run. She noticed a few tiny scraps of paper on the floor. Magazine page scraps? Her mind whirled. Then, as her driver braked hard for a sudden stop, Duke's collar slid out from under the driver's seat! Now she got it: her *driver* had kidnapped her dog! She knew then that she would get her pet back, but she'd have to play it cool to bring him safely home.

As instructed, Jennie left the ransom money in the designated spot. The next morning, indeed she found Duke tied to the tree. Then she called her driver to come to the house. When he arrived, she promptly fired him. Needless to say, her family kept very close tabs on their beloved pet going forward!

Though relieved we came to Shanghai dogless, my kids still wanted a pet. Fortunately, Carly Weiss had founded the SCAA. On their website, I found two cats that sounded like a good fit for my family. I talked to our ayi. To my delight, she had no problem with taking care of two cats and wouldn't charge us extra. So, Mr. Zhao drove the kids and me to the cats' owner's apartment in Puxi.

When we arrived, we met Etienne, a tall, dark-haired Belgian man who was relocating to Dubai. We spent the next thirty minutes chatting, while the kids and felines bonded. "Well, it looks like both the kids and the cats are happy, so I guess we'll take them," I announced.

"Great!" Etienne replied. "I'll help you get them into the carriers." And that was that. We now had two new furry family members.

On the way home from Puxi, it occurred to me: what language did these animals understand? They had a Belgian owner, who lived with a Chinese girl-friend. Flemish and Mandarin? Would they respond to English? It struck me as a very Shanghai expat thing that at about a year and a half old, the kitties were on their third language! Regardless of potential language barriers, my family enjoyed our new pets—even ayi. Starsky, Mr. Personality, left us with some memorable stories. He liked to jump up high to get the toys we placed for him. Sometimes, we put a toy or a treat on one of the lever-style door handles in our house. What the cat learned from this was that he could open the doors and let himself out of the house. At first, we thought this was cool. Then one of our neighbors, a charming Norwegian man named Karl, began asking around the street about an all-black cat. My heart skipped a beat when he revealed that Starsky had been not only letting himself out of our house, he'd been letting himself *into* Karl's.

"I'm so sorry," I said, completely embarrassed, "that sounds like our cat."

To my horror, my neighbor then calmly reported that the felonious feline helped himself to snacks in their kitchen and occasionally made off with the children's toys! "I am SO sorry!" I replied, mortified. "I'll try to make sure ayi keeps an eye on him and keeps the doors locked."

"No matter," he chuckled, good naturedly. "Don't trouble yourself. My family enjoys his visits. He is welcome any time."

I exhaled a deep sigh of relief that he reacted with such kindness.

Leave it to a kitty to figure out how to live the good life!

When we left Shanghai, we concluded—for a variety of reasons—that it would not be in our pets' best interest to bring them to the US. Naturally, I asked Karl if his family would like to adopt our cats. The Andresens had grown very fond of our crazy Starky, who now spent about half his time at their house. Thus they happily accepted. Now as the cats turned four years old, I realized they were adding a fourth language to their repertoire—Norwegian! Moving every few years and adding new languages, like their expat owners? How Shanghai!

LIFE'S A BALL, A RABBI,
DOUBLE BEIJING, & PHUKET REPEAT

In April, Planet and I planned to attend two more formal events—something else that never would have happened to me in Shaker Heights! Since all I had in formalwear was my Aussie Ball dress and my Chinese skirt and top, I actually had nothing appropriate to don for the American Chamber of Commerce (AmCham) Ball or the SAS Spring Gala. In Shanghai, Women's formalwear seemed elusive. I didn't want to risk the Dong Jia Du—always hit or miss—and for no good reason, I didn't feel like using Mrs. Wang. Hence, I paged through the *Passport to Shanghai*. A woman named Ya Cheng had strong recommendations. Why not give her a try?

On appointment day, Mr. Zhou wound down the narrow lanes of the former French Concession and into a maze of hutongs in search of Ya's house. A middle-aged Chinese woman with her black hair tied in a tidy bun and a neat housedress greeted me when I finally arrived. The seamstress, I soon discovered, had trained in Paris and spent time in Switzerland as well. I also quickly learned that Ya spoke no English. I dusted off my rusty French, reverting to my shaky Mandarin when French failed me. Frenchdarin, anyone? Nevertheless, I managed to communicate why I had come. I had seen a stunning Armani-style top at an upscale shop in XinTianDi. I wanted to copy it and add a matching skirt. Ya suggested we visit the store together.

Inside the boutique, Ya had me try on the top and then carefully examined me in it. Yes, she could not only copy it, but she seemed excited about the project. Then we returned to her house to look at fabrics and take measurements. I chose a bright blue material I thought suited me very well. The seamstress shook her head. "*Bu ke yi*," (can't) she said. I couldn't imagine what the problem was. Eventually Ya managed to express that this was *not* my color. She pulled out a fabric color wheel, then pointed out the shades she thought would flatter me. She recommended a blue-grey that I never would have chosen. I definitely appreciated Chinese honesty in this situation. Between that and her European training, I knew I should trust her.

When I picked up my formal silk skirt and blouse two weeks later, I was thrilled with both Ya and her handiwork. The color and the outfit looked great on me! Though not as convenient as Mrs. Wang, I recommended my new tailor to everyone. She was definitely worth a trip into the French Concession's mysterious hutong labyrinth.

By now, the SAS Spring Gala committee had launched into a flurry of last-minute activity. We spent the Friday before the event at the Spanish-style compound preparing the event room and prizes. It seemed unreal how easily and quickly major events were accomplished in China. The committee handily solicited plane tickets; fancy hotel stays in exotic locations like Cebu, Philippines and Phuket, Thailand; paintings; and Chinese antique-style furniture. The silent auction items included everything from oriental rugs to pearl jewelry. Instead of a raffle, guests could buy a balloon for about $5. When popped, a ticket inside revealed a smaller prize, like costume jewelry, household accessories, silk photo albums, candles, etc. When the big day arrived, we enjoyed a lovely buffet dinner, great auction action, and dancing. We also raised a substantial amount for charity. Another highly successful community service event in the books!

Soon after, I again donned the beautiful ensemble Ya Cheng had crafted for me, and Planet and I made our way to the Jin Mao Tower (our third time this year) for the AmCham Ball. We took a neighbor (also a potential client for Planet) and his wife. By this time, we had learned that most Shanghai balls ran under a similar format. The event began with an elaborate buffet dinner, followed by a keynote speaker, a silent auction, a live auction, and finally dancing.

As with most balls, this event served as a fundraiser for a local organization—this year, Shanghai's Special Olympics organization. Planet and I were pleased to do our part while enjoying another lovely evening out meeting more members of the expat community.

Jewish Life and a New Rabbi

That spring, no one seemed to know quite how to pull together a Purim event in Pudong or had the energy to try. Therefore, we skipped the holiday entirely. But on Passover, fortunately, my family found no lack of options. The Neidermeyers graciously hosted the first seder. About twenty people attended, with everyone contributing food dishes. We all felt grateful to have each other and to share this unique experience. On the second night, which we rarely ever celebrated in the US, Chava invited us to her home. She too had a crowd of about twenty, as her husband's family had journeyed from Israel for the occasion. The family members had great personalities and spoke English well, so everyone had a pleasurable and memorable time.

Apparently, among the Jews we had met recently, several had petitioned the Puxi Rabbi to work his magic and try to get a Rabbi for Pudong. Well, soon we received a minor miracle: the worldwide Chabad organization very generously sent us a Rabbi! Even better, the new Rabbi Rosenberg was Puxi Rabbi Rosenberg's brother. His wife, Rachel, it turned out, hailed from suburban Cleveland.

Motivated by appreciation, I volunteered to host a welcome party. Because my house wasn't kosher, the guest of honor planned to bring all the food. As a hostess, that felt oh so wrong! Yet, I understood the necessity. On party day, the new Rabbi sent an "advance team" to prepare my kitchen. I had no idea what that meant, until his Chinese helpers arrived and began draping aluminum foil over every surface in my kitchen!

I happily envisioned that when Rabbi arrived, he would bless our family mezuzah (a tiny scroll with certain Torah verses on it that Jews put on the doors of their homes) and install it on the doorframe of our adopted house. I would feel so much better about living here with our mezuzah finally placed.

When Rabbi arrived, he said he'd be delighted to perform our ceremony. I handed him the mezuzah. He looked at it carefully.

"No, I cannot do the ceremony," he said, handing the symbolic object back to me.

I looked at him, puzzled. "Why not?"

"Your scroll is not kosher."

What? I had no idea the scroll had to be kosher. No!

"Um, how do I get a kosher scroll?" I asked, secretly very annoyed. Though I knew he was right, it also felt wrong for him to deny the hostess something so simple.

"You have to order it from a place in California. They can be expensive," Rabbi advised. "Or I can get one from Israel, but it might take longer."

Well, that's what happens when you send an Orthodox Rabbi to lead a reform community. And that was that.

Rabbi and I made our way back into the kitchen to check on the food preparations and wait for our guests. About thirty people turned up, which seemed a good sign. As the event wrapped up, many people remarked that they liked our new clergyman and felt thankful they no longer had to trek to Puxi or hold their own services in makeshift places. We felt exhilarated to play a role in building Pudong's first Jewish community. In fact, the entire Pudong Jewish community eagerly anticipated that in two years, my friend Dena's son would be Pudong's first ever Bar Mitzvah—history in the making!

Though grateful to have our own Rabbi, a Lubavitcher serving a group of reform Jews was definitely a different experience—good and bad—than most of us were used to. One of the best parts was that he held open door Shabbat services. Any Jewish traveler who found him/herself in Shanghai on Shabbat could join Rabbi's family for dinner. What a wonderful concept! Imagine having Shabbat dinner with Jews from anywhere and everywhere in the world…in Shanghai. On the flip side, it seemed crazy that the Rabbi actually flew in a kosher butcher once a month so that the community could have kosher meat. It also seemed extravagant (and somewhat absurd) that his wife flew to Hong Kong every month for her ritual bath, since Shanghai had no mikvah.

When the high holidays arrived in fall 2006, we hoped to hold services in the beautiful old 1920s temple at the Bund, Ohel Rachel. But the government imposed so many rules and decided to charge such high tariffs, Rabbi found it impossible. What a shame—though not a big surprise. So, Rabbi cheerfully held services for dozens of worshippers from around the world at the Hotel Sofitel. Following orthodox rules, however, Rabbi set up seating for men on one side of a wooden partition and women on the other. I really did NOT like sitting apart from my husband and son. How could I complain, though? We had the privilege of attending services without spending hours in traffic.

All the parents felt fortunate that the Rabbi's wife—along with a helper or two— set up a Hebrew school for the kids. I marveled at the Rebbetzin: here she was only in her late 20s, 7,000 miles away from home, teaching her Chinese helpers to cook kosher meals, building a Jewish community in China, pregnant with her third child, and teaching Hebrew school on top of it all! Although this brave young woman's life couldn't have been easy, she set a good example, and I appreciated her boundless positive energy.

As our new Hebrew school had only seven students that year, it had a cozy, private school vibe. The kids got significant personal attention for the language study lessons and found the workbook fun. Fortunately, they also enjoyed the religious studies. The Rebbetzin had a genius token economy, where the kids could earn raffle dollars for good behavior and progress in their studies. At the end of class, they could buy prizes. Alexis earned a bag of Israeli potato chips one week, and Anders purchased some Israeli candy. As if all this wasn't excellent enough, the best part was that the classes were held at SCIS, the school in The Pearl compound. Hebrew school had come to us!

With Rachel's arrival, our community also founded a Rosh Chodesh (women's friendship and learning) group. We rotated meetings among each other's houses, enjoying getting to know each other, learning, making arts and crafts projects, and sometimes just enjoying an in-home spa night together. I felt fortunate to now have a Jewish social life similar to the one I had enjoyed in Shaker Heights.

The Beijing Antiquing Trip

In early April, eleven SEA members—including Bonnie Douglas and I—set off on a rare shopping-in-Beijing adventure organized by Carly Weiss. Our shopping bonanza weekend began at one of her Tibetan carpet sources. From the City, we drove for about an hour to a multi-room shop where we spent about four hours enthusiastically watching several young men flip through piles of brightly colored tribal designs, both new and antique. Some of us had difficulty choosing from so many alluring choices, but eventually everyone came away with a carpet, or two, or three…or more. Thinking this was a unique opportunity, I bought a traditional Tibetan lion rug and a supposedly rare blue cloud rug for Anders' room, a red tribal patterned rug for Planet's and my home office, and a blue and white Tibetan lion rug for the master bedroom dressing room. I couldn't wait to get my textiles back to Shanghai to liven up the house and make it feel more like my own.

About a week later, the carpets arrived at my house and I unrolled them. I stood there, shocked by the layers of ground-in filth. They looked like they had been ferried here by camel through a Beijing dust storm! As I unwrapped the blue and white lion rug, I discovered sizable dark stains in two of the corners. The room where we had shopped was dimly lit, but still, I think I would have noticed these blemishes. When I unbound the patterned rug for Planet's office, I spied a pink stain in one corner. What in the world happened to these rugs? Had we shoppers had been tricked in the showroom, or had the transportation company ruined the rugs enroute to Shanghai? Anything seemed possible. Complaining to the rug vendor was probably futile, so I simply sent the carpets out for cleaning.

Given the Chinese's excellent reputation for cleaning, I couldn't have been more surprised by the results. The blue lion rug returned with the stains darkened, plus white spots where the cleaner had tried to remove some other stains I hadn't even seen! The pink stain on the red tribal rug remained exactly the same. Only the blue cloud rug looked clean. What now? I guessed I'd just have to get the rugs worked on again when we returned to the US. *Grr!*

In the same shop where we bought rugs, the SEA group also shopped for Thangkas like I'd seen in Carly's apartment. As our group browsed through the brightly painted canvases, two of them caught my eye. I purchased these treasures, and back in Shanghai, I hung one Thangka in the office. The other found a home in the foyer. Between the rugs and the art, bit by bit, our rental house grew a little homier.

That evening, our tour guide extraordinaire treated us to another one-of-a-kind experience: a thirty-minute tour of Beijing's main historic district in

Madame Mao's own 1970s Red Flag limousine! I could hardly believe we were really cruising the neon-lit streets of Beijing in this four-wheeled piece of history. Carly explained that this iconic vehicle was now owned by and displayed at the Red Capital Club—a notable restored historic courtyard residence, whose restaurant had recently earned a place on Conde Nast's "sixty hot tables for the millennium" list. In the club-style room where we sipped our aperitifs, waiting as we took turns riding in the car, signs on some of the chairs warned guests not to get comfy in them. Purportedly, the ghost of Marshall Lin Biao occasionally showed up and didn't take kindly to finding someone else's tush parked in his favorite seat. *Ha, ha.*

Our dinner plans didn't include the uber-trendy Red Capital Club dining room, however. Instead, our evening's grand finale took place at the Grand Hyatt, where we enjoyed a nine-course meal starring Peking duck and beggar's chicken. I felt indulged watching as the waiter hammered the beggar's chicken open, the lotus leaves releasing an appetizing licorice fragrance, before we tucked into the tender, flavorful meat. I normally don't care for duck, but as the Hyatt chef prepared it, I could easily have eaten seconds of the succulent delicacy.

The next morning, the group rose early to visit one of Carly's antique Tibetan furniture sources. Of special interest there were hard-to-find document carriers and cabinets. At the warehouse, I gave the goods my "would it fly in Ohio?" test. If I couldn't picture it looking fabulous in my Shaker Heights home or liking it ten years from now, I passed on the item. I watched as the rest of the group went crazy over the cabinets. In the meantime, one of the Guy Tais discovered a creepy tribal headdress covered with Barbie-doll-head-sized, manufactured skulls. He popped it on and lurked around the warehouse in it, sneaking up on unsuspecting ladies while we shopped. They were generally not amused.

Since none of the furniture or accessories passed my purchaseability test, I focused on small accent pieces. I left with a red document case adorned with the Tibetan lion, plus three hand-painted drums. I entertained ideas about placing a round piece of glass atop the largest drum, turning it into a conversation-piece side table. When everyone had finished paying for their treasures, we moved on to our night's lodging. We relaxed and chatted in the van for about an hour until we arrived outside the Red Capital Ranch (same owner as the Red Capital Club). Carly picked up her mobile phone and made a call. Moments later, two young women clothed in long, brightly colored traditional Tibetan dresses scurried out to open the mammoth wooden entrance gates. The van rolled into the estate, which looked like a small village, complete with a miniature river running between the main lodge and the ten individual guest villas. A segment of the magnificent Great Wall towered above this exceptional property.

The driver deposited us at a Manchurian-style hunting lodge, which housed the reception desk, the restaurant, and the cozy Tibetan Tiger Lounge. As we waited our turn to check in, the young Tibetan girls served us tea while Carly explained that the property originally belonged to a local warlord. In more recent history, her friend had brought his own, modernized vision of the property to life here.

After check in, we each explored our own intensely charming stone and wood, feng-shui décor villas. Each accommodation had been carefully named after a natural element—such as lake, wind, or thunder—and a plaque outside each door detailed its special powers. I sucked in the fresh, country air, so revitalizing after big city pollution. I felt very cozy in my little cabin and relished the tasteful blend of trendy and natural in the stone bathroom while I showered. How exciting to spend the night in the shadow of the Great Wall, I thought as I soaped up and imagined life here in a bygone era.

That evening, we gathered before the Tibetan Tiger lounge's floor-to-ceiling windows to enjoy a fantastic sunset over the Wall, while the fireplace logs crackled in the background and a young Tibetan lady came around to give us brief foot massages. We sipped hot cider spiked with rum and contemplated whether we were actually in Shangri-La, rather than just an hour outside Beijing.

We tore ourselves away from the fireplace with difficulty. Yet, no one wanted to miss the multi-course Tibetan meal next on our agenda, since none of us had ever tasted this cuisine. At dinner, some of the more interesting dishes included mountain grasses with peanuts, deer satay, and deep-fried white bean paste with crispy white noodles in honey sauce.

That night, I slept like a newborn in this unique and refreshing setting. In the morning, I woke to a large, country breakfast that included impressively fresh, delicious homemade yogurt and granola. After the meal, about half the group wanted to hang around the property, but the rest of us set off for a quick trip to the legendary Wall. As Carly informed us, though the Wall was accessible from the Ranch, the section was very steep, and it might take us an hour and a half just to climb up the hillside before reaching the hiking portion. As a result, our hostess hired a van to drive us to the well-known Ba Da Ling section instead.

We opted to take the cable cars both up and down in the interest of time. Rumor held that this section of the wall was the less crowded and less touristy. Indeed, we seemed to have the place almost to ourselves. We found the section in excellent shape and the views truly outstanding. We only had about forty-five minutes to explore, but it proved enough, as this section was also very steep. As we happily hiked and snapped photos in the warm April sun, I felt awestruck by this architectural marvel, stunningly accented at the moment by a backdrop of white dogwood trees in full bloom. I fantasized that next year I'd join the group of Shanghai runners tackling the Great Wall Marathon.

On return from the Wall, our whole group set out for the last stop on our shopping tour. Today's adventure was a Ch'ing Dynasty (1644-1911) reproduction furniture source near the city. The government had decreed that only items made after 1911 could leave the country, so we couldn't purchase real antiques. Nobody seemed to mind, maybe because reproductions would be just as nice and considerably cheaper. As we cruised through the site, most of the cabinets, altar tables, chairs and looked like the standard fare found throughout Shanghai, and the prices smacked of expat gouging. Nevertheless, a few of the ladies bought several pieces. Nothing I saw, however, passed my test.

Two elements rendered this portion of the trip notable, however: dogs and the toilet. As is common in Asia, the furniture venue consisted of several buildings set up in a U-shape with a courtyard in the middle. In the dusty enclosure, someone had set up a large kennel, attempting to raise and sell German Shepherds. A man saw me resting in the sun, contemplating why the dogs were there while I waited for our group to finish shopping. He made a beeline over to me. He'd sell me a dog for only 8,000RMB (about $1,000!), he enthusiastically informed me. I nearly laughed aloud, the price was so outrageous! Remaining polite, I smiled and replied, "*bu yao, shi shi*" (no thanks). Owning a dog as a pet was growing fashionable now for wealthy Chinese. I wondered how much he'd ask a native to pay for a dog.

As the disappointed pet breeder shuffled off, I realized I needed the bathroom. I wandered toward the back of the compound, where I encountered a man who pointed me toward a brick shed. As I walked, the foul stench grew stronger with each step—clearly an impending "China moment!" I peered inside the hut, but couldn't make out anything resembling a toilet. Of course, the shed had no electricity, and only a few rays of daylight streamed in from the small hole cut into the door. Holding my breath, I waited for my eyes to adjust. There it was: a round hole in the ground, about half the size of a toilet bowl, with a wooden lid covering it. Nervously, I gripped the toilet cover's protruding long wooden handle. There was no telling what might lurk inside…a snake? Rats?

I prayed nothing would take a bite of my rear as I proceeded with my business. I finished and turned toward the hole to replace the lid. Then I saw them. Pigs! The facility emptied out into a pig pen, and the animals had gathered for the…feast! I guessed that whatever solid waste the swine didn't devour, the farmer used for fertilizer. Neither presented a particularly attractive picture. Well, I respected that nothing went to waste in rural China. But for me, this was definitely one of those times when I certainly would have much preferred a well-placed bush! Out I ran, sucking in fresh air as fast as possible, making my way back to our group. And with that, our wonderful, unique Beijing antiques adventure drew to an end.

Return to Beijing

I returned to Beijing the very next weekend. Only in Tai Tai life, right? This time, my family and I toured the city with our charming new Korean friends, the Parks, whom we'd met in Bali over winter break. Dan and Ka Hee had heard that the overnight train from Shanghai to Beijing was a fun low-budget experience. Dan and Planet thought the kids would love it. Hence, on the appointed evening, we met the Park family at Puxi's main rail station. We didn't have to wait long to board the two private sleeper cars we reserved. The kids buzzed excitedly as we settled in. Each family had brought part of our picnic dinner. The Parks provided some delicious Kim Bap, and we contributed several types of salads. While we ate, the kids figured out the sleeping arrangements: Anders and Diana with us, Rebecca and Alexis with Dan and Ka Hee. After dinner, the kids went to their respective cars to cozy up for the remainder of the approximately twelve-hour trip.

We had been warned that the more hours into the trip we waited to use the bathroom, the fouler it would become. Thus, we made sure the kids used the facility before bed. When I ventured in for a late-night pit stop, I had to work around mysterious puddles and tissue paper lining the floor—the rumors held true. Fortunately, the rest of the trip flew by smoothly, with no drama in either car. We arrived at the Beijing train station about 8:00 am, feeling reasonably rested and anxious to start our adventure.

The first order of business was to taxi over to the Grand Hyatt to drop off our luggage, then meet up with the driver Planet had arranged for us through his office. We exchanged pleasantries with Mr. Yu and explained that our first stop today was the fabled Summer Palace. Once there, we took in the jaw-dropping, colorfully decorated rooms, elegant furniture, and remarkable artifacts. We even found a place where the kids could dress up in old royal robes and headdresses, while we parents snapped away with our cameras.

As we made our way over to the lake to rent a boat, we noticed the throngs of Chinese tourists, finally allowed to enjoy a foray into their own history. But they noticed us, too. Suddenly, it seemed, everyone wanted a piece of Anders. Every few feet some family wanted to have their photo taken with my blue-eyed, platinum-tressed child, or some grandmother stretched out a hand to determine for herself whether his wild, curly blond mane was real and if it indeed felt like silk. The more Chinese tourists fussed, the more upset my son grew. We had heard that Westerners with big, round, blue eyes and blond hair received a great deal of attention in Asia, but this seemed beyond normal. Finally, even I grew concerned, as we had hardly made any progress toward the lake.

My developing "Chinese" mentality caused me to begin harboring visions of charging gawkers 10RMB to take a photo and 20RMB to touch his hair. Instead, the Parks proposed a better idea. They arranged our group in a protective shield formation surrounding Anders. The Chinese tourists still gaped, but remained mostly deterred from turning Anders into the latest side attraction. Now, we easily reached the lake and managed to spend the rest of the afternoon boating around without incident.

When we returned to the hotel, Planet got directions to the legendary Peking Duck restaurant, Li Qun, that his work colleagues had recommended. Getting to this establishment constituted an adventure in itself. We walked along city streets until we came to the designated hutongs. At last we had come to the tricky section, winding our way through the nameless alleys without any familiar landmarks (though I'm told that nowadays, cute duck drawings on the walls mark the way). Along the way, a multitude of rickshaw men tried their best to get us to buy a ride with them. We had been tipped off that these were con artists, who, if they didn't simply charge an outrageous sum, would bring the unsuspecting to some other restaurant and assure them *it* was Li Qun. Thankfully, we had been given good directions and Dan's Chinese was excellent. We reached our destination without any issues.

Though the rich and famous frequented the place—photos of politicians and diplomats from around the world lined the walls—the décor appeared strictly no frills. The white plaster building stood crammed to overflowing with basic dining tables; patrons; and bustling, matter-of-fact waiters. Across from the entrance, a wood fire blazed, over which ten plump ducks crackled and dripped. A bucket full of drippings lay neglected in one corner of the cooking area. Planet and I felt excited that our very own Anthony Bourdain moment had arrived!

Our two families got settled at our table and then got down to the serious business of eating. Encouraged after last week's experience at the Hyatt Beijing, I had to try the duck here. Maybe I'd become a fan. I placed some meat in a paper-thin pancake, then added a dash of scallions and a dollop of delicate plum sauce. I rolled it all up and popped the treat into my mouth. Delicious!

My kids had never tasted duck, yet Alexis enjoyed her "pancake," and Anders actually downed three helpings. In addition to the main course, Dan ordered several other dishes, ensuring everyone would have a chance to sample other local-favorites. This meal proved some of the best Chinese food I had ever eaten. It seemed amazing that eight of us shared a duck, about six other dishes, and drinks, for about $20! (Sadly, I'm told that Li Qun is now overrun with expats and tourists, and the prices and staff attitudes have changed accordingly.)

After dinner, we took the kids for a quick swim before bed. The magnificent hotel pool area resembled a tropical jungle river, complete with a series of massive stone columns anchoring the sides, plentiful palm trees and ferns, and Polynesian-style white stone statues. Some of the columns had rock formations, while others had fountains. The low lighting changed colors every few minutes, so the ceiling resembled an amazing sunset. We could easily have been walking into a movie set or a themed hotel in Las Vegas. At any moment, we half expected crocodiles and an explorer's river boat to show up. The hot tub, also notable, lay bubbling under a rocky overhang, as though it were a lava or quicksand pit hidden in a secret cave. The kids went wild over this water wonderland. While they played, we adults relaxed, savoring the excellent chocolate pastries the Parks had brought along from their favorite Japanese bakery in Shanghai.

In the morning we made short work of the Hyatt's outstanding brunch buffet, as we needed an early start. Mr. Yu arrived right on time to drive us to the Mu Tian Yu section of the Great Wall. Even on a Sunday morning, impressively-thick traffic clogged the roads, and it took us nearly two hours to get there. As we tumbled out of the minivan, we discovered the steep uphill hike to the entrance. All along the way, vendors called out from their little tents, hawking all manner of touristy mementos. Finally, we reached the Wall entrance. We walked nearly an hour in one direction, in awe of this stone fortress. Several times we found ourselves facing amazingly steep steps. We were getting quite a workout as we explored forts and lookout towers, gazing out at the beautiful landscape and Dogwood trees in full fuchsia blossom. I thought back to my Sunday jogs in Shaker Heights: I never would have imagined I'd one day take a Sunday stroll on the Great Wall!

As we made our way back down, the kids spied a luge. They mysteriously grew much too tired to walk any more. Sliding back down to the base of the  park looked like fun, so the adults gave in. The luge route appeared long and relatively steep, yet we practically we had to pull a Fred Flintstone, pushing our sleds along with our feet and hands to keep them moving. As we neared the bottom, two savage-looking men dressed in Mongolian warrior costumes popped out of the bushes, emitting fierce roars, nearly scaring me out of my skin. Quickly they made it known they wanted 20RMB for guests to take a photo with them. We passed on that opportunity.

On the return trip to Beijing, traffic had died down significantly, leaving us plenty of time for our next stop, the Forbidden City. Thankfully, Anders received no celebrity attention there, and we wandered unhindered among the multitude of splendid buildings, opulent rooms and majestic courtyards, contemplating China's amazing history. Here, our busy weekend in the capital city drew to a contented close, and we caught an evening flight back to Shanghai.

Even the Best Laid Plans...

Clearly, travel remained a staple of Asian expat life. When spring break arrived, I looked forward to exploring more of Asia. Friends kept telling me how much they loved a place called Kota Kinnabalu in Sabah, Malaysia (Borneo). In addition to the natural beauty and interesting culture, Sabah remained the only place in the world with two orangutan rescue refuges. I thought the kids would love it. Since it was our first year abroad, however, I didn't know how quickly flights out of Shanghai booked up or that travel plans sometimes brought surprises.

I spent a few afternoons researching Kota Kinnabalu and excitedly booked our trip. But then American Embassy travel advisory emails spread doom and gloom, the negativity mushrooming as dark and thick as the clouds in the Shanghai skyline. According to the Embassy, terrorist groups—most likely

Philippine Muslim rebels—planned attacks on places frequented by tourists and potentially intended to kidnap tourists. An epiphany struck me: Americans are incredibly privileged: in the US our trips are spoiled usually only by the most mundane of reasons. When Americans head off to Florida, we rarely have to worry about hurricanes; if we zip off to Montreal, we're unconcerned about a potential crowd of *fleur de lis* protestors; potential subway bombings while we take in a Broadway show generally aren't on our radar. Here in Asia, however, serious risks seemed more a part of daily life. In this part of the world, disasters (like the tsunami of 2004) and political unrest (like the bombing in Bali) regularly derailed trips. Now, I fretted. Though the rebels supposedly targeted the more remote areas of Sabah, what if they *did* plan to attack the more touristy areas, as they had in Kuta, Bali? I decided I shouldn't take a chance.

As a result, I needed to develop a Plan B before the flights out of Shanghai for spring break were all booked. What to do? Planet and I discussed the issue until we finally arrived at a conclusion. Since we had enjoyed our time in Phuket, Thailand so much, why not take the kids back for another week?

During our second vacation to Phuket, thankfully, nothing eventful happened. One thing we learned, however, was that the expatriate world gets increasingly smaller the longer you remain part of it. Noelle Hamburger called to say her family was going. But since we were leaving after they were, could her driver drop off some fabric market purchases for me to bring along for her? Every time we went to the beach or the pool, we ran into at least one family that we knew from our compound, from SAS, from the expatriate organizations, or from Planet's company. In a way, it felt reassuring to actually know other travelers. I liked chatting with familiar people and having readily available playmates for the kids. On the other hand, occasionally I wanted a complete break from everything that made up my Shanghai Tai Tai life. Sometimes I just didn't feel like having to socialize; I just wanted to relax with my family, read, and decompress. But that's the way the fortune cookie crumbled on this side of the Pacific.

章
18

COMMUNITY SERVICE, CHINESE JUSTICE, & IMPENDING SUMMER

By spring, my confidence in community service grew, and I found myself volunteering to chair SAS's Teacher Appreciation lunch. It felt great to have a vision for an event and find approval for implementing it.

First, I asked teachers to have the pre-K and Kindergarten students make placemats. I assigned other grades to bring in flower arrangements to decorate the tables. The kids brought in so many flowers that we gave away sixty-two bouquets to the teachers—way more than expected! I arranged for the orchestra to provide music, and the parents kindly brought in most of the food. Of course, what would a Shanghai event be without shopping? Eight parents set up booths selling various gift items.

I found organizing the event a significant amount of work, but it was a well-deserved labor of love for the teachers. The event came off beautifully, and I was glad I played the leadership role. Early on, I learned that anything the expat community wanted done, they had to do themselves. Nearly everyone had to contribute in order for clubs, activities, and events to succeed. Now, I saw that volunteering was also essential to enjoying life in Shanghai. The more I got involved, the better I felt about living there.

Naturally, life kept moving at its whirlwind pace. Before I could blink, elections for next year's PTSA board were announced. Nothing was ever apolitical, and with several key board members moving on from the city, everyone waited to see who would run. Well, I knew what I wanted, and I moved fearlessly forward. I quickly found myself elected communications VP. I gravitate toward this position whenever I'm new in town because it allows me to quickly learn what's going on in the school and the city and to immediately make acquaintances with a variety of people. The Vice President role was undertaken by a charming lady from Hong Kong named Happy Hong. After the election, however, the Board still needed a President, a Treasurer, and a Secretary I panicked. How would two of us handle the work of an entire board until others stepped into these roles? People told me not to worry, but I thought they were crazy.

"Sometimes you just have to wait and see who shows up in the fall," the PTSA moms said. Others said people were waiting to see if their friends would sign up. Hmm. The revolving door and the clique thing again. Well, Happy and I had no choice but to wait and see.

Chinese Justice—A New Mindset

The Chinese sense of justice and ethics seemed both vastly different and unpredictable to my Western sensibilities. Fortunately, the country enjoyed a very low crime rate, which consisted mostly of pick pocketing and minor stealing. Perhaps a holdover from the traditional social organization, with local governments and leaders having jurisdiction over their small territories, any type of formal legal system seemed non-existent. Laws seemed to exist, made up on the spot, to benefit only Chinese citizens in any given situation. People were also tried by juries of their peers at accident or crime scenes, not so different from social media judgment in Westernized countries. Fortunately, Planet and I heard about local scams and how to avoid them from friends and from the American Embassy newsletters. The few experiences I had with Chinese crime and justice, however, made me glad to be American—even though our country seemed grossly over-legislated in contrast.

My first experience happened at MegaFit. I wasn't a fan of the hair dryers provided in the gym locker room. Their power was so wimpy I could have drunk an entire cup of tea and taken a nap in the time it took my hair to dry. So, I brought my own device. One Friday morning, I accidentally left it there.

My friends felt sure my dryer—like anything else—would be long gone, stolen. When I went back on Monday, however, and asked at the desk for it, a clerk said they actually had it.

The now frightened-looking desk clerk called the security guy over. They began asking me questions. What color was it? *Oh, good grief! Who remembers ridiculous details like this?* I racked my brain…dark grey with some bright green? Apparently, I got the grey part right, sort of. It was actually silver (close enough) and white. The clerk looked at the security agent, who nodded. She handed me back my hair dryer.

When I shared this story, my veteran expat friends surprised me by saying that if I had provided *completely* the wrong color, the guard or front desk ladies could have justified taking the dryer home themselves. *Whose mind works that way?* I had just learned that the rules about finders/keepers had some unusual twists here. Another time I opened up my gym locker to discover someone had left a very nice watch. It never occurred to me that I shouldn't bring it to the front desk, where I assumed they had a lost and found. But friends who heard the story tsk tsked.

"The staff will sell that in a heartbeat and swear they never saw it!" they opined.

Well, what should I have done? Apparently, the solution was to put the word out on the Tai Tai grapevine and/or place an ad in an expat paper to find the owner. OK. Another lesson learned.

During our second year in Shanghai, my friend Jennie Kowalski moved into a new house in a largely still-under-construction new development in Jin Qiao. Her younger daughter unwisely left her scooter in the driveway one day. Come early evening, Jennie's husband, Sam, just happened to look out the kitchen window and saw a truck pull over. Out jumped a construction worker. Quick as lightning, he snatched the scooter, tossed it in the back, and took off. Sam flew out the door and chased down the truck, shouting loudly. The workers knew they'd been caught red-handed. The truck pulled over and the much-embarrassed thief had no choice but to return the item. But lesson not learned. The Kowalski's son had a nice skateboard ramp. It was awkwardly large and heavy enough that they decided not to lug it in and out of the garage on a daily basis. After all, it wouldn't be something a construction worker could just toss onto a truck in seconds flat. One morning, however, the skateboard ramp vanished. The moral of the story: Chinese construction workers will steal *anything* they can find a way to move. The only surprise here was that it took them more than a day to figure out how to pilfer it.

I, of course, experienced my own theft situation. One spring day, I attended an SAS Spring Gala meeting at another compound's restaurant. From there, I went to the popular Dragon Fly Spa for a massage. Relaxed and happy from my excellent day, I reached into my purse, planning to phone Mr. Zhao to come get me. I shuffled. No phone. I rifled. No phone? One more scrounge. No phone!

I told the front desk woman that I needed to look around the massage area because my phone was missing. She let me. It wasn't there. I told her to ask the masseuse. Of course, *she* hadn't seen it. By now I was so irritated that I allowed myself to go "ugly American" on Miss Front Desk.

"Give. Me. My. Phone. Back. NOW!" I hissed, sinister as the Wicked Witch of the West.

She returned a quintessential Chinese poker-faced blank stare.

I glared daggers back.

"My PHONE. Go and get it from the masseuse and her accomplice. NOW!" I barked, with all the drama I could muster.

"Madame, we don't have your phone. Please leave your name for the manager," she replied, calmly and coolly.

I left my name, home number, and cell number.

In the meantime, I found Zhao napping in the Chrysler in the Jade Leisure Center parking lot. I explained to him what had happened and asked him to drive me back to the place where I'd had lunch. While we drove, I used his phone to call the restaurant to say that I'd lost my mobile and told them exactly where I'd been sitting. When I arrived, the hostess said they hadn't found it, but I was welcome to look. I scoured the booth. On my return to the parking lot to find Zhao, I had an epiphany: if my phone *had* been there, my phone call had told someone exactly where to find it! I cursed myself for thinking like a newbie instead of an Old China Hand! The next day, I received a phone call from someone higher up the food chain at Dragon Fly. The woman interrogated me sharply. Then she accused me of "changing my story" and hung up in a huff. The Dragon Fly staff had now added insult to injury. But the story didn't end there. A few days later, I received another call from someone in an even higher position than the first caller. This woman treated me even worse. She acted like *I* was the criminal.

"You change your story every time!" She insisted, rather loudly for a Chinese.

Now I was so angry I could have taken on a Tibetan tiger. Clearly, I wasn't going to get my phone back, and I now understood that these calls allowed the company to absolve themselves and save face. At this point, I just wanted the fiasco to end.

But no. I received a third and final call from the spa chain. This woman had the nerve to ask, "Why did you bring a valuable item like a phone with you?" *What!* What adult on Planet Earth is *ever* without a phone? The situation had grown absurd. Now she was basically calling me, in a subtle Chinese way, stupid. Then she, too, launched into the "you keep changing your story" strategy. I would never get my phone back; Dragon Fly would never admit they harbored a thief or buy me a new phone. Finally, that was that.

As I shared my story, expat friends told me that the Chinese find nothing wrong with stealing. Their philosophy is that if you're dumb enough to be stolen from, you deserve it. Strangely, there also seemed to be a warped kind of logic behind clothing pilfering and grocery money skimming. Chastain's wife, Madeline, noticed that her ayi made off with a pair of her jeans. When Madeline confronted her, the ayi said, very matter-of-factly, "but you had five pairs." Somehow, it seemed rational in the ayi's mind. Since no one *needs* more than one pair, and my friend had an outrageous five pairs, why should she mind ayi taking a pair? Amazingly, Madeline said she knew of several other women whose ayis had helped themselves to their clothing items using the same type of rationale. Tai Tais also discussed how since there were no receipts at the fresh markets, we'd never know definitively how much our ayis spent buying our fruits and vegetables. The standard practice was for the ayi to say she spent less than she did and pocket a few RMB for herself. When opportunity knocked, I guess, they just couldn't resist. Based on this information, I found the new mindset I had to learn distasteful.

Bittersweet

The end of the international school year brought a mixture of stress, relief, and sadness. Families busily prepared to return to their home countries for the summer, which was a little hard on all the kids. Alexis and Anders wouldn't be going to summer camp with their friends, like they did in Shaker Heights, and they wouldn't see their Shanghai buddies again until August. In some cases, the kids wouldn't see their friends at all, as a percentage of families finished up their Shanghai tenure in June. Thankfully, all the expat kids stayed in touch with friends around the world through Facebook and the Club Penguin game.

The Tai Tai crew shopped and attended closing, thank you, or bon voyage events; collected gifts for friends and family at home; and squeezed in quick last visits with friends. At year's end, the meaning of friendship stared everyone down. It was the season to give thanks for the people who had shaped your life that year and to feel curious about those who would magically appear the next fall, starting the mad college freshman cycle all over again.

I couldn't believe how much I had learned and survived since August. It seemed such a crazy life, and yet, I was slowly growing comfortable with its complexities. Still, I couldn't wait to escape back to the US, back to a life that was familiar and low stress!

章
19

THE SHANGHAI ANTIDOTE

In nearly every Shanghai expat family, the wives and children returned to their home countries for the summer while the husbands remained on the job in China. Many expats needed to spend a certain number of weeks or months per year in their home country to maintain citizenship. Others said that Shanghai was simply much too hot, too humid, and too boring in the summer. Really, there was almost nothing for the kids to do and no one there to hang out with. Everyone seemed glad to visit with family and briefly enjoy their homelands.

After spending the school year in a Chinese city of 17 million, I felt determined to spend our first summer back in the US somewhere that represented the complete antithesis of that environment. Though I would have loved to return to my house in Shaker and have the kids attend their regular summer camp, Planet had insisted on selling our house and cars and leaving Ohio permanently. As a result, I could spend the holiday in any town, anywhere. So, I chose Nantucket and Martha's Vineyard. I had never been to the two legendary Massachusetts islands, and they seemed like the perfect antidote to my mega-metropolis blues.

As you know, air travel isn't often a joy, but sometimes the reasons are unexpected. On the three-hour flight from Shanghai to Tokyo, the kids and I sat behind a Chinese family whose infant cried non-stop the entire flight—no exaggeration. I breathed a sigh of relief when we landed and headed for our next flight. Soon, we boarded the flight to Detroit and got comfortably settled in our seats. Just then, who should we see taking their seats in the row directly in front of us, again? No! The same exact family who sat in front of us on the last flight! Except this time, they proved they had only given us a small taste of the hell they could unleash. As soon as the flight took off, the infant began to bawl. It seemed physically impossible, but this baby wailed the entire way to Detroit, except for a single two-hour interval, when, mercifully, he napped. With the infant finally asleep, I looked forward to some peace. But the approximately ten-year-old boy sat awake watching movies. He didn't just laugh, he shrieked loudly and hysterically, as though enjoying an amusement park ride. In the meantime, the mother had smuggled a smelly, dried fish in her carry on. When she whipped it out for the family to snack on, we nearly gagged as the briny stench drifted toward us. And let's not forget the father's contribution. He had to be the one contributing the death farts wafting in a noxious cloud above our seats for at least half the trip.

Thirteen hellish hours later, as glad as I was to be back on US soil, I didn't land in the best mood. Now, half dead from sleep deprivation and noise and air pollution on the plane, we still had to fly from the Motor City to Boston. From Boston, we would rent a car and drive about an hour and a half to my in-laws' home in Worcester, Massachusetts, spending a few days with them before traveling on to the Cape.

With the kids and their grandparents happily re-connected, we went on to enjoy two weeks of pure Heaven in Nantucket in a wonderful, old, sea captain's grey salt-box house. As I lay in bed in the master bedroom, I gazed out the enormous picture window. I felt tremendous joy at the view—nothing but blue-green ocean. If I opened the window, I could take in the wonderful, soothing sound of waves crashing and inhale the fresh salty air. One night, I watched a thunderstorm create an incredible light show—thrilling! I felt my Shanghai stress melting away.

While on the island, the kids attended sailing day camp. (Finally, water that wasn't polluted and off limits!) While I waited for them, I spent my time reading, walking on the beach, and biking the myriad trails—basically healing from the year's traumas and trials. I couldn't have been happier and wondered how other people grooved on the "energy" of major cities. I felt incredibly thankful to be on a peaceful, charming island. The fewer the people I saw, the better.

The kids quickly made friends at camp. One night, the mother of a brother-sister pair the kids befriended invited us to dinner. On the weekend, we let the kids have a sleepover. I thought many people might envy that mother's life. Her husband worked for a major investment bank in New York City. In addition to their home in the city, they had a large, homey "cottage" on the island. The mom and kids lived on Nantucket all summer, while the dad flew in for the weekends. This mother had the best of both worlds—city and country—and the wealth to get the most out of both. So, it surprised me when she remarked that she envied *my* life. It was "more interesting."

After two idyllic weeks, the kids and I drove our rental car onto the ferry back to the mainland. From there, we caught another ferry to Martha's Vineyard. There, we spent two outstandingly pleasant weeks on a small sheep farm, belonging to an aunt of Planet's work colleague. The owner allowed the kids to give the animals their breakfast, which they adored. During the day, Alexis and Anders attended an arts camp run by a delightful aging hippie. Though vastly different from the sheer physicality of sailing camp, the kids liked the games and learning various art techniques. It's possible, however, that Anders enjoyed the tire swing in camp director's yard more than learning to paint or decoupage. I thought about how none of this was happening in Shanghai—ever!—and felt glad for the kids to have these experiences to balance their other life.

Planet, his parents, and his sister came out to join us for a week over July 4. We all agreed the Edgartown Independence Day parade showed some of the best small-town spirit we'd ever seen. Throughout the week, Planet and I absolutely loved biking the island's trails and shopping the farmers-market-style small grocery stores for fresh fruits and vegetables. No sending ayi to haggle, and hooray for the USDA! We also loved buying fresh fish for dinner down at the pier—no sending Mr. Zhou to the market or trying to figure out how to translate fish names.

One day while we were driving the kids home from camp, we saw a typical road sign—"Xing". Alexis had never noticed one before.

"Mommy, why does that sign say 'shing?' We're in America!" she asked.

Great question! I felt proud that my kids had become excellent observers of the world around them. I loved how Alexis' comment revealed her blending and analysis of the two worlds she now straddled. I complimented her, then I explained with a giant grin on my face that in the US, "Xing" meant a crossing.

When our time in Martha's Vineyard ended, we reluctantly said goodbye to the sheep and the lovely town. Next, we flew to Colorado. We spent a week hiking and biking at Beaver Creek, where I cherished the sheer majesty of the mountains, the lush meadows, rushing streams, and pounding waterfalls. I breathed the sweet, incredibly fresh air. I never took Colorado air for granted, but after a year in Shanghai, it meant more than ever. *Recycle, lungs, recycle!* I listened carefully to the energetic sounds of rushing water, the animals, and the night. The sheer number of visible stars in the night sky amazed us. *How would I ever leave this magical place? How did anyone manage to live anywhere else? Shanghai was so NOT me!*

Following our week in Beaver Creek, Planet had to return to Shanghai for work, and the kids and I spent our last two weeks in St. Paul, Minnesota visiting my family. Soon, the day I had been dreading arrived. Though I believed my summer spent absorbing nature rejuvenated me enough to handle another year in China, it just made me sad. I lost it in front of the kids and cried for nearly an hour as our Asia-bound flight left Minneapolis airspace, kicking off year two in the Middle Kingdom.

章
20

FALL, ROUND TWO

When we returned to Shanghai in August 2006, I hit the ground running. First on my list, preparing for the PTSA kick-off meeting. That fall, SAS enrolled a whopping 150 new families—enough students to finally add grade 11. That also meant that the following year, we would have enough students to complete the school with grade 12. This good news saved a number of my neighbors from having to send their high school kids all the way down to the Puxi campus and endure the challenges of having kids on two different campuses. The increased enrollment also meant that Happy Hong and I had to gear up for a larger-than-usual first PTSA meeting. My partner argued her English wasn't good enough and she didn't like public speaking, so I found myself default MC. We booked the cafeteria, laid out our agenda, and expected about seventy-five parents to show up.

On meeting day, however, the people just kept coming. By start time, about 125 parents had packed themselves like sardines into the now way-too-small room! I had never addressed a crowd that large, but the meeting went very smoothly. Well enough, in fact, that within the next month we recruited a President. What a relief! And as soon the other moms observed that our new President, Hollee, was a competent, likable, veteran leader (she had recently moved from Manila, Philippines, where she chaired the American Women's Club), we filled the remainder of the board positions quickly. From this experience, I learned "wait until fall and see" *was* a Shanghai PTSA thing.

Of course, the PTSA had no shortage of excellent events planned for the 2006-2007 school year. Over the past year I had grown comfortable with living a life of community service and more confident. Somehow, I had developed a vision for the Fall BBQ. Though I wondered if I might be insane, I volunteered to chair this enormous, flagship event. In addition, I couldn't wait to participate in Santa's Workshop again and possibly some other events, too.

After the PTSA kick-off meeting, Dena Morgan, who was new to SAS sought me out. She was an American with three kids (her daughter was in Anders' class that year) and also a new member of the Pudong Jewish community. Someone had told her to introduce herself, and I was soon glad. She and I remained friends throughout my time in Shanghai and had many excellent Tai Tai adventures.

Our year was also off to a great start in the Alexis friend department. Our prayers were answered! A new IBM family from Massachusetts moved into our compound. I nearly danced for joy when I discovered that their daughter, Kylie, was in Alexis' class. The girls instantly became good friends. *Goodbye, Bianca!*

BBQ for 1,000

The outset of my year was consumed by the SAS Fall BBQ project. I thought it would be wise to have co-chairs, so I recruited two friends, Diana Barrington (a Brit now living in the US) and Suzette Madden (originally from Shanghai, but now living in the US). The event had such complexity I thought we'd have greater success if we divided and conquered. Luckily, many of the PTSA ladies had worked this event for years and knew exactly how to successfully pull off their venues—the games, the vendors, the performances, and such. Three of us plus our excellent committee leaders and their helpers really formed a dream team.

In 2005, 750 people bought the BBQ dinner, but this year we expected 1,000! It seemed mind-boggling to plan not just the event, but a meal for a small army. We decided to offer an upscale lunch (instead of a dinner) using a more reliable vendor than last year (who would not run out of food!). We also included a skate park and skateboarding show, an acrobat show, a bouncy house and giant inflatable slide, fourteen games, a bake sale, and a shopping boutique. Whew!

Because it was the Shanghai expat community, donations to our event began rolling in. I easily got Guilia's husband—who worked for a major multi-national food company—to donate bottled water. When another woman's husband got wind of it, he couldn't let *that* company remain our only beverage donor. Suddenly, one of the world's leading soft drink companies was also donating water. When Guilia's husband found out the major soft drink company was also donating water, he had to one-up. The next thing I knew, his company was donating ice cream, too. OK! I wondered who we could offend for our next donation!

Naturally, both husbands demanded that their water products be stored and served separately (because of brand competition). I put huge notes on both stacks of drinks to that effect. We nearly had an international incident, however, when some "helpful" soul we tasked with setting up a water stand put both brands together, despite the note! I rushed to do damage control, but not without a tongue lashing from Guilia.

We also inherited a smorgasbord of bakery and sweets. At MegaFit, Planet and I met a young chef named Patrick. He had the good fortune to wing off to Switzerland for culinary training, and then landed a plum job as the pastry chef and chocolatier at the Hotel Intercontinental. Like any industrious, savvy Chinese yuppie, Patrick, used his good fortune to open a bakery, chocolate, and sandwich shop in Jin Qiao, near the gym. I tried to return the generosity he showed to my children (and the general guanxi) whenever we visited the Intercontinental Hotel's brunch by inviting him to host a booth at the BBQ to introduce his wonderful bread, pastries, and chocolates to the SAS community. I could not convince him that I really didn't need him to donate 1,000 items. He insisted. Unfortunately, his store failed about a year later, and I felt terrible that my efforts to help him earn SAS expat business for his shop proved useless.

Overall, the 2006 Fall BBQ resulted in SAS Pudong's biggest, most profitable community-builder/fundraiser ever. Everyone had a great time, and I remain forever grateful to Diana, Suzette, Guilia, Dena, and all the other wonderful PTSA moms who guided this event to its outstanding conclusion.

Intellectual Life Goes On

Despite co-chairing a major event, I couldn't neglect my true love—books. All summer I looked forward to a new year of AWCS book club. I guess I was on a roll with leadership, as I found myself chairing the group for the new year.

I started by having each book club member send me a list of three reading recommendations, each with a short description. I shared the list with everyone, then I tallied up each woman's votes for which books they wanted to read. We planned to cover the top ten. We voted to read the following novels:

TITLE	AUTHOR
Desert Queen	Janet Wallach
Riding the Bus with my Sister	Rachel Simon
Wild Ginger	Anchee Min
Shanghai Boy, Shanghai Girl	George Wang & Betty Barr
The Forest Lover	Susan Vreeland
A Short History of Tractors in Ukrainian	Marina Lewycka
Red Poppies	Alai
Operation Yao Ming	Brook Larmer
A Thread of Grace	Doria Russell
Leaving Mother Lake	Yang Erche Namu & Christine Mathieu

Over the course of 2006-07, I enjoyed all of these books, but especially the China-related ones. I appreciated developing a greater sense of the country's past and Chinese women's perspectives on it. Those books made enough of an impression on me that I reviewed most of them for the *Courier*.

Getting Crafty

In addition to book club, one of the most interesting social events I attended that fall was the Cartonnage class given by a charming Dutch lady named Amalie in her luxurious mansion in the most exclusive section of The Pearl. This tawny-haired artist, aged late-forties, had four children at SAS. She spoke six languages, and this was the fourth country her family had lived in. She had recently moved from Jakarta, Indonesia, transferred for her husband's job with a major worldwide electronics company. Although the Vander Veldens identified as Dutch and held Netherlands passports, I'm not sure any of her kids were actually born there or had ever lived there. The concept made quite an impression on me, and I felt slightly envious. Amalie had European sophistication, beautiful manners, and a truly cultured interest in art. She often arrived at events in dramatic dresses accented by remarkable jewelry. While many people would simply come off as dilettantes dressed that way, it suited Amalie well and enhanced her allure. As we learned that afternoon, two of her favorite hobbies included quilting and cartonnage. Only after we both moved to Chicago in 2008, however, did I discover what a highly accomplished quilter she was.

When I arrived, four other ladies already sat waiting in Amalie's kitchen. We paid her 100RMB (about $14.50) as a materials and instruction fee. Cartonnage, we learned, was the ancient art of traditional French box making. When we got down to business, Amalie explained that we should use our X-Acto knives to cut our cardboard pieces to the required size; next, paper the pieces; and finally, glue the pieces together. It seemed simple enough. I decided that I should make a scrapbook for all the photos I was gathering from my Asian adventures. I admired all the beautiful, colorful paper Amalie had brought from Italy and France for us to use as she spread it out on display. I pictured myself proudly pedaling home with a unique treasure an hour from now, then enjoying the oohs and ahhs from Planet and the kids around the dinner table. Maybe I'd even have time to make a small gift box as well.

I lifted my knife and slipped it into the cardboard. Oh, oh, oh! The tool wouldn't move smoothly or precisely! If I had a paying job cutting cardboard to make decorative boxes, I would probably have ended up fired within hours! Only with much guidance from Amalie was I able to cut in a straight line to the right length and width. It required much more patience than I would ever have guessed.

After what seemed like hours, my pieces lay ready for papering. I measured, I cut, I laid the lovely paper pieces on the cardboard cut outs. Trying to line up the paper, fold it, and glue it onto the cardboard took me nearly an hour. I looked at my watch: it took a miserable, nearly two hours to reach the final stage of gluing the whole book together. With an embarrassing amount of help from Amalie, I finished my scrapbook, complete with decorative beads dangling from the ends on a satin ribbon. It was lovely. Thankfully, no one but my new Dutch friend would ever know how much sweat and brow ruffling it had caused!

章
21

THE BOOK THROWER

O ne thing we learned very quickly in Shanghai was to expect the unexpected. While most of our SAS experiences were positive, one of the situations we faced in the fall of 2006 remains deeply disturbing. Certainly, we never expected to have such a negative school experience as we did our second year at SAS.

That year, Alexis had a teacher named Mrs. Cooper. Alexis was always a very sensitive girl on a good day. She's the girl who would come home and cry because a classmate got in trouble. So, at first, we were unsure what to make of her concerns. Almost from the start of the year, our daughter came home talking about how loud Mrs. Cooper got and how she "yelled" at the kids. Our radar was turned on, but had not approached alarm level yet.

Then one day, Alexis came home and said that the feisty teacher had thrown a workbook at a student. Apparently, he had broken some rule, and the teacher sent the book whizzing through the air at him while loudly voicing her disgust. Planet and I remained unsure what to do. But then, Alexis came home in tears. The same incident had repeated, but this time the book had nearly taken off her nose enroute to the offender. After consoling her, I started asking around about the teacher. I could hardly believe my ears when some of the parents filled me in.

"Ooooohhhhh!! Her!" one said.

"Oh, last year two families left the school because of her," offered another.

"Oh, she used to be in Kindergarten, but the kids were terrified of her, and so many parents complained, they moved her to fourth grade," noted a third.

"Isn't she the one the kids can hear yelling all the way down the hall?" someone else commented.

"Oh, the so and so's son used to hide in the bushes every day. He was too afraid to go to school and be in her class," said another.

The list of scandalous reports went on and on. *Everyone* seemed to know a Mrs. Cooper horror story!

The next day when I went to SAS to work on a PTSA project, I popped into the elementary division principal's office. As we talked, he had the nerve to tell me there had "never been a complaint" about this woman. I thought my head might explode as I listened, but I also knew that a principal had to support his staff. He said the first step was for me to sit down and have a conversation with her. Well, my motherly instinct told me that a meeting with her would be a waste of time, but if that's what it would take for something to be done, I'd do it.

I made an appointment with Mrs. Cooper, and early the next week we met.

"I just can't imagine WHY you're here today," the teacher cooed with phony honey dripping from her voice. "Your daughter is SUCH a lovely girl...so SMART...and doing SO well in my class."

The back of my neck prickled.

"Well, Alexis has come home from school very concerned. She's a sensitive girl, and she says you get very loud in class," I began.

Mrs. Cooper's arm flew across her chest. "Oh," she blurted out and began speaking very quickly. "Well, I guess I do get a little loud. Ha, ha. All of us teachers do. Ha, ha. In fact, one night we all went out, and we were having such a good time...we got really loud, and the restaurant had to ask us to leave. Ha, ha, ha," she babbled nervously.

Who admits something like that? Especially when trying to smooth over a parent?

"Well, that may be, but Alexis says that you get mad and yell at the kids."

The perpetrator fabricated a shocked look on her face. I hesitated, not quite sure how to say what I needed to voice next.

"She said you...threw a book at a boy."

"Ooohhh…did I?" She fudged. "I…I don't remember that…ha, ha. Are you SURE?"

The conversation went on with her blathering nonsense and skirting the issue, until finally she looked at her watch.

"Oh, just look at the time! I'm really sorry I can't talk longer, but I'll miss the teacher van back to Jin Qiao!" And with that she started packing up her gear.

I sighed. "OK, well thanks for your time." *Now what?*

Well, I had done what the principal had asked. So, I immediately set up an appointment with him. Sitting in Mr. Hyde's office the next day, he again gave full support to the teacher. But I still needed my child moved out of that classroom.

"If this had happened in the US, this would be a lawsuit," I reminded him. In the US, especially at an expensive private school, I would only have had one conversation with a principal before my child would have been moved into another class. Yet, here we were, with him giving me a hard time. What was up with that?

"Just so you know, it's not our policy to change classrooms. We just can't have parents picking their kids' teachers. You can see how complicated that might get," he argued. "But since you're on the PTSA board and obviously do so much for the school, I'll do it just this once, and ONLY FOR *YOU*. And you have to promise not to tell *anyone* that I moved your daughter."

I couldn't believe what I was hearing. I clearly had stumbled into something bigger here. Why was he protecting this expat version of Cruella DeVille? Don't tell anyone? Like kids wouldn't notice a student was gone from one class and suddenly present in another? Like parents wouldn't get wind of it from the kids? The news would be hot on the expat grapevine without me ever saying a word! But Mr. Hyde wasn't done. "In return for my helping you, Alexis will need to see the school psychologist for some counseling."

Huh? "Um…Ok." What else could I say? This whole conversation had been so weird, I thought I'd count my blessings. Sending Alexis to see the counselor seemed a small price to pay in order to get her moved. In my parental mind, I thought maybe Alexis might benefit from some support for her trauma.

How wrong I was! Alexis came home after her appointment extremely upset. She explained through her tears that the psychologist had spent the entire session trying to convince her that the book throwing incident had never happened! I was floored! As I thought back to my conversation with Mr. Hyde, my temper flared. Now I knew why he wanted her to see the counselor!

Clearly the school was bizarrely bent on protecting this terrible creature. Thus, I told Alexis that what the counselor said was *absolutely wrong* and she had every right to feel disturbed by the psychologist's behavior. I promised her she would never have to see the counselor again. I seethed with anger at the additional mental damage done to my child. Just what was going on at SAS behind the scenes?

The worst part, however, was that Mrs. Cooper learned nothing from this incident. She kept right up with her bad habits. The next year, big gossip circulated among the expat community before the kids had even been back to school for a month. A nice Mormon family with six children, fresh off the plane from the US on their first adventure abroad, enrolled at SAS. One of their sons had the misfortune to find himself in Mrs. Book Thrower's class. Immediately, he got on her bad side. A text sailed through the air. BAM! It hit him, square in the face! He was actually injured.

When the father went to Mr. Hyde to complain, the principal refused to move the boy out of her class. Mr. Mormon reminded him that aside from the absolute unacceptability of the situation, he was paying *six* tuitions at the school that year (roughly $135,000). What do you think the principal did? He stood his ground. *Wow!*

This, however, wasn't the end of the story. When word got out among the expat community, the gossip mill ramped up, and all the old horror stories made the rounds again. The third-grade parents grew so outraged, they actually got up a petition. They insisted on having the angry instructor replaced, and they threatened to bring a lawsuit because their children felt unsafe.

I could hardly believe my ears when I heard Mr. Hyde's solution: instead of getting rid of Mrs. Hot Head, he hired a teaching assistant to "help monitor" the classroom. *Absurd!*

Naturally it wasn't the outcome anyone wanted. In disgust and disbelief, the victim's beleaguered family took their injury, their insult, and their six tuitions and left as fast as a Chinese family on a moped. What a horrible introduction to Shanghai!

I never learned what kind of fantastic behind-the-scenes story kept the school covering up for the evil Mrs. Cooper and made them willing to not only lose six tuitions plus pay an additional staff member salary, but I'm still dying to know. It must be a doosie! Anyone who knows the real story, please IM me!

22

EXPATS BEHAVING BADLY

One thing about China is that it remained a land of contrasts and extremes, and most certainly a place that lent itself to indulgences of all sorts. While most families enjoyed the super-affordable luxuries of an ayi, a driver, and exotic vacations, some expats also engaged in a significant amount of other more questionable activities. Ironically, while the women's sources of bliss generally involved the plentiful spas, inexpensive shopping, and gourmet lunches, the Tai Pans and Guy Tais found themselves just as often solicited for or indulging in other types of more dubious pleasures.

In Robin Pascoe's book, *A Moveable Marriage* (2003), she notes that fifty percent of expat marriages don't survive, a fact confirmed in the literature Planet's firm provided to us as we considered our move. In July of 2005, I had only a vague idea of why so many relationships bit the dust abroad. It didn't take long after arrival for me to clue in as I watched people around me living out their own versions of "what happens in Vegas stays in Vegas." The problem was, however, that what happened in Shanghai often didn't stay in Shanghai; bad behavior sometimes left a devastating trail of destruction.

You could argue, of course, that in general fifty perfect of marriages fail, and you'd be correct. So, what was different about China that ramped up the statistic within a statistic? Think about how a stranger sitting next to you on a plane often tells you his or her life story, embellishing the tale with way more details than you'd ever really want to know. The same factor works when people move abroad. You're removed from your regular life, from your family and friends, your religious institution, your usual job, and etc. Everything seems different. You are yourself, and yet, you're not. Somehow, this fuels a sense of freedom to say and do things you probably wouldn't in your own hometown. To enhance the situation, there are elements in Shanghai's culture that seem to promote this mentality and behavior. Namely, the way Western males appeared as low-hanging fruit to ambitious Chinese females.

To provide some background for why some foreign men made such easy targets, take the fact that when a marriage moves abroad, a couple suddenly finds themselves away from all the regular background influences that help hold a relationship together: family, religious institutions, community, and regular routines. Without these censors, anything could happen. In such isolation, marital flaws may magnify. Sometimes, a couple's old issues suddenly saddled with the new ones simply becomes the last straw. In addition, a marriage often experiences stress from a spouse's extremely demanding new job responsibilities. People based in China but working for home offices in the US or Europe often have to adjust to 24-hour work cycles: while the work day ends in Asia, it's twelve to fourteen hours earlier in America, and business is just ramping up. So, people regularly end up on conference calls at odd times.

The trailing spouse has her (or his) own set of stressors: she can't work, she's trying to create a friend group and make a rental house feel like a home, she's learning to manage household help and a driver, helping the kids transition, and dealing with her husband's new work situation. For some relationships, these challenges become a deal breaker.

As if all of this isn't enough, there's one more major issue that takes down many a marriage: business entertaining. Strip clubs and prostitutes are an extremely popular form of keeping clients and colleagues contented in China. Companies hide the issue very carefully. Even foreign businessmen who don't groove on that scene still feel pressured to go out, because it's what clients or colleagues want to do and that's just part of getting a deal done. Prostitution— often disguised as "karaoke hostesses" or massages with offers of a "happy ending"—runs rampant.

Let me solve the mystery of Asian hotel in-room phone call hang-ups for you: prostitutes or their pimps trolling for business. They hang up when a woman answers instead of a man. Strolling through the hotel lobby on your way to the elevator, you've probably passed by several ladies of the evening. You just didn't notice because unlike in the West, the women look respectable and are unlikely to be drug addicts. Ditto for the nearest bar. The abundant cornucopia of willing women can easily make a man feel like a five-year-old in a candy shop. Even if a guy would never consider indulging in this type of behavior at home, here he's in a fantasy world where seemingly everyone around him is indulging.

Pressure to conform also comes in the form of girlfriends/mistresses. Americans don't tend to indulge in clandestine affairs of the heart at quite the rate Europeans and Asians do, but suddenly, because a guy's business associates and clients from Europe or Asia all have girlfriends, he's considering the idea. In many parts of the world, being able to afford a mistress is a status symbol, like proving you can afford to wear a Rolex and drive a Ferrari. Even the best of husbands can feel tempted by the "coolness factor" of a Chinese girlfriend—especially if he knows the extra-curricular relationship has a finite end because he'll only be in Shanghai a few years. Away from the prying, ethical eyes of friends and family, it starts to seem like a short-term, well-deserved, harmless indulgence.

One of the dangers of a job transfer to Shanghai, however, is that for a variety of reasons, the male ego has reason to swell. Sometimes a Western man's job is much more interesting than it is at home. He gets treated as a "foreign expert," and Chinese colleagues defer to him. Even though his salary may not be considered that great at home, here the man is viewed as wealthy. Suddenly the bald, forty-five-year-old who looks like he swallowed a VW Beatle and couldn't get an attractive woman to look in his direction if he was on fire has Chinese women viewing him as a prize, flirting, willing to date him, or even just have sex with him. The tech nerd who couldn't get a date at home now has an attractive Chinese girlfriend. Or two. Or as many as he can afford to keep happy. Before you know it, a man can hardly see for all the stardust glittering before his eyes.

Let's weigh the options: 1. Go home to a wife who may be depressed or resentful, or even if she's not stressed out, definitely does not look at you with all the excitement of a first date or like you're Brad Pitt 2. Have drinks and enthusiastic sex with your attractive Chinese secretary, who gazes at you throughout the day like you can leap the Pearl Tower in a single bound. You start to see where this problem begins.

The problem with Chinese females' interest in expat men possibly begins with the one-child policy. This has led to an abundance of Chinese men, most of whom have been catered to as "little emperors" and now believe that they are gods. This doesn't exactly make them delightful dating partners. White men, however, are seen as (and often are) more educated, more cultured, and better mannered. Foreign men don't tend to patronize them like the patriarchal Chinese men, and young, educated Chinese women don't have to pretend to be demure and ditzy. With expat men, Chinese women feel flattered that someone they consider superior is interested in them. In addition, common stereotype holds that all Western males are rich, automatically rendering them desirable. Chinese women know that foreigners are easy targets, and they don't give two hoots if a man is married as long as they get what they want. So, even if a foreign man wouldn't consider indulging in such behaviors at home, temptation in Asia remains strong. And there you have it! The encounter can be a one-off, a long-term affair, or sometimes the Chinese woman even wins the marriage lottery.

As a case in point, my friend Chastain happened to observe another Guy Tai he knew at the popular local western supermarket. In the check-out line, Mr. Hot-to-Trot flirted with the average-looking twenty-something check-out cashier. She perked up, her internal radar suddenly on alert. A white foreigner paying attention to her? After a few more minutes of chatter, Mr. Indiscretion discovered that Miss Opportunist was good to go for a quick romp at his apartment. The price? A new winter coat.

Let your imagination run wild about how often this type of transaction occurs! The women seem to view these flings as practical—just another business deal. And why not? It's a win-win: everyone ends up with exactly what they want. At the other end of the spectrum, Chinese women seem to have no issue with becoming mistresses if it gets them a swanky apartment, a car, and plenty of spending money. In return, the guy gets to indulge his sexual fantasies with someone who treats him like he's George Clooney even though he more closely resembles Peter on *Family Guy*.

Some Chinese women want to date a foreigner because they think he can advance their career or they want opportunities to travel. Some hope their lover will pay their university bills. Beyond being a mistress, some Chinese women hope the Western man will divorce his wife and marry them. Some just want a US green card, with or without the title "Mrs." To get what they want, Chinese women will pull out all the stops to charm a man. It often works.

Occasionally, the repercussions of these Shanghai indulgences had unintended, negative long-term consequences. I knew or heard of numerous Western men who dumped their wives for their Chinese girlfriends. While most of the men skipped deliriously off into the sunset, the consequences of dalliances or divorce wreaked havoc for on wife and kids.

At the start of our second year abroad, I heard a somber story about a family in my compound. At the end of their summer back in their home state, the wife prepared for the family's upcoming move to Singapore for the start of the school year in August. Her hubby had other ideas. He broke the news that *he* would be moving to Singapore…without them. He planned to divorce his wife and move there with his Chinese girlfriend, instead. It was truly sad how many times I heard similar stories.

Even remaining in a marriage sometimes had surprise consequences. One day while attended a luncheon, the woman seated next to me shared a tragic story about a Tai Tai friend whose husband loved to indulge in business "entertaining" and viewed the Asian philosophy as his license to partake. About a year into their Shanghai stint, the wife began to have a mysterious discharge and abdominal pain. When she visited her doctor, she expected to hear that she had some type of cancer. No. It was something much simpler: Gonorrhea. Gonorrhea? She put some clues together and figured out exactly what kind of business entertaining her husband had been doing. In fact, her medical condition was so advanced, he had to have been "entertaining" for years—clearly without the courtesy of using a condom—before they ever arrived in China. At this point, the doctor advised her only option was a hysterectomy. When the woman confronted her unfaithful spouse, he grew angry, telling her to "buck up and quit whining. You live a good life!" For real. And with that, another expat marriage went the way of the tragic statistics.

Sometimes, happily, karmic justice prevailed for the wronged wife. An acquaintance, Milena, discovered that her husband of twenty-some years had added a Chinese girlfriend to his extra-curricular activities. Ms. Expoiter boldly demanded an apartment, money, and whatever else suited her fancy of the moment. She grew very insistent about his getting her a US visa. When the US government denied her application, she demanded that Mr. Sideline marry her. Well, either love is terribly blind or men are terribly stupid when they're having a lot of crazy good (even if it's "she wants something") sex. Mr. Sex-Struck desired this Chinese schemer so much that he divorced Milena and married her. Now Mrs. Taking Advantage insisted that they move to the US as soon as possible. So, Mr. Misguided applied for a US Visa for her. They believed that now, married to a US citizen, the government couldn't turn her down. But, the Visa application came back denied. Again!

In the end, Milena got her husband fired from his company for violating the morality clause in his job contract. Mr. Cheater and his new wife then remained stuck in China. How did she like him now, when he no longer had a good expat package for her to take advantage of and gain "big face" for but found himself completely unemployed? I'm guessing she'll dump Mr. Too-Late-to-Be-Sorry the moment she finds a new dupe with a high-paying job and the kind of US government immigration connections to get her that coveted Visa. Word to the wise cheater: wipe the fairy dust from your eyes, and be careful what you wish for! And Milena? She laughed all the way back to the US (divorced trailing spouses get sent back to their home country) and lived happily ever after in a charming beach town.

章

23

CHANUKAH & A TRIP DOWN UNDER

One of the aspects of living in Shanghai that I appreciated most was how SAS embraced the student body's diversity. Instead of sterilizing the school of religious holidays, they invited the parents to come in and teach about their own specific traditions. I guess the theory was that when you live in a miniature global village, learning about all religious traditions promotes understanding and respect and helps students get along with their classmates better. The kids could then see that people from around the world tend to have more similarities than differences.

So, in December 2006, when the parents were invited to come in and make presentations on whatever winter holiday traditions their families celebrated, that sounded like a license to pull out my candles and dust off my dreidel! I signed up to give the Chanukah presentation in both Alexis' and Anders' classrooms.

On the appointed day, I passed out the traditional chocolate gold coins as I told the students the story of Chanukah. Then I led them through the math problem of how many candles I would need to buy for eight nights of menorah lightings. I finished by teaching the kids to play the dreidel game. It proved a bigger hit than I could have imagined. With a significant stash of candy at stake, the ecstatic children would have played all afternoon. But all too quickly, our time together drew to a close, satisfied grins on all faces. I went home very happy that so many kids had a chance to learn about Jewish holiday traditions. I think the students had even more fun than I did!

The Land Down Under

That year, we stayed home to catch our breath during October's Golden Week school holiday. Thus, our first family trip during the 2006-07 school year took place at winter break. As a result, our plans were big. Planet had always maintained a fascination with the "land down under," and this year we made his vacation dream come true. Thankfully, the kids were growing into excellent travelers, and they endured the 10½-hour flight to Sydney, then a ninety-minute flight to Brisbane, like troopers.

We spent the first week of vacation at a resort in the fabled Gold Coast. Nothing particularly interesting or eventful happened that week, although we came with an impression of the area as a downscale, 1960s version of Florida. After a quiet week of family time, we switched to the hullabaloo of the big city. In Sydney, we met up with Dena Morgan's family for a trip to the zoo. We had a great time enjoying the balmy, sunny weather and the animals. As you might guess, the highlight of the day was the koalas. At this time, you could actually have your family photo taken with a koala perched delightfully on his bamboo tree. Holiday card, anyone? This is still one of my favorite family photos.

My family spent the rest of the week exploring the city. Since we were already a week into the trip, when we reached Sydney, Planet had to look for… you guessed it…a laundromat! There cannot possibly be another husband in the world who'd want to do laundry while on vacation! Fortunately, the rest of the trip proved less taxing and more fun.

One evening, we had dinner with the family of one of Planet's work colleagues and then wandered around an amusement park. On New Year's Eve, Planet had scored us tickets to a big music and fireworks event in the big park just outside our hotel. We ended the trip with a day at Manly beach. The kids spent hours mesmerized by a waterspout, then recovered by having their first scoops of Gelato. As we flew back to Shanghai, enlightened and relaxed, I realized my children were racking up stamps on their passports faster than a Tasmanian devil spins, and I felt grateful they had the opportunity to learn about so many places.

章
24

THE VARIETY OF SECOND SEMESTER

What is there to do in boring, cold January with one's post-winter-break blues? Brunch! The City took the Sunday mid-day meal seriously, and the expats relished taking advantage of this. From dim sum shops to the major hotels, brunch never disappointed. Three of our favorites were the Yi Café, the Westin, and the Hotel Intercontinental.

Our first Shanghai Sunday brunch experience took place at the newly opened Yi Café at the Pudong Shangri-La. Reg and Marilyn raved about it, so Planet, the kids, and I met the Bixbys and their son there one afternoon. We quickly discovered for ourselves the reputation was well deserved.

The Yi Café's concept involved "eight crazy chefs," each responsible for a station presenting cuisine from a particular world region. We cruised past sites set up for Indian, Chinese, American/Australian, Italian with made-to-order pasta, Sushi and cold seafood, Southeast Asian, Middle Eastern, salads, and more! Clearly, this enormous buffet required a strategy, and we needed to prioritize! Though I could have eaten my weight in grilled lobster tails, I wanted to save room for the incredible dessert room. About thirty kinds of bite-sized pastries, cookies, sweet breads, and rolls stood beckoning in precision form. A cooler held multiple flavors of ice creams and sorbets, with waffle bowls and about a dozen types of candy to put on top in addition to rich, creamy hot fudge or high-quality caramel. Small Shangri-La signature gift boxes stood at

278

the side, waiting for the kids to fill them with the large variety of candies—a great souvenir for later. Chocolate fountains in pink, green, white, and milk chocolate streamed enticingly. Wooden skewers lay waiting for diners to kebab them with marshmallows, angel food cake, and fruits. The room was pure sugar-lovers' Heaven!

A few delicious hours later, our group managed to waddle away from our table. My family had joined the ranks of the Yi Café's fan club. Considering the massive quantity of delicious gourmet food, we thought the price of 258RMB (about $36) per adult seemed extremely reasonable.

We thought the Yi Café was THE brunch in Shanghai, until Chastain invited us to join a group of friends at the Westin. Similar to the Yi Café in its international cuisine offerings, but taking the "outrageous brunch" concept to a new level, this lavish affair sprawled over *two floors* and offered an all-you-can-drink alcoholic-beverage option. The drinks included Tattinger champagne, wine, and cocktails, and since everyone knew the steep prices of alcoholic indulgence in Shanghai, diners usually left this event as drunk as they were full. This dining experience also stood out by offering a kids' buffet, complete with toys and free babysitters.

Even with a strategy, I found it challenging to navigate through the vast reaches of this culinary extravaganza. Sampling even half the delectables could take hours. The enormity of the brunch also had a unique drawback: when a friend went off to the make-your-own bloody Mary bar, s/he might not return for fifteen minutes, at which point I might be off to explore the desserts. This made socializing challenging. Even so, the Westin's brunch made a welcome addition to a foodie bucket list. At this time, the brunch cost 488RMB (about $70) or 588RMB (about $84) with the adult beverage option (an incredible bargain given Shanghai drink prices). Though pricey, you could pay double that much at fancy hotels in the US for a brunch half the size and half as good.

More often, however, my family and I frequented the Hotel InterContinental's brunch. The buffet existed on a significantly smaller scale than the swishier hotels, but the price also reflected that. My favorite thing about this brunch—other than having our pastry-chef friend, Patrick, spoil us—was the Movenpick Swiss ice cream. It tasted so rich and creamy compared with US ice creams. I could have skipped all the food items and just made a meal from the mango ice cream.

This hotel's brunch featured large, impressive chocolate sculptures Patrick created, and when our friend knew we were coming, he kindly made chocolate bunnies and other treats specifically for Alexis and Anders. He stepped away from the kitchen to deliver them personally, which thrilled the kids. What could be better? Well, our friend went over-the-top by making sure they also left with treat bags full of wonderful sweets!

Patrick had recently married Gracie, who worked at the InterContinental as a banquet sales manager. Fortune had smiled on the couple, and they followed the Chinese rule of finding multiple ways to making money. They had recently saved enough money for Patrick to undertake his dream of owning a bakery (in addition to his hotel job, of course). His croissants emerged from the oven as buttery and flaky as any in France. A perfectionist, he purchased chocolate only from the world's best-quality suppliers. His hot chocolate rivaled anything served in Zurich or Amsterdam. He sold lovely European style sandwiches, and of course the shop's front shelves stood stocked with plenty of chocolates. To our surprise, we discovered Patrick's high standards also applied to serving foods and beverages. Certain sandwiches simply could not, and would not, as Planet learned, be served cold—or hot. Chef would not let customers add something to a sandwich that his training suggested should not be on it. One day, I stopped by for lunch after MegaFit, and he even refused to serve me a hot chocolate with my tuna sandwich. When I asked why, he said, "It simply isn't done!" Never mind what I *wanted*, I'd been schooled.

Even though, sadly, Patrick's shop closed before reaching its second anniversary, we continued to enjoy Patrick's company at MegaFit and at the hotel's excellent brunch.

Chinese Hawaii

We had heard through the expat grapevine that the south-China island, Hainan, was the "Chinese Hawaii." What better place to spend the Chinese New Year school holiday?

On trip day, Mr. Zhou pulled into our driveway, right on time as always, to ferry us to Puxi's Hong Qiao airport. We realized we'd been spoiled by our regular thirty- to forty-five-minute commute to the Pudong airport when it took us an aggravating seventy-five minutes to reach the Hong Qiao terminal. Even so, we still had an hour to kill before our flight. We could relax a little. Or so we thought…

When we approached the ticket counter to check in and deposit our luggage, the agent informed us our flight to Sanya, Hainan Island, had oversold. Since we hadn't called last night to confirm, we had lost our seats. *Confirm! What?*

Thankfully Planet was an old pro at managing travel issues. He quickly negotiated both a concrete confirmation *and* an upgrade to first class on the next flight out. That plan, however, involved driving back across the entire city, in heavy Shanghai traffic, to the Pudong airport. I sat sweating on the edge of my car seat, squeezing my hands together, all the way to Pudong, willing us to arrive on time. It seemed a miracle that we found ourselves stepping out of the car after only forty minutes and boarding our flight on time. What a stressful start to our vacation!

When we finally arrived on Hainan, I immediately understood why it had grown so popular. The island lay just under four hours away by air (off the coast of Vietnam), and the scenery indeed resembled a lush, South Pacific island, full of palm trees, colorful flowers, and crystal-clear turquoise water. As far as the hotel property was alluring and magnificent.

Of course, we had already learned that no expat can vacation in Asia without running into familiar faces. At the hotel, we saw Guilia with her two boys in tow, the younger of whom was Anders' classmate and good friend. We then discovered Kilty, another SAS mom, with her son, Shane, whom Anders had befriended through Cub Scouts. And finally, we spied…NO!…Bianca! I crossed my fingers and hoped for the best.

In the morning, the kids and I prepared to hit the beach (unfortunately, Planet had a big project underway and needed to spend most of the day in our room working). When we stepped onto the sand, a few SAS families had already set up camp. Soon, the kids spied a banana boat buzzing by. We moms quickly agreed to share the cost of letting the kids ride it. The boat driver asked a whopping 340RMB for four kids for twenty min, plus 115RMB more for a fifth kid (about $12 each, plus a crazy $16 more for the fifth). Guilia self-assigned to take him on. With fantastic Italian bravado, she worked him down to almost half that amount *and* extended the ride time to thirty minutes. I admired her work! Soon, the kids were flying around on the giant fruit, shrieking with delight as the driver whipped them along the shoreline and then good-naturedly dumped them, thrilled, into the balmy South China Sea.

When their banana boat time ended, the kids ran in and out of the water and played games in the sand, while we moms chatted. I noticed ethnic minority ladies walking up and down the beach carrying baskets bursting with all types of pearls. A few other women had baskets filled with large, beautiful seashells. As the skeletally thin, black-haired women in their long dresses and traditional bamboo sun hats swished by me, I did a double-take at the ruby-red stains smeared across their lips and teeth.

"What is going on with the pearl ladies' teeth?" I asked the Tai Tai crew.

"It's some type of a berry they eat. It decreases their appetite and gives them a good buzz," Kilty offered.

I looked at her quizzically.

"It's a digestive aid, I heard," Guilia jumped in.

My head whirled as I tried to conjure up a vision of their lives. I couldn't blame them for wanting a cigarette-style buzz—lots of people need that or coffee to start their day. But why would they just leave long red smears on their faces, especially before interacting with guests? It seemed as baffling as the filth in the lovely, old apartment building I'd toured with Gang of One in Shanghai. I wasn't sure what this revealed about Hainanese culture.

At the resort, we saw few other tourists. However, I noticed several beach loungers near us filled with massive bodies...sprouting embarrassingly bad hair dye jobs in unnatural shades of dirty blonde, Barney purple, ketchup red, and Little Mermaid orange. Though the women seemed to range from about 175 pounds to 350 pounds, they all sported *thong* bikinis! *Yikes!* Their spouses looked equally ridiculous with their pot bellies overflowing from their tight European designer speedos, jabbering self-importantly on their mobile phones.

The beefy women looked like they were getting serious about buying pearls, and Bianca's mother Isabel caught me staring.

"They're Russians," she informed me.

Several hundred of my brain cells blew up. I had expected to encounter Japanese or Australians, maybe. But a beach full of *Russians* in China? "How do you know?" I asked.

"We lived there. I learned to speak Russian."

This impressed me. The intel could work to our advantage. "Will you ask them what price they're paying for pearls?"

Maybe her Russian was rusty, or she didn't understand their dialect, but Isabel shook her head, no. This left me baffled, but I couldn't press her.

The other ladies and I looked at each other with wizened glances, ready to form a "Tai Tai Team." Even without data from the Russians, we knew that negotiating as a group, we could get a good deal. Guilia self-appointed as lead bidder. We chose our merchandise, then our Italian version of William Shatner worked her magic like this was Priceline. When we had our pearl price down to about $12.00 per strand, I knew I had beautiful, outstanding holiday and birthday gifts covered for the rest of the year! Score!

The warm sun and our shopping spree had left me thirsty. Anxious to practice my Mandarin, I hailed a waiter and ordered a diet Coke. The young man stared at me, utterly uncomprehending.

"Did I say that right?" I asked, looking at the moms for guidance. They nodded in approval.

Then I heard another waiter talking to the Europeans. He was speaking… Russian! Waiters in Hainan who spoke Russian and not *putong hua* (common language)? I thought that all Chinese spoke Mandarin, the country's official state-approved language. Sadly, I resorted to English. It worked. The waiter scribbled something on his pad and scurried away. Huh. Who knew Hainan was a Russian vacation hotspot!

The remainder of the week, the kids had a ball kayaking, riding the banana boat, and playing at the beach and in the pool. Bianca even remained drama free. We returned to Shanghai rested, relaxed, and ready for another round of expat life.

Shanghai Literary Festival Part Two

All year, I eagerly awaited the next Shanghai Literary Festival. In March 2007, I listened, spellbound, as Yang Erche Namu regaled us with the highly memorable details of her autobiography, *Leaving Mother Lake*. Though Namu's autobiography covered the fascinating years from her birth to her days at the infamous Shanghai Opera School, the life that unfolded after her opera career seemed even more remarkable. Not long into her singing career, Namu went deaf in one ear and had to abandon the career that she had attained at great personal cost. Well, she'd always wanted to be a model, so off she went to Paris. Voila! When she grew tired of—and too old for—modeling, she decided to become an author. Who goes from singer to model to author in one lifetime? This woman had re-invented herself as many times and as successfully as Cher! I wanted to be her some day!

Namu was not only talented, she was kind. She attempted to give back to her community by providing money for schools and medical care. She also established an artists' hotel. Anyone could stay there for free, if they agree to create a piece of art and donate it to the hotel. This talented woman never wished western ideals of success or culture for her hometown, only that the villagers' lives would improve through having access to key necessities. Unfortunately, when *Leaving Mother Lake* achieved fame in China, entrepreneurs capitalized on the people's misguided interpretation of the matriarchal tribe's "walking marriages." Suddenly, the railroad reached the village, which previously took three days on horseback to reach. Men ventured out into these hinterlands in droves, assuming that since the tribal women didn't marry—simply changing lovers at will—their chances of scoring a hook up were good. When outsiders realized that wasn't exactly how the sexual process worked for the native women, prostitutes came streaming into town like spawning salmon to capitalize on the opportunity. What a pity that Namu's dreams of improving her community brought as much negative change as positive.

Leaving Mother Lake, however, remains a fascinating study of the Mosuo tribe and one of my favorite reads of all time. I wish all high school students could read it as part of the curriculum. I truly admire Namu, and I highly recommend her story.

Emerging writer Gao Xiaolong, whose book *Death of a Red Heroine* my AWCS book club had recently read, gave an inspiring talk. Later, I also found myself speaking to Amy Tan as she autographed my copy of her latest endeavor, *The Opposite of Fate: Memoirs of a Writing Life*. I enjoyed her thoughts on writing, especially the essay on the anxiety of penning a second novel. So, I remarked that if I ever taught a writing class, I would use this book—or at least that essay—since I thought it offered particularly valuable advice. She actually glared at me and gave no response. She rolled her eyes, plopped the pen down onto the page, signed, and thrust my book back at me. *Really?* Despite her behavior, I enjoyed reading all of her books and devoted a whole-page summer reading write up in the *Courier* to her work. Perhaps I should have mentioned *that* to Miss Curmudgeon fan hater.

Shanghai Fashion

Children with blonde hair and light eyes could easily stumble into successful modeling careers in Shanghai. My friend Bonnie's daughter had jobs nearly every weekend. The pay hovered around $100 a session and generally seemed fun for the kids. So, I asked Bonnie to help me get my much-noticed son into the field. I entertained grand visions of stashing away some money for his college tuition. The booking agent seemed happy to hear from me, and she had a catalogue job coming up soon.

A few Saturdays later, Mr. Zhao drove Anders and me into Puxi to the shoot for an adorable line of European children's clothes. The on-site coordinator introduced herself and handed me the first outfit. The parents stood undressing and dressing their children in one big room. As I tried to help Anders undress, he suddenly grew enormously uncooperative. Oddly, he insisted on hiding over in a corner and dressing himself. Ok, fine. But then he kept hesitating to get undressed. Moments later, the coordinator trotted over, searching him out. The other kids had finished dressing and were making their way onto the shoot scene. What was the problem?

"Anders, you cannot behave this way. You wanted to model. Here we are. Get dressed. Everyone is waiting for you," I urged.

"Mommy...." he murmured, a pained look on his face.

"What IS the problem, honey?"

Finally, he confessed, nervously. "I'm not wearing any underwear!"

Oh, good grief! Why did he have to pick *today* of all days to experiment with not wearing underwear!

"Oh, Anders. Today was really *not* the right day to skip putting on briefs. You've made a commitment, so you're going to have to finish the job. I'll stand in front of you so no one can see you, ok?"

"What if people can still see me," he moaned, mortified.

"No one can see you. I'm going to stand right in front of you. You *have* to put on the outfit. *Right now!*" I stated firmly, wrestling him into the pants.

When we arrived on set, an assistant stood posing another blonde-haired blue-eyed boy and girl in the "out in the country" setting. All three children looked like they inherently belonged there. The outfits were irresistible. The photographer began shooting, and moments later the first scene was complete.

I breathed a sigh of relief as the coordinator motioned us back to the dressing room, where she quickly handed out the next outfits to the young trio. Maybe Anders would behave better now that we'd gotten the initial shock out of the way, he'd met the other two kids, and he understood what modeling was about.

Wrong! My son put up the same resistance as with the first outfit. In fact, he dawdled and resisted with each clothing change. At one point, Anders even held everyone up while he took his time in the bathroom...pooping! It didn't take me long to figure out that my son would go down in history as having the world's shortest modeling career!

At the end of the shoot, the coordinator strode over to us.

Surprisingly, she spoke softly and kindly to the child who probably represented her least-cooperative model ever.

"Even though things did not go so well with you today, I'm still going to give you the full pay. I want you to feel good. Maybe another time you can do better."

"Thank you," we both answered simultaneously.

But this single foray into modeling was enough for Anders. Even the thought of a cool $100 couldn't motive him to try it again. There went my college tuition fantasies! Since my son's first modeling job was also his last, thankfully I'd always have the beautiful photos the kind coordinator sent me.

Photography and modeling brings me to how in general China seemed like a land of fashion don'ts. Take Mr. Zhou's prominent right pinky nail, for example. The fabled talon extended about an inch and a half and he had filed it to a point, like a miniature sword, which he wielded with great pride and care. My kids, fascinated, one day asked Zhou why his nail was so long. I couldn't wait to hear the answer, but Zhou just smiled and didn't say a word. Maybe he didn't know the English words to explain. Curious, I asked around. Apparently, this fashion statement was to Chinese men what whiter-than-white skin is to an Asian woman: it shows that a man is a sophisticated urbanite, a non-manual laborer. I suspected it carried a more nefarious meaning, like maybe membership in a gang or secret society. Others thought it indicated wealth or intelligence. One person answered snarkily that it's simply useful for favored Chinese male hobbies. "You know…cleaning their ears, opening cigarette packages, and picking their noses!"

One of the fashions I found strangest was seeing people out and about in their pajamas. Among countless examples, a PJ-clad vendor watched over his fruit stand, while another night-dressed man buzzed by on a motorcycle. *What?* When I asked around, people told me that the Chinese had been so poor for so long, that they wanted people to know that they could afford a luxury like pajamas. To prove it, they wore them out in public. Well, now I understood why Xiao Mei frequently wore furry pink bunny pajamas during the day, even in hot weather!

One day when stopped at a traffic light, I looked over and saw a woman passenger in a sedan wearing a flowered shirt under a bright, striped blazer. Her hubby was wearing a bold striped shirt under a loud plaid jacket. *Help, call the fashion police!* Maybe the bold colors and patterns were a backlash again the Mao era's drabness? Whatever the case, growing up, we had the concept of matching and blending beaten into us. I recall we even had a brand called Garanimals that made it easy for the smallest children to accomplish this task. We Americans for the most part match, match, match.

Though she was in her forties, Xiao Ting remained fond of her red plastic Mickey Mouse house slippers. Xiao Mei wore t-shirts that had either badly translated English phrases on them, or had a bunch of Western alphabet letters just thrown on for good measure that said nothing at all. One day she appeared in a t-shirt that read, "I'm the little brother." I laughed when I saw it. Then I tried to kindly explain the situation to her. I don't think she got it.

Of course, the ever-present surgical masks were a fashion staple. The surgical mask could be worn anywhere, any time, it seemed. It wasn't clear whether the people wearing them in traffic simply feared pollution and fumes or had other reasons. And finally, the Chinese male's most popular, indispensable accessory: the cigarette. Smoking was expensive, and terrible for your health, so Chinese men smoked like chimneys apparently to prove both their manliness and their financial success. One day as Mr. Zhou motored me to Puxi, rolling happily down Hunan Lu, I looked over and saw an armored car next to us. I noticed that the two back windows were open. Besides security issues, what was wrong with this picture? A single arm stretched out of each window into the air, a lit cigarette dangling from each hand. And now the question presents itself: doesn't all the smoking make wearing a face mask ridiculous?

Orangutans, Waterfalls, & Headhunters

By the May school holiday, the US government had ceased ominous travel warnings for Kota Kinnabalu, and the kids and I were finally on our way to orangutan country! (Planet, unfortunately, had to remain in Shanghai for work.)

When we arrived at the Shangri-La resort, the desk clerks seated each group of guests in the lobby lounge area, serving us a welcome drink while they checked us in. I sipped my peach tea happily. It's slightly sweet and slightly salty flavor, and the green plum floating at the bottom of the glass made it easily the tastiest peach tea I'd ever had. We had arrived late in the evening, so we gave ourselves a quick tour of the resort, then called it a night.

Very early the next morning, we awoke to a single, mournful bell signaling the Muslim call to prayer. It reminded me of how vastly different this country was from my own homeland in every way, from landscape and weather to culture and religion.

After enjoying the wonderful buffet breakfast, we made our way over to the small orangutan refuge nestled on the far end of the property. There, we paid about 70 Malaysian Ringgits for the three of us (about $10) to visit. The staff seated us in a small room where we watched a twenty-minute video on the animals and the attempts to preserve the species. Then guides ushered outside to the animal sanctuary.

The weather that morning registered about 95F and one-hundred percent humidity—perfect weather for jungle creatures, but for humans, not so much. While we watched the orangutans play in the trees, within a few minutes an infant and a middle-aged woman both passed out from the intense heat. Staff rushed in, attending to the fallen, while the rest of us spent about thirty more minutes watching the animals eat their morning meal and play.

As the gamekeepers parceled out the food, a band of Macaques came around and attempted to steal the food. Alexis stood riveted, fascinated, especially when the staff fed the youngest animals from baby bottles. One keeper explained that when the young orangutans—bred onsite here—grow old enough, they get transferred to the much larger Sepilok reserve, where they are taught to survive and then released into the wild.

Very pleased with our primate visit, we returned to the main resort area to cool off at the vast, inviting beach. It seemed nothing short of miraculous that the resort had managed to commandeer so much oceanfront. Hurray, no trash, pollution, or dangerous tides prevented us from completely enjoying the beach here! As we shifted our feet through the warm, soft, mushroom-colored sand, a soothing, temperate breeze wafted over us. The kids and I waded into the water and found it warmer than bathwater—nearly hot. The gentle, salty waves felt good lapping over our sweaty bodies. Soon, an afternoon rainstorm rolled in, but Alexis had always adored rain, so we voted to stay outside. Call us crazy Americans, but we got our thrills experiencing a tropical downpour on an exotic beach that, amazingly, we had all to ourselves.

At 8:00 am the next morning, a small motorboat glided onto the resort beach to pick us up for a tour. The kids loved being out on the water in a boat, scouting for birds, animals, and sea creatures. They shrieked with glee when the driver hit the gas hard and we bounced over the waves.

Our guide did an excellent job providing cultural information about the people who live on and along the water. He seemed to relish sharing information about his country and the ethnic group we'd soon encounter—the Bajau, also known as Muslim "sea gypsies." This tribe lived in tiny, brightly painted one-room homes suspended over the water on stilt-supported platforms.

When we arrived at our designated stop in the "sea gypsy" village, we stopped for a coffee break at a local home. The stilt house, as with all the others in the area, was a one-room affair. Before we could enter the home, the guide directed us to take off our shoes and place them on the shoe rack standing just outside the door. A jar of water had been carefully placed there with a ladle. So, we followed tradition and washed our feet.

Once inside, a middle-aged gypsy woman crouched over a log fire. We formed a circle around it and settled down onto the straw-mat floor. The guide informed our group that the females among us must sit with our legs bent to one side, rather than cross-legged, for modesty and manners. The gypsy woman then turned, reached over to a small rack, and handed each of us a huge green coconut with a straw poking out. The raw coconut milk had a subtle salty, sour flavor. It tasted nothing like the stuff sold in cans at the supermarket or the dried flakes for baking.

Then the woman placed a frying pan on the fire and added oil. Before long, hat-shaped doughy cakes crackled and grew browned. Anders got really excited

about the idea. How could the host resist his platinum curls and heart-melting blue eyes? Before we knew it, my son became the sous chef, helping to fry our snacks. Then he proudly assisted our host in passing around a basket of the hot, fresh pastries, while a young Bajau girl served us strong, delicious local coffee, sweetened with condensed milk. Next, a basket of banana chips made its way around the circle. Oddly, the chance to try a local hand-rolled cigar completed our snack stop.

When we returned to the boat, we glided down a coast lined with bamboo huts and colorful houses on stilts on our way to a market. Once there, the kids and I enjoyed browsing through the vibrant stalls offering children's trinkets, carved wood pieces, jewelry, handicrafts, colorful tropical-print clothing, and t-shirts. Surprisingly, the vendors wouldn't bargain. We didn't like any items well enough to pay tourist prices, so we left the market empty-handed, but not disappointed.

As if we could possibly be hungry after our sea-gypsy snack, the next stop on the itinerary was lunch in a bamboo restaurant on stilts. The kids had grown so comfortable with Asian food that they didn't even blink when the waiters passed around a variety of Malaysian dishes. While I sampled the curries, the kids happily spooned up wonderful coconut rice steamed in a banana leaf and savory noodles. Our favorite dish was the savory scallion and egg pancake. We hoped we'd come across some of these items again one day soon back in Shanghai.

When our bellies couldn't hold another morsel, the guide ushered us back onto the boat. The kids and I felt peaceful, enriched, and relaxed, the hot, dewy air blowing against our bodies. It seemed really cool to arrive back at the Shangri-La in a boat, a magnificent, intense, yellow and orange sunset serving as a backdrop. I declared our first Borneo adventure a success.

Our second Kota Kinnabalu adventure took place off-roading through the tropical rainforest. Promptly at 8:00 am, our guide, Rayyan, stood patiently waiting for us in the hotel motor court next to his sturdy, four-wheel-drive jeep. The kids' eyes brightened with anticipation and excitement as we clambered into our seats. When we reached the national park, Rayyan maneuvered the four-wheeler onto a rugged dirt road. We bumped and bounced along. The steeper the road grew, the more my anxiety about toppling over the cliff on the left side multiplied. While the kids loved the amusement park quality of the trip, my awareness that my body could only take so much increased. I distracted myself with the gorgeous, lush scenery, glad the kids were enjoying themselves. Fortunately, before long we came to a river, where Rayyan had planned a short hike. We disembarked from the jeep and strolled past a small farm until we reached the designated path. I hoped Rayyan knew what to do if we encountered one of the many varieties of native, ginormous man-eating snakes! The path was muddy and quite slippery. Just as I finished telling the kids, "take your time. There's no rush," though walking extra carefully, I slipped and fell on the camera! No more visual documentation of our trip! I sighed disappointedly as the strong, nimble guide helped me get back to my feet.

When we reached the river, a rope swing hung from a tree, and Rayyan encouraged the kids to spend some time launching themselves into the water. They needed no prompting. After roughly half an hour, the guide let us know the time had come to venture deeper into the jungle. Back in the jeep, we jolted and veered for about thirty minutes until we reached our lunch stop. There, we heard water roaring, as intense as Niagara Falls. In another "pinch me" moment, before us a massive, incredibly powerful waterfall pounded into a straight-out-of-Paradise emerald-green lagoon.

Rayyan pulled a traditional Asian lunch box from the rear of the jeep. His wife had prepared an our meal, now divided among the stacked woven-wood compartments. The boxes held white rice, fried chicken, tropical fruits, stir-fried vegetables, and some type of Malaysian cookie. The guide spread a blanket on the ground and laid out bottled water and sodas. As we finished up our meal, rain rolled in. Within moments, we found ourselves running toward the off-roader, as a few gentle drops quickly morphed into a roaring South Asian gully washer. The guide gently explained that when the downpour ended, the increased water levels would make a swim at the waterfall too dangerous. What a shame our tour had come to a premature end. Still, we had experienced many new and once-in-a-lifetime things in an overall satisfying day.

Our third and final tour in Kota Kinnabalu remains the most memorable of that trip and one of the most unusual experiences of our lives. Borneo has a long, notable reputation for its head-hunting culture. So, of course we had to visit a traditional head hunter village/museum. To begin, our guide strolled us past a series of bamboo huts, then stopped midway before a tree. She pulled off what looked like an extra chubby caterpillar. Poof! She popped the greyish insect into her mouth live and swallowed!

"Would anyone like to try one? They're nice," she beckoned. My kids looked stunned. Apparently, the locals regularly ate this common worm as a snack. No takers? No surprise. The guide kept going. A moment later we arrived at our first activity: learning to shoot poison darts! The woman handed us each a round, hollow bamboo stalk, about three feet long. She grabbed a dart and proceeded to show us how to blow it from the pipe. Targets had been set up attached to trees at the far end of the clearing. Excitedly, the kids picked up their weapons and ammunition, and let the darts fly. They loved it!

Before long, the guide steered us toward a row of bamboo long houses resting atop tall stilts. Inside the first house, we found a series of museums exhibits. The eaves lay lined with bleached skulls. I felt slightly taken aback when I considered just how many skulls it took to go around a room! Some had even been decorated with henna designs. I looked at the kids, observing their reactions. They appeared to take the room's décor in stride. *Whew!*

Here, we learned the purpose of the head-hunting practice. In contrast to, say, displaying a severed head on the tower gates of London to make a political statement, Southeast Asian tribes collected their enemies' craniums for other reasons. Some say warriors sought an enemy's head to obtain the life force within it. The fiercer the enemy, the more power the warrior who killed him gained. In some tribes, a young man could not become an official member or marry until he had collected a head. Still other natives believed that the head would ensure the dead person would be his slave in the life to come. Sometimes heads were taken in retaliation or for retribution. Frighteningly, the guide informed us that some rural Southeast Asian tribes collected heads until the 1970s! Fortunately, as the tribes continued to modernize and align more with contemporary society, the practice diminished. Scientists don't know, however, whether the practice has died out completely in some of the more remote villages. *Yikes!*

From the plaques in this museum, I learned that lining the walls of a Kota Kinnabalu long house with heads represented the high point of tribal decorating savvy. The more heads adorning a home's walls, the higher the family's status. The skulls, they believed, provided power and strength to the males, so the more the better. Of course, the more masculine power male family members had, the more desirable they appeared to potential marriage partners. Finally, the crafty craniums supposedly worked as charms, protecting the home from any dangers lurking outside.

That also brings us to tattoos. In Borneo, tattoos have traditionally held great meaning. A man's first tattoo often signified his tribal affiliation. After that, battle's intensity, or the special meaning of a head taken might necessitate commemorating the experience with some ink. Carrying captured heads around on a belt or a stick was obviously impractical, so tattoos made sense, allowing a warrior to easily display the story of his successes. Whatever the tattoo, a warrior had to *earn* that particular design. No one's painting an *Entegulun* on a man's hand unless he has severed a head. It makes the reasons for getting tattoos in the West pale in comparison. Oh, and another reason the tattoos were earned through bravery: they were made the original way, using sharp sticks dipped in ink!

From this sobering, slightly creepy experience, the guide led us into another long house for our final activity. There, we marveled while locals dressed in historic clothing performed traditional dances. The men wore red headdresses made of printed cloth and feathers, long ribbons trailing down their bare backs. Around their necks hung a variety of necklaces: beads, animal teeth, and…a miniature skull! They wore black loincloths and brightly colored ribbons around their waists, long knives hanging from one side. The women wore black dresses, their headdresses displayed a tribal motif, and long feathers shot up from the backs of the headwear. Colorful necklaces dangled from their necks, and tribal-motif sashes adorned their waists.

The kids watched spellbound, until suddenly one of the warriors let loose a chilling whoop. He raced from the stage, stopping in front of me. He screamed an ancient battle cry into my face. *Oh, no! What next!* Then he grabbed my arm and pulled me toward the stage, motioning for the kids to join me. We didn't dare refuse!

The two women on stage had laid down two six-foot long bamboo poles. Now, the women picked up the front ends, and the two men picked up the rear ends of the poles. The fierce-looking yeller motioned for us to dance, jumping in and out of the bamboo poles. Alexis and Anders laughed joyfully, taking this all in as a wonderful new game. Make-the-blond-tourists-dance served as the show's grand finale; then my new ferocious warrior friend changed his expression to just-plain-scary, and waved goodbye. I could finally exhale!

As we waited for our hotel van to return, the kids noticed an ice cream cooler. I would have expected guava and papaya, but instead the popsicle flavors included avocado, durian, purple yam, and red bean. I knew enough to advise the kids against Durian—which tastes like old, sweaty gym socks. They felt unsure about avocado, but were game to try red bean. I think the treats cost the equivalent of about five cents each. As they enjoyed their treat, I hoped my children would always  remember the unusual, exciting, interesting things we had experienced and learned today and throughout our visit to Borneo.

You Just Have to Cross Two Oceans

For summer 2007, I had to get creative again about spending the majority of the summer abroad—a great "Tai Tai life" problem to have! The kids had been learning about Europe in school and were curious about their paternal grandmother's birthplace—Munich, Germany. The Firm's expatriate package allowed each of us to fly business class round-trip to the US once per year. As I investigated what we could do with that budget, I discovered that I could actually save the company money by booking "around the world" economy-premium tickets instead. Though this type of ticket had a variety of combinations, one package stood out: all we had to do was cross two different oceans. A plan came to me: we'd fly from Shanghai to Germany, then from Europe to the US, and then back to China, crossing both the Atlantic and the Pacific. Ta da!

The kids and I would first spend a week at an all-inclusive family style resort called Centre Parc in a forest just outside Hamburg, tour Munich for a few days, then head over to the States to spend two weeks at Hilton Head Island, South Carolina and three weeks in Beaver Creek, Colorado. Planet would stay in Shanghai with the rest of the expat dads for the majority of the summer, but take vacation time to join us for parts of our Hilton Head and Beaver Creek weeks.

In early June 2007, Alexis, Anders, and I boarded a Lufthansa flight to Frankfurt. After an uncomfortably warm, but otherwise uneventful twelve hours in the air, we arrived in Germany. After living in Asia all year, it seemed strange to see a sea of blondes and brunettes hair scurrying through the airport as we made our way down to the taxi stand. The next surprise: every cab was a Mercedes. Inside the car we not only found seatbelts, but they functioned! The friendly, helpful drivers even had navigation systems—no simply pretending to know the city, grunting at clients, and leaving female clients off in the middle of the road! Our trip seemed off to a good start.

The next morning, as we ambled through the lobby on our way to breakfast, a cacophony of familiar sounds reached my ears. *Mandarin? What?* We stepped into the dining room to discover a bus load of Chinese tourists chattering like magpies over the savory but mysterious German deli meats, cheeses, salads, yogurt, and bread. I nearly laughed aloud over the irony: I had just made my summer escape from the Middle Kingdom, in search of what Europe had to teach us, and now we sat surrounded by familiar faces and tones!

After breakfast, we journeyed to Centre Parc. At the resort, we checked in, then followed the site map to our "hut." We unpacked, then took a walk around the property. We discovered a bowling alley, a large lake with paddle boats and canoes and a zipline running across it, a rock wall, a game room, and a pool with multiple slides. Even an ice cream parlor stood waiting for our pleasure. Of course, Alexis and Anders enjoyed all of the activities, but the bowling alley provided a memorable, unique experience. The alleys had computer systems that allowed for players to choose from about six different types of games, complete with fancy animation on the board. In addition, the soda fountain had drinks not found in the US. The orange-flavored Coca-Cola quickly emerged as a favorite. It felt good to spend time outside in the clean, fragrant air. Thankfully, our Shanghai-saturated lungs had once again entered the summer recycling phase.

Next stop, Munich. There, we spent a few wonderful days wandering the streets and squares, carefully making sure to spend time in grandma's childhood neighborhood and taking photos of her family's apartment building. We took bus tours of castles and the enchanting town Rothenberg-ob-der-Tauber.

After Germany, we spent two wonderful weeks in Hilton Head, where both Planet's and my family visited us. Then we went on to enjoy three exhilarating weeks in Beaver Creek. At Hyatt camp, the kids went off-roading, horseback riding, camping, rafting, and the whole western shebang, while Planet and I hiked and biked. I was so happy, I nearly forgot I had to return to China. All-too-quickly summer break ended, and we found ourselves back on a Shanghai-bound 747 for another year's adventures.

章
25

THE LAST HURRAH

Fall Part Three

How could this be our third fall in Shanghai, already? When we arrived in 2005, I thought I'd never feel at home in China, and yet as we returned to 110 The Pearl in August 2007, I felt like a veteran, seasoned in all the aspects of daily life that gave me migraines in year one. I now loved having a live-in ayi and a driver, and I'd grown accustomed to the pampering and copious socializing.

As traumatized as I was moving the China, I could hardly believe that now it was our turn to leave. In early summer, Planet's firm had decided to down-size him. Thankfully, he soon received a job offer back in the US. We picked Chicago as our new home, and Planet would start in January.

Naturally, I went into overdrive trying to pack in as many Asian adventures as possible. Everything I did until the day we boarded a stateside-bound plane felt bittersweet. It caused me to focus on where I'd been over the past two years and what the future might hold. I had grown to appreciate some things about the China experience. One of the best aspects of living here was the strong sense of community among the expats. The socio-economic markers that so obviously divide people in other parts of the world did not exist here in the same way. As you already know, our housing situations were pretty much all the same, and our cars were nearly all blue or silver minivans. We all had drivers and ayis. Life in the expat community felt quite egalitarian, as people gladly associated with or socialized with people they may never have ever crossed paths with in their home countries. I wondered what kind of community would I find in my new Chicago neighborhood.

The closeness of the Shanghai expat community seemed a rare gift now. Any time I made the trip into Jin Qiao, I could count on seeing at least three people I knew somewhere in the Jade Leisure complex. I could sit and have a coffee in the Starbucks and leave with a lunch date. If I went to an exercise class at MegaFit, I might leave in another woman's van for an afternoon shopping adventure. There was no such thing as a "quick" grocery run, as I had to budget time to spend a few minutes chatting politely with every acquaintance I encountered. And as you already know, we couldn't even vacation without running into at least one neighbor or SAS family.

I knew I would sorely miss the small, close-knit community and meeting women from around the world on a daily basis. What could ever compare to the rich, international social life I'd led as a Shanghai Tai Tai? I knew I would also miss the way that most of the expat community consistently treated one another kindly and with the best of intentions—it renewed my faith in humankind. I could only hope Chicago would prove a typical, friendly Midwestern city with strong midwestern values

In the meantime, I volunteered for the PTSA, wrote copious articles for the *Courier*, participated in my intellectual club, and led the AWCS book club.

Using the same process as the previous year, the book club developed a great reading list for 2007-08:

BOOK	AUTHOR
Death of a Red Heroine	Qiu Xiaolong
The Seasons of Beento Blackbird	Akosua Busia
Fahrenheit 451	Ray Bradbury
The Nanny Diaries	Emma McLaughlin and
Nicola Kraus	
The Reluctant Fundamentalist & Holy Cow: An Indian Adventure	
	Moshin Hamid &
	Sarah MacDonald

A Long Way Gone	Ishmael Beah
Life of Pi	Yann Martel
Nobody Said Not to Go: The Life, Loves, & Adventures of Emily Hahn	
	Ken Cuthbertson
Diplomatic Baggage	Brigid Keenan

Looking at this list, clearly one of the best things about joining an international book club was reading books I might not otherwise pick up, reflecting a wide range of genres, backgrounds, and intellectual levels. In addition, I enjoyed these titles more than I might have because of the global perspectives provided by the group members. I knew I'd always have fond memories of this group.

Philippine Paradise

Of course, I took advantage of travel opportunities. For Golden Week, the kids and I (Planet stayed behind for some work obligations) journeyed to Cebu, Philippines. While I found the check-in process at the Kota Kinnabalu Shangri-La a wonderful stress buster, the Cebu Shangri-La took the experience one step beyond: guest check in at the airport! When we arrived at the Cebu airport, we only had to find the hotel's desk. From there, we handed off our luggage to the agent and walked outside to the resort van. Even better, when we arrived at the resort, each family was met by a hostess who led us to our rooms, where she completed the check-in process in the room. At this gorgeous resort, the main attraction for my kids was the adventure zone: a three-story climbing structure and ball pit featuring three different slides. Young visitors could also choose from a variety of organized activities. The activity center was supervised by the most charming staff we'd encountered yet in our travels.

Since Alexis and Anders had found nirvana at the adventure zone, I decided to seek my own at the resort's Chi Spa, where I had one of my life's best spa experiences. The spa's main check-in area resembled a tiki hut, beautifully decorated according to Feng Shui principles. A wonderful woody-spice aroma wafted through the air. Small gazebos stood all around a pool filled with artistic spraying jets. Oversized chairs, like giant burnt-orange bean bags, furnished some of the huts, while wooden benches with colorful pillow rolls decorated others. Inviting loungers adorned the pool deck. All this ambiance would have sufficed, but I booked a unique and amazing water shiatsu massage.

For the treatment, my therapist led me to a small, individual pool, shaded from the sun by a wooden canopy. He put floats around my ankles and handed me ear plugs. Then he began the session by having me float on my back. He grasped me around the arms and chest and gently floated me around the pool. Soothing, celestial spa music played softly in the background both above and below the water. I felt relaxed immediately in this womb-like setting. After a few minutes, the therapist began to massage my spine, including my tailbone. He followed this with a technique that swayed my body from side to side, which felt like a good stretch. As the man continued to mold my limbs into a variety of surprising positions, I learned how the force of the water contributed to each stretch. Several times, the therapist lifted me up by the back. Now I understood why the spa offered only a few appointments for water shiatsu a week: it clearly required a highly trained, strong man. My mind drifted pleasantly off into its own Shangri-La, and the treatment ended much too soon. After, a hostess appeared to serve me a post-treatment glass of watermelon and lime juice. I left Chi feeling peaceful and truly grateful.

My second trip to the spa was also a unique and wonderful Asian experience. The two-hour massage included water garden privileges plus the sauna and steam room. While I signed up and paid, the desk clerk served me lemon water, accompanied by a chilled, lavender-scented towel rolled up on the bamboo serving tray. As at the Westin's Banyan Tree, the sign-up process involved a survey to determine which of the traditional treatment elements would best suit me. The questions included items like my favorite color, preferred weather, etc. It turned out that my ideal element is wood. That result determined the scent for my treatment room, the type of massage oil, and the drink I'd be served following the massage.

Then, my therapist led me down the lushly landscaped pathway to my own individual villa. When I entered the villa's main room, the woman brought over a tub filled with hot water. She placed my feet into the water, then poured coconut milk from a small pitcher and tossed in rose petals and jasmine blossoms. As my feet soaked in the luxurious blend, the therapist served me herbal tea. The room smelled, of course, like a smoky, wood-burning fireplace as the result of my spa survey. The therapy room itself was beautifully decorated with carved wood beams, a domed ceiling, and lemongrass wallpaper. Brass animal candle holders lit the room, and lovely copper bowls with fluted pedestals held scented oil.

About ten minutes later, the masseuse removed my feet from the bath and dried them. Then she applied a warm, fragrant bolus bag to my feet and legs. Two hours flew by, and before I knew it, I heard her chiming the miniature brass cymbals to signal the end of the session. To ease me back into reality and enhance the benefits of the procedure, the therapist served me more tea. Afterward, I went outside to enjoy the water garden, contemplating how Asian spas possess an ambiance and provide experiences like nowhere else in the world. I would miss them terribly!

One of the other great experiences at the Shangri-La Cebu was snorkeling. We quickly learned its reputation was well deserved as the kids and I donned our snorkel gear and padded into the bathwater-warm, crystalline water. We brought some bread with us from breakfast to lure the fish.

The moment the crumbs hit the water, loads of fish zoomed over to us. The kids laughed excitedly as pale-yellow fish with neon pink stripes and huge black eyes swam curiously by them. I spied a zebra-striped species with a neon yellow tail and fins dotted with black polka dots. *Gorgeous!* A small silvery fish with yellow fins wiggled by, as a girl standing near me triumphantly held up a big orange starfish. Orange and white clown fish and an azure blue fish with two black strips near the top and a bright yellow tail circled the scene. We saw cantaloupe-colored fish with large black eyes and white fish with neon yellow stripes, pink eyes, pink fins and tails. My favorite of all, however, was the neon yellow and blue striped fish with feathery fins in a matching pattern and neon pink eyes. I couldn't believe how many different types of beautiful and unusual fish just casually showed up in one lagoon. I had never seen such amazing patterns and bright colors, and it seemed a wonder they actually occurred in nature. No wonder people loved to dive here!

Another aspect of the Cebu trip we will always remember was how genuinely happy, caring, and hospitable the warm, wonderful Filipino people were.

Sometimes, staff would just stop and chat in a way that made you feel they really did want to know about you, your life, and your hotel experience. The towel ladies at the pool insisted on carrying guests' towels and totes to their seats and laying everything out for them. They insisted on moving guests' chairs and adjusting everything perfectly. One morning at breakfast, while I watched in fascination as three old Asian ladies squeezed lime juice over their oatmeal and then topped it with pickled vegetables, our waiter randomly decided to entertain my kids with a couple of magic tricks. Another day, I paid one of the eager adventure zone staff to take Alexis, Anders, and a couple of their new friends to the Karaoke room.

As the week flew by, Alexis and Anders developed a burning desire to own a stuffed parrot like the club mascot, Polly. Before the trip ended, a thoughtful staff member managed to score a Polly for each of them! I left highly impressed with the value Asian people placed on relationships and community. They truly cared about others. I hoped my kids would always remember their time in Cebu and the Filipinos' kindness.

New Zealand: The Last Hurrah

Winter break 2007 arrived as quickly as the construction of a Pudong high rise. The impending departure day for our last Asia-Pacific adventure had all of us packing enthusiastically—a welcome distraction from the heartbreak of saying our goodbyes. As our Asian grand finale, we planned to spend three and a half weeks touring New Zealand before repatriating.

On Sunday, December 9, Mr. Zhou skillfully maneuvered the Shanghai Hi-Ho Silver to *Pudong Ji Chang* (Pudong airport) one last time. With mixed emotions, we bade our loyal driver a grateful goodbye and good luck. Then we checked in our Tumis and strode toward the gate, bound for Kiwiland.

Twelve sky hours later, we landed in Auckland, on New Zealand's north island. Since we were traveling with a fourth-grader and a fifth-grader, we made our first stop there the Sea Life aquarium. The museum offered many excellent displays, especially the sea horses and the "petting zoo" of rays and other docile sea creatures. But as with nearly every tourist, our favorite part of the museum was observing the numerous, outstanding King and Gentoo penguin exhibits—species native to New Zealand. Alexis and Anders could hardly get enough of these adorable, rare creatures.

The next day we journeyed to Rangitoto Island. The first step was to ferry across the Hauraki Gulf. When we disembarked, we boarded a four-wheel-drive tram that brought us to the volcanic peak. As we drove, our guide explained the island's lava-laden history and how the volcanic activity created an interesting topography and rich soil supporting a plethora of plant life. We all loved the "New Zealand Christmas Flower," also known as Pohutukawa. The flower grows on a type of myrtle tree and looks like a feathery red version of a thistle— or the trees from Dr. Seuss's *The Lorax*. The flowers bloom in December and January, and according to Maori (New Zealand natives) folklore, they represent the blood of a young warrior who died while attempting to avenge his father's death.

One of the highlights of North Island was Planet and the kids' outing to Waitomo Caves. There, they abseiled down one-hundred meters to enter the extensive system of underground caves. Once they reached the bottom, they jumped into a black-water boat to tour the labyrinth of waterfalls and limestone formations. Lighting, courtesy of an army of glow worms, added a magical atmosphere to the outing.

Our North Island experience ended at the resort I enjoyed the most—the Huka Lodge. This charming resort stood near Lake Taupo, on the bank of the Waikato River, just downstream of the legendary Huka Falls. The pastoral setting, with its rich, dense Granny Smith apple-colored grass balanced by the blue-gray rushing water, really spoke to me.

From Auckland, we boarded a flight to Christ Church to begin our South Island adventure. Our most memorable Christ Church tour remains our visit to the International Antarctic Centre. It's difficult to say whether we enjoyed the "storm room" or the Little Blue (Kokora) penguins the most of all the excellent exhibits. The storm room—kept at a brisk minus-eighteen degrees Fahrenheit—attempted to re-created conditions in Antarctica. The museum lent visitors parkas and boots to brave the frosty air. Once inside, guests could climb on an ice slide, create a windstorm, or take shelter in an igloo. The adorable Little Blue penguins onsite had all been rescued. As with the Borneo orangutans, the museum sought to preserve the species and provide refuge. We could have spent hours observing these charming little animals.

My family also learned what it's like attempting to reach the continent of ice, about life at Scott Base, and about current research projects going on there. I found the entire prospect of Antarctica daunting, and I knew I wouldn't be signing up for the increasingly-popular tours any time soon. With the addition of the museum's new 4D theater and the Husky snuggling room, I felt like I'd already had the whole Antarctica experience—and stayed significantly warmer and safer! Outside the museum, we took a ride on one of the Hagglund vehicles, a crucial tool in Antarctica. They resembled the Snowcats used in ski resorts for driving on ice and snow, but they were different because they can conquer crevasses and even drive through water in extreme Arctic conditions.

Our first stop outside Christ Church was the charming Victorian town called Dunedin. The town's beautiful, embellished train station and elaborate gardens spoke of its fortune. After a quick stop at a sports museum, we drove to Larnach Castle, the day's ultimate destination. The estate consisted of the castle, extensive planned gardens, and a number of service buildings now converted into guest lodgings. The kids loved the idea of staying in a real castle, but for Planet and I, it was all about the stunning view of Dunedin and the Peninsula.

The next morning, we scheduled a tour of the Cadbury chocolate factory, which began operation there in the 1880s. Inside the plant, we followed our guide through a series of shaky wooden staircases into the various chocolate processing rooms while she explained the history of chocolate candy and of the Cadbury company. At one point, we found ourselves walking through a giant vat, where old chocolate still clung to the walls, suddenly starring in our own version of *Willy Wonka*. This tour wasn't nearly as extensive as the one Planet and I had taken at the Cadbury factory in Tasmania, Australia, but it made for unique fun, provided some helpful educational and historical information, and gave the kids a great story to tell.

As with any tour, our journey ended in the gift shop. Again, we may as well have been hanging out with Mr. Wonka in this festive, childhood fantasy room. Of course, we let our absolutely delighted kids choose a few sweet souvenirs.

Though it may seem difficult to top this portion of the trip, the most wonderful thing about New Zealand was the plethora of natural beauty and the endless list of interesting, unusual things to do. One of the most popular touristy things to do, believe it or not, was to rent a camper. So we did. Planet felt a little nervous about not only piloting the enormous vehicle but having to drive it British-style. Planet popped the key into the ignition and moved to put the big rig into gear. A look of panic I'll never forget crossed his face. He had just discovered that not only would he be driving a moveable hotel on the "wrong" side of the road, he'd be maneuvering a *manual transmission*!

Planet made the best of things, and after a few test laps around the parking lot, we were underway. We headed up the North Otago coast, toward the Moeraki Boulders. The Moeraki Boulders are one of those amazing natural wonders everyone should see. Formed from mudstone, they have been shaped by the sea over an estimated four- to five-and-a-half million years. Some of the boulders stand over six feet in diameter. According to Maori legend, the smooth black rocks resemble an eel basket remnant from a boat wreck. The rocky shoals of Shag Point reveal a canoe's hull, and the reticulated patterns on some of the boulders look like fishing net remains. Whatever the case, we spent a lovely, sunny day by the waterside, having a wonderful time collecting colorful, amazingly smooth, round, flat rocks. I bought a rare-wood bowl in one of the towns, and it now sits in my family room filled with these special-memory, unique stones.

After returning the camper, we stayed at my favorite place on the South Island: the stunning eco-tourism Wilderness Lodge at Lake Moeraki on the banks of the Moeraki River. One of the best aspects was that the Lodge offered a rare opportunity to observe native Tawaki penguins—the ones with the feathery yellow eyebrows, also known as Fiordland Crested Penguins—in their natural habitat on Moeraki's beaches. The Tawaki are the only penguins who live in the rainforest, and the Wilderness Lodge had gone to great lengths to help protect these animals and promote their survival.

At the Tawaki penguin habitat, our excursion started at the hatchery, where we viewed eggs and some adorable babies. Next, we observed mothers tending their young in hillside nests. I couldn't believe we observed these delightful creatures within touching distance! Finally, we watched the fathers fishing in the sea and comically waddling back to their families. What wonderful creatures!

As unforgettable as our Tawaki penguin day was, we had one other remarkable experience at the Lodge. As an unexpected surprise, the hotel manager invited us to feed the river eels. With some hotel staff, we made our way to a nearby portion of the river, carrying buckets stocked with large chunks of lamb. Apparently, these species were struggling to survive, so they received a little boost from their human friends. I shuddered to imagine eels that could scarf down meat the size of a small chicken.

At the riverbank, suddenly the water turned from clear to brown. Three-feet long, murky fawn-colored, evil-looking water snakes appeared, their demanding, wide mouths open, wriggling with expectation above the surface. Powerful enough to climb a New Zealand waterfall, clearly they could easily tear a human arm off in seconds flat with equal ease. Now I understood why we had carried huge meat chunks and felt grateful for the long-handled hooks we used to feed them. I came away mildly horrified. You couldn't pay me enough to get in a small boat or raft on a New Zealand river now that I knew what lurked under the water! The kids, having no proper sense of danger, thought giving these fierce, strange-looking creatures their dinner was awesome.

From Lake Moeraki, our next stop was my favorite town in New Zealand: Queenstown. With its alps, extreme sport opportunities, old mines, hot springs, and charming houses, it struck me as the Southern Hemisphere's version of Colorado. Here, we had the opportunity to try out a luge track and bungy jump at the sport's original site, the Kawarau bridge. While the local hot springs didn't impress us much, we enjoyed the scenic drive to check out a winery, where we had a pleasant tour and lunch. The kids also got to try a new, crazy sport—ZORBing. At this site, Alexis and Anders jumped inside the clear plastic balls (about eight feet high), then the guide started the ZORB rolling down a hill. Laughably, they looked like giant hamster balls rolling around. When the ZORBers landed at the bottom of the hill, more guides stood waiting to help with commemorative photos.

I wished we could have lingered over Queenstown's magic, but we had booked a fjord cruise on Milford Sound.

When we arrived at the small ship, and everyone had boarded, the crew offered passengers an opportunity to take a raft exploration side trip. Out on the water, we paddled around looking at rock formations and the stunning scenery around the fjord. After dinner, we had an "it's a small world" experience. In the main room, a few kids had gathered around the piano, skillfully pumping out a variety of Christmas and other tunes. I don't know why, but I decided to speak to them. Not only was the family from my hometown, but I had gone to school with their mother! She came from a family of extremely accomplished violinists, so no wonder the kids showed such talent. What a coincidence!

After the cruise, our next stop was the Franz Josef Glacier. Since I'm the one voted most likely to slip and fall into a ravine, never to be seen again, Planet took the kids on this adventure. They took a short helicopter ride to the glacier, where they hiked and explored for a thrilling hour and a half. The venue is definitely another New Zealand must do.

Next up, Kaikoura, town of the legendary dolphin swim. On our tour, we motored out to sea in a small boat with only a few other people. When we reached the designated spot, I eyed the azure blue water in amazement. As though they were simply an average school of minnows, the area surrounding the boat grew gray-white with gentle, curious dolphins. The guide explained how to interact with them, making various sounds and movements to attract them and keep their interest. Guests were allowed about thirty memorable minutes in the water with these playful, enchanting finny new friends.

Our tour of South Island ended where it began, in Christ's Church. But we had one final adventure. We rented a large, attractive house with Bonnie Douglas's family. We spent our first day hiking in the local recreation area and attempting to buy UGG boots. To our disappointment, the trendy footwear wasn't any cheaper than in the US. When evening fell, Bonnie and I cooked a big New Year's Eve roast beef dinner while we waited for another SAS family we knew—who were also traveling in New Zealand—to come join us. While we prepared, I felt conscious of the fact that in all likelihood, our three families would never be together in the same place at the same time again—a classic expatriate situation. I made sure to savor that evening.

All too quickly, three and a half weeks sped by. Amazingly, every day was different but equally outstanding. I felt grateful for all the time we spent in New Zealand and believed we had started off 2008 auspiciously. On January 2, we found ourselves Chicago bound, winging toward the next chapter of our lives. What this new year would bring was anyone's guess. Regardless, we'd always be thankful for the special memories of our incredible Asia-Pacific friends, experiences, and travels.

章
26

WE INTERRUPT THIS LIFE...AGAIN!

With our New Zealand extravaganza complete, I could hardly wait to be back in the USA! Fairly vibrating with anticipation, I had no clue how challenging repatriating actually is. No matter how much someone may look forward to returning home, grief comes as part of the package, as does your countrymen's lack of understanding of what you've been through and are now dealing with. Losing a life that had grown familiar, a circle of friends, a strong sense of community, and a shared adventure all counted for much more than I realized.

In Shanghai, every day brought a new adventure—or two or three. When I left the house in the morning, *anything* could happen! Life back in the US quickly grew familiar and mundane. While the stability provided comfort, it also seemed boring.

In Chicago, we purchased a home half the size of our house in Shaker Heights, which cost us double the price and triple the taxes! *Scandalous!* In addition, Dobby the House Elf did not appear to cook and clean, no matter how much I willed it. I had to pay for several hours of strictly house cleaning what I paid for a month in Shanghai for a helper who did *everything*, twenty-four hours a day, five or six days a week. The first few times I drove, I felt like a nervous teenager again. A drive into the city took anywhere from thirty to ninety minutes, throughout which I had to sit behind the wheel and pay attention to traffic. No reading or making notes! I had to remember to fill the gas tank, pump gas myself, keep the car clean, take it for service, and wash it myself. Mr. Zhou would spontaneously combust to hear of Chicago parking prices!

At work, Planet returned to routine status as another cog in the wheel. Here, he blended in with the rest of the employees. He received no special treatment or reverence, as foreigners did in China. Work life reverted back to the usual projects, dramas, and politics.

The kids faced a special challenge: they arrived at their new schools in January, when friend groups and routines were already long established. They were also coming into schools where the vast majority of the kids had known each other all their short lives. I am forever grateful to the thoughtful, compassionate fourth-grade teacher who had each of her students write to Anders, introducing themselves and asking at least two questions about him. When my son arrived in his classroom in January, the kids already felt like they knew him and vice versa. My daughter's fifth-grade team also gave her great support, and she enjoyed the attention of being the new girl—who, can you believe it, moved here from *China*!

However, my kids discovered that American education focused more on reading and writing, so they were ahead in math and science, but behind in language arts. They knew where countries in Asia lay on a global map, but they struggled to learn the geography of the US states. They couldn't locate Iowa, and they found the fifth-grade map-of-the-states test very difficult. Strangely, they also found their new language requirement—Spanish—hard!

The other thing Alexis and Anders found challenging is how many safety issues kids have to pay attention to in US—even in the most expensive zip codes. In Shanghai, the kids roamed freely in our compound, protected by guards and the watchful eyes of our neighbors. In the US, they felt curbed, and for a while mystified, by re-learning American safety protocols. In Shanghai, the foreign strangers they met were all safe and even desirable to know. For the most part, the expats all served as one another's extended family. In America, we had to re-learn "stranger danger."

Another challenge came in the form of chores. In China, ayi cleaned their rooms and did all the chores. In Chicago, I had to re-teach the kids why they had to keep their own rooms clean, make their beds, help me prepare dinner, and take out the trash. As you might imagine, we experienced some re-adjustment pains!

The most difficult part of being back in the US for me was that no one understood that repatriation was actually challenging, and no one besides other expats gave a fiddler's fart. No one wanted to listen to stories about living abroad (no matter how interesting or amazing). They couldn't relate to how annoying it was to have to drive myself into the city or how frustrating it was that not everyone was a potential friend. "But you're *back*!" people announced, as if the US was the only country in the world—or at least the only one that mattered. They were mystified that I couldn't just jump right in and pick up where I left off. Feeling homesick for aspects of Shanghai life baffled them. *What's to miss?* They imply. Ah. That's just it.

Shanghai Is a State of Mind

Adjusting to life in the US came to us in pieces, over time. With each friend we finally made, each trip to the grocery, each dinner cooked, each gas tank filled, and each sidewalk snow blown, life slowly returned to our new normal. Yet Shanghai never left us. Wherever we turned, before long something would happen or we'd see something that served as a reminder of our lives abroad. We gravitated toward Asian people when we went out. We had to resist breaking into Mandarin when we interacted with anyone who looked Chinese. Though, sometimes the wait staff in Chinese restaurants humored us, after they got over the initial shock that the blonde-haired, blue-eyed diners just ordered in Mandarin. No one but our family (or others who had lived in China) understood what we meant when we experienced a "China moment."

It seemed that elements of our lives in China would always remain part of our lives. I had only to wander through my house to conjure up a Shanghai state of mind.

An intricately carved antique Chinese wedding bed serves as the showpiece in my family room. At our house in The Pearl, the piece held court in the bay window of my living room. There, ayi served tea to me and my girlfriends as we gossiped, worked on community service events, and plotted shopping adventures. In the afternoons, my children favored doing their homework in the "tea house." Although an ayi no longer serves the drinks and snacks here on Chicago's North Shore, my new friends' faces express delight when I invite them to try out my prized Chinese antique. There, I serve them wine in the beautiful and inexpensive glasses I bought during my glass factory shopping adventure with Chava. But I no longer bother to tell people the stories about how I acquired the tea house or the goblets; I simply smile knowingly to myself. In my kitchen, I recently packed up the red and black rooster place settings I used as our dishes in China for my daughter to take off to her college apartment. As I carefully wrapped plates in packing paper, I remembered the day I purchased them, when Chava took me on my first trip to the Hong Qiao Flower Market. I think I paid about $1 each for the cute be-fowled plates and bowls, when shopping at such bargain prices was still a new thrill.

My guest room closet remains stocked full to bursting with the plethora of silk cosmetic cases, phone cases, candles from the Pudong candle factory, silk CD cases and photo albums, authentic green tea, antique Japanese obi tea boxes, pearls from Hainan, and a wide array of jewelry I either won at events or bought in Shanghai's omnipresent markets. Countless hours and exciting adventures went into compiling this stash, and now I have a plethora of great gift options on hand.

When I walk into my daughter's bedroom, my eyes rest on her bedroom set. I recall the day I went to Jisheng Wellborn furniture to pay the balance on the set, anxiously guarding the ridiculously large stack of RMB bursting from my purse. Next to the bed lays the beautiful blue and pink Oriental rug I won as the door prize at the SAS fundraiser my friends and I organized. My mind whirls back to all the fun we had the evening of the event and saw all our hard work come to fruition.

In Anders' room, the Tibetan "cloud" rug brightens up the décor and the supposedly rare Tibetan tiger carpet adorns his bathroom floor, bringing back memories of my antiquing trip to Beijing. In my own room, my closet remains full of clothes gathered at many stalls throughout the fabric markets. I still dream about how much fun I had designing my own clothes and seeing my flights of fancy stitched into reality. Playing clothing designer, and the low prices I paid for my creations, remains one of the things I miss most.

Sometimes it seems like I may have simply dreamed my China days, while dozing off in a lounge chair in my back yard on a sunny day. If it weren't for the treasures spread throughout my home and the fact that I sometimes understand random snippets of Mandarin, I might believe it never happened. These things reassure me that in some way, my remarkable Shanghai expat days will always be a part of me.

Thankfully, Amalie's family moved to Chicagoland at the same time we did. Through her, I learned of an international women's club for women. Luckily, these women understand perfectly why I miss ayi and Mr. Zhou, they're willing to hear a China story 1,000 times if necessary, and they know what I mean by a China moment. The group also satisfies my need to continually meet women from around the world and to embrace international diversity. We hold monthly lunches at different ethnic restaurants, host potluck meals centered around foods from our home countries, and have a book club—similar to the SEA's—where we enjoy the advantages of international perspectives. I would be significantly less well-adjusted to Midwestern life and happy without this connection to one of the best parts of my Tai Tai life. Had I not lived in China, I wouldn't have the privilege of participating in this wonderful international women's club.

When we left Shaker Heights, I felt devastated to give up my "Better than the Brady Bunch" life. Then, I couldn't imagine I'd benefit from living in China. But now, I realize that taking the road less traveled has actually made all the difference. When I think about how much richer I am for all the experiences my family and I had (good and bad), the friends we made, and the places we traveled during our China years, I realize that the "gift" I thought I was giving to my husband and children became a gift to myself as well. Though I went so reluctantly, I'm truly thankful I became a Shanghai Tai Tai. Shanghai won a place in my heart, and any time I need her, all I have to do is look at the Asian artifacts in my house to channel a Shanghai state of mind.

Think of my story next time you're relaxing in your Shanghai hotel room!

ABOUT THE AUTHOR

Shelly Aschkenase is a globe-trotting writer, editor, and educator. Her passion for applying economic theories to literature compelled her to earn a Ph.D. in Modern American Literature from Georgia State University. The groundwork for that mission was laid while studying for a B.A. in Economics and English at Wellesley College. She hails from St. Paul, Minnesota's strong Nordic stock, where, like F. Scott Fitzgerald, she attended St. Paul Academy. In her free time, she can usually be found on a bike or hiking trail contemplating how best to wrangle words into meaningful experiences.

Made in the USA
Monee, IL
24 March 2020